'The greatest little river in the world'

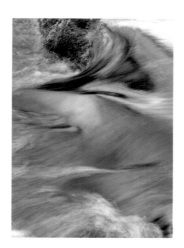

THE GRETA

The story of a Lakeland river as it flows through the life
and times of Keswick and its people

KEITH RICHARDSON Colour photography by Val Corbett

Keith J. Richardson

RIVER
GRETA
WRITER

River Greta Writer
Windebrowe Avenue
Keswick
Cumbria
CA12 4JG

www.rivergretawriter.co.uk

THE GRETA
The story of a Lakeland river, The Greta, as it flows through the life and times
of Keswick and its people.

First River Greta Writer edition: 2012

A catalogue record for this book is available from the British Library.
ISBN: 978-0-9559640-3-9

Printed and bound by The Amadeus Press, Cleckheaton, West Yorkshire.
Design and pre-press by Malcolm Rigg, Keswick.

CONTENTS

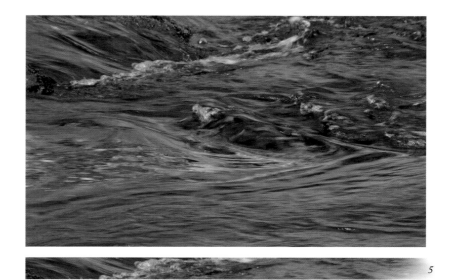

FOREWORD

This is the book that deep down I always wanted to write.

Which is not to say that I did not want to write any of the other books I have written and published under the River Greta Writer banner; nothing could be further from the truth. It is simply that this book, *The Greta*, is arguably the most personal and is about the river with which I have had a close affinity all my life, including the years of my childhood when I lived for the best part of 10 years in a terraced house half a dozen paces from the bank of the river at Low Briery, then a working bobbin mill and farm and now a holiday village; which in a nutshell, I guess, tells you a lot about the changing face of the Lake District.

During the research and writing of *The Greta* some people queried how it would be possible to write an entire book about a four-mile stretch of river? No fewer than 272 pages later I have hopefully provided the answer to that question in a publication that has a greater pagination than any of its predecessors in the series of Lakeland books that comprises *Ivver Sen*, *Joss* and *Jack's Yak*.

My attachment to the Greta was obvious through my choice of name for the publishing company, River Greta Writer, that I established in 2007 following a working life as a local newspaper reporter on *The Whitehaven News* and, later, newspaper and magazine editor with *The Cumbrian Gazette* and *Cumbria Life*. The words River Greta Writer had a certain ring to them and were symbolic of my sense of freedom after deciding to go it alone.

In cutting loose and setting out as a full-time writer and publisher it was not my firm intention at the outset to write a book about the River Greta. I had been writing pieces about the river at regular intervals and while the idea of at sometime writing a book was washing around in my thoughts – like a twig caught up in a whirlpool on the beck – it only became a definitive statement of intent two years ago when I began my research in earnest.

It is a book that I have inadvertently been researching all my life simply by living close to the river. Like many other people I probably took the river for granted and I suspect that this is a river that has far greater significance for the people of Keswick, and the thousands of visitors the town and area attracts each year, than they themselves might realise. To consider the town of Keswick without the River Greta is unthinkable.

It is always there, ever flowing, never ceasing, always constant, high, noisy and raucous or low, soft and musical on its journey from its source and tributaries in the fells and, ultimately, after joining the River Derwent, to the sea.

I love to listen to the Greta at night, while walking home, when the town is largely silent and the full volume of the river's passage under Brundholme Woods is much more noticeable. It was not without good reason that the poet Robert Southey labelled the Greta 'the loud lamenter' and its Old Norse name 'grjot a' translates to 'rocky river.' When the river is in spate you can actually hear the boulders rumbling along its bed.

There is always something special about walking by the river, to take in the distinctive aroma of the beck and to stand on its pebble strewn bank among clumps of the prolific greater woodrush and the occasional golden burst of marigold, watching trout rise or the white-fronted dipper bobbing and weaving on a stone in the middle of the fast-flowing current before hurtling, a brown blur in a rush, up and down the beck at astonishing speed. The river has many qualities.

To spend time with the river is to relax. Yet it is also inspirational, emptying the mind of troubles and allowing more positive thoughts and ideas to flood in. It is also a great place to sit, to look and, that apart, to do absolutely nothing.

As I worked on the book and developed my ideas, a number of specific themes or subjects began to rise out of the maelstrom and became chapter headings. In the order in which they appear in the book they were the river's source and tributaries; the memorial stone at the foot of Skiddaw near Whit Beck, a tributary of the Glenderaterra; the river dwellers, the people who have lived or still live on its banks; the old stone bridges over the river; the days of water-powered mills and industry; a childhood at Low Briery; wild swimming; Southey and Coleridge and Greta Hall and the family currently living there; flooding down the centuries; wildlife; fishing and fishermen; pollution and, last but not least, The History Files – the latter devoted to how the river ran through the life of the town from the late 19th Century (1877) to the early years of the 20th Century (1910).

It soon became clear, especially when interviewing people who live in houses near the river, that the Greta runs not only through some of the most magnificent scenery in the UK – if not the world – but that it also flows through the landscape of our lives.

Writing this book also brought home the importance of the cycle of water and the vital importance of clean water; after all the river has been polluted in the past from the lead mines on Blencathra and with sewage and other rubbish from the town. Good, clean water is, like the river, something that we may be in danger of taking for granted and we pollute water anywhere and anyhow at our peril and must always be mindful of any development that might compromise the quality of the Lake District and its rivers and lakes; now or in the distant future.

For instance, I have serious concerns about a proposal to bury long-lived (as in thousands of years) high level radioactive waste in a massive underground repository in Cumbria, in a geologically questionable location to the west of the county and probably beneath or near the Lakeland fells from which springs the water that is essential to life. Such a proposal, if it goes ahead, inevitably raises the awful spectre of the possibility of water pollution in centuries to come from a potential radioactive graveyard.

On another level I have worries about the future of wildlife on the Greta. The otter on the river has experienced a welcome renaissance but the threat to the Atlantic salmon is very real and the numbers of fish currently running the river to spawn are diminishing at an alarming rate. It is a problem that is not specific to the Greta but is a wider environmental issue and one that, in my view, needs urgent attention.

The book *The Greta* is a celebration of the river and the vale and the town through which it runs. I only hope that the people who live in and visit Keswick and the Lake District National Park of the future – at a time when it will hopefully be a World Heritage Site – will be able to appreciate and enjoy the river as much as I have done. And that the wildlife, such as the otter, the heron, the dipper and the trout and salmon will all be around to do much the same.

If they are then the River Greta will be just fine and should be able to continue on its endless journey from the mountains to the sea for thousands of years to come.

Keith Richardson
September 2nd, 2012.

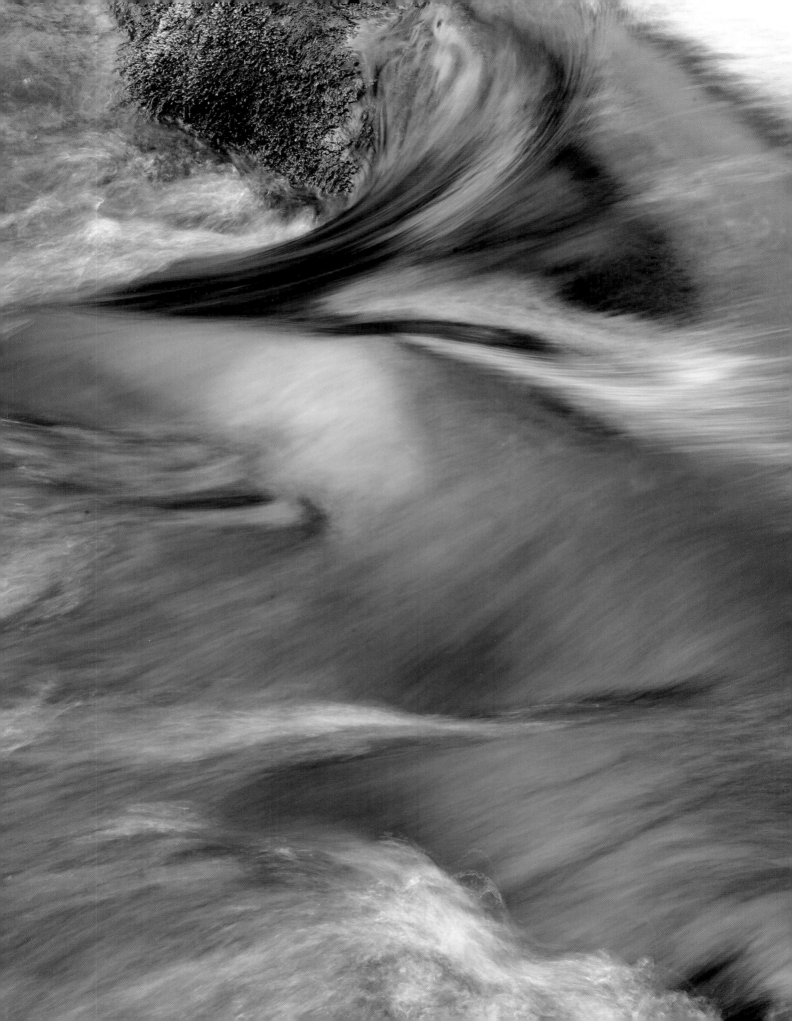

Source and Tributaries
THE GREATEST LITTLE RIVER IN THE WORLD

The source of a river is the beginning of a world.

The source itself may not be anything to look at, no great shakes and all that, but the river-to-be announces its arrival with a burbling, almost joyous gush of pure water springing out of goodness only knows where, some hidden subterranean depth of unfathomable mystery. Alternatively it can just sort of come together, almost like casual acquaintances meeting in the street and heading off in the same direction, an accumulation of surface rainwater soaked up in the moss, sedge and grass of a high Lakeland fell, cutting a channel and transforming itself into a stream, a beck and, ultimately, a river. And there is, of course, no turning back once the downhill race is underway; no turning back until, that is, water's never-ending climatic circle kicks in and returns the water to the beginning to start all over again.

Over the years explorers have gone to incredible lengths to identify the precise source of great rivers such as the Nile, the Amazon or the Ganges. And then to marvel, having found the source, at how from a very small, understated beginning in the middle of nowhere the first pure outpouring will grow into a stream and then gradually spread and swell and gather momentum into a vast expanse of water – a life source for man and beast, flora and fauna – on its long journey to the sea. Fast, busy, eager, ambitious and energetic in its youth and slow and more leisurely as it ages and thickens at the hips, the journey of a river stands comparison with that of our own lives. We start in total innocence, in floods of tears, and end, or at least we hope we do, although there is no absolute guarantee, with a degree of wisdom as life, and its many streams and rivers, continues its eternal and mesmerising cycle. And we have not even touched on the Universe.

In comparison with many rivers on Planet Earth the River Greta is a relative trickle, albeit a very lively and beautiful one that flows – on its short, fast, snaking, four-mile ride to the

Facing page:

Where waters meet. The rivers Glenderamackin (left) and St John's Beck meet under Threlkeld Bridge to form the River Greta. A man rides over the bridge on his horse against the backcloth of Clough Head.

The Glenderaterra.

River Derwent – through some of Lakeland's most amazing scenery. It is, certainly, to my mind, and for all sorts of reasons, the greatest little river in the world.

The Greta is, of course, a significant tributary of the River Derwent, the source of which can be found high in Borrowdale volcanic as opposed to the Skiddaw slate through which the Greta and its own tributaries and headwaters have cut their way over thousands of years. It is accepted in some circles that the single source of a river is not where its name begins but is, in fact, the furthest point on the map away from where it ends – irrespective of the tributaries and the becks of other names that join forces to become the river in question. So, in the case of the River Greta your starting point in the search for its true source is the place we know as Cement Point where the Greta ends and it joins the River Derwent at the foot of Keswick, a couple of hundred yards or so below where the bottle green water of the Derwent emerges from Derwentwater.

Travel the Greta up stream from Cement Point and after four to five miles of twists and turns through spectacular countryside you will come to Threlkeld Bridge, or New Bridge as it was known. It is directly beneath the twin arches of the bridge that the River Glenderamackin and St John's Beck merge to form the River Greta. That is the exact place where the River Greta begins but it is not, strictly speaking, its source. To find the source you need to follow, not literally, although it is good to do so on foot, the respective courses of the River Glenderamackin and St John's Beck (at one time known as The Bure) as they go their separate and very different ways. You will then discover that the greatest distance from the Greta's end lies in the direction of St John's Beck and that the source of the River Greta is high in the fells above Thirlmere reservoir in a mountain cove that opens up atop the waterfalls of Wyth Burn.

Both the River Glenderamackin and St John's Beck start their lives high in the Lakeland fells and, irrespective of the pleasant surprise that waits at the top of Wyth Burn, the Glenderamackin is arguably the more dramatic location of the two. There the small beginnings of the river rise out of the fellside of Mungrisdale Common under the imposing heights of Sharp Edge on Blencathra. In this high and

St John's Beck and walkers cross the packhorse bridge near Bridge End Farm.

solitary mountain fastness the Glenderamackin feeds also from a small stream, Scales Beck, that slips out of the dark, forbidding and 'bottomless' basin that is Scales Tarn, situated directly below Sharp Edge. The bottomless reference is a gross exaggeration on my part; this tarn just looks as though its depths descend to the centre of the earth. The Glenderamackin then surrounds Souther Fell – and its legions of ghostly Roman soldiers that have been seen down the years – before turning back on itself in a great big U towards Threlkeld and its union at the old stone bridge with St John's Beck to form the Greta.

The Poet Laureate Robert Southey (1774 – 1843) of Greta Hall, Keswick, visited Scales Tarn and Blencathra on one of his daily walks and wrote: 'Wild it is as ever was chosen by a cheerful party to take their merry rest upon a summer's day. The green mountain, the dark pool, the crag under which it lies, and the little stream which steals from it, are the only objects; the gentle voice of that stream the only sound, unless a kite be wheeling above, or a sheep bleats on the fell side. A silent, solitary place; and such solitude heightens social enjoyment as much as it conduces to lonely meditation.'

Southey, however, did not have much faith in the more fanciful theories about the undeniably dramatic nature of Scales Tarn. 'Absurd accounts,' he wrote, 'have been published both of the place itself, and the difficulty of reaching it. The tarn is said to be so deep that the reflection of the stars may be seen in it at noon day . . . and that the sun never shines in it. One of these assertions is as fabulous as the other and the tarn, like all other tarns, is shallow.'

He was certainly more impressed with the view from Blencathra: 'Ascending toward the brow of the mountain, you look back through the opening, where the stream (Scales

Looking across at a wintry Lonscale Fell and Skiddaw from the slopes of Blencathra. The beginnings of the Glenderaterra flow through the valley bottom.

Previous pages:
It all begins here.
The starting point for the
Glenderamackin, tributary of
the River Greta, under the
impressive ridge of Sharp Edge
on Blencathra. Scales Tarn is
hidden behind the ridge to the
left of the picture.

Top:
The Glenderamackin near
Mungrisdale.

Bottom: Looking across at the
valley through which the
Glenderaterra flows.

Beck) finds its way, to a distant view of the open country about Penrith with the long line of Cross Fell bounding it. When the brow is reached you are on the edge of that bold and ragged front which Blencathra presents when seen from the road to Matterdale or from the Vale of St John's. A portion of the hill (Hall Fell it is called), somewhat pyramidical in shape, stands out here like an enormous buttress, separated from the body of the mountain on all sides by steep ravines. These have apparently been formed by water spouts bursting what was once the green breast of the mountain, and thus opening water courses which the rain and storms have continually been deepening. In looking down these ravines from the brow you have a sense of perfect security; there is not even an appearance of danger, and yet if the whole depth below were one precipice, the effect could not be grander. At the foot is the cultivated valley, where the Glenderamackin, collecting the waters of Blencathra, winds along to join St John's Beck, and form with it the Greta. In front are the Ullswater mountains. The vale of St John's and Nathdale open into the subjacent valley; you look over Nathdale Fell which divides them, and, beyond it, Leatheswater is seen, in its length, extending between Helvellyn and its own fells. Derwentwater is to the right of this, under the western side of these fells, and the semi circle is everywhere closed by mountains range behind range.

'My friend, William Westall, who has seen the grandest and the loveliest features of nature in the East Indies and in the West, with the eye of a painter, and the feeling of a poet, burst into an exclamation of delight. Those who perform the whole excursion on foot, may descend in a south westerly direction, to the Glenderaterra, cross that rivulet by a wooden bridge and return to Keswick through Brundholme Wood, by a very beautiful road, commanding views of the Greta and its manifold windings below, and, farther on, of the town, the lake and the whole line of mountains from the Borrowdale Fells to Wythop.'

I have walked the routes of the Glenderamackin and St John's Beck from their respective sources to the point where they join forces to create the Greta at Threlkeld Bridge. Both streams are attractive in their own way, the Glenderamackin, into which flows Troutbeck and Mosedale Beck, which I have also followed, is in more of a hurry and has a dark, shallow bottom; while St John's is a much gentler stream for the most part, idling its way through the beautiful vale of St John's and is probably the more pleasing on the eye of the two. The original starting point for St John's Beck was Leathes Water, in what Southey described as 'a beautiful sylvan spot.' This was in the days when Thirlmere was in fact two entirely separate lakes, Leathes Water and Wythburn Water, with a Celtic-style wood bridge, supported by stone columns, spanning the stream that linked the lakes in the centre ground. The valley was flooded, amid much controversy, in the latter years of the 19th Century to form one great stretch of water, the Thirlmere reservoir of today, to provide drinking water for Manchester.

Nowadays the water leaves Thirlmere to enter St John's Beck via a somewhat daunting cavern cut into the rock at the dam end of the reservoir and through which the overflow from the lake roars and tumbles its way straight down, hundreds of feet, to the valley floor. From there it takes a more conventional route to the Greta through beautiful pasture, under a timeless packhorse bridge and past neat little stepping stones near Bridge End Farm.

William Wordsworth (1770 – 1850) wrote in 1835: 'The Cumberland Greta, though it does not, among the country people, take up that name till within three miles of its disappearance in the River Derwent, may be considered as having its source in the mountain cove of Wythburn, and flowing through Thirlmere, the beautiful features of which lake are known only to those who, travelling between Grasmere and Keswick, have quitted the main road in the vale of Wythburn, and, crossing over to the other side of the lake, have proceeded with it on the right hand.

'The channel of the Greta, immediately above Keswick, has, for the purposes of building, been in great measure cleared of the immense stones which, by their conclusion in high floods, produced the loud and awful noises . . .'

Top: Stepping stones over St John's Beck.
Bottom: The old Celtic-style bridge that once separated Leathes Water from Wythburn Water (now Thirlmere reservoir). Picture courtesy of The George Fisher Collection.

Previous pages:
An ice and snow-covered
Tewet Tarn in winter with
Lonscale Fell and Blencathra
(right) beyond. A little stream
from the tarn flows into the
Naddle, a tributary of the
Greta.

Below: Tewet Tarn as seen from
the heights of Blencathra.

Walking up Wyth Burn, just beyond West Head Farm, the stream rises through cascades and rowan-occupied pools with steep fells on either side, into a boggy land, appropriately called The Bog – almost like a forgotten world – where it widens into some significant pools. When I visited, a dipper was searching for food in the sunshine, on the fringe of the water where the stream widens into a pool. In this environment it is entirely feasible to imagine encountering a prehistoric monster grazing on the fellside; such is the atmosphere and other worldly remoteness of the place. All around are drumlins, known collectively as a swarm, and testimony to the glacial power of the Ice Age. Beyond The Bog Wyth Burn flows beneath Ash Crags and it is here, on a tributary of Mere Beck, on the eastern slopes of High Raise, that the source of the Greta is to be found as it rises out of the fell 2,350 feet above sea level.

On the opposite side of Dead Pike another stream runs into Thirlmere. This is Raise Beck which charges headlong past the large mound of stones on Dunmail Raise that divides the old counties of Cumberland and Westmorland and is reputed to form a burial mound and the resting place of the last King of Cumberland, King Dunmail, who was defeated by Edmund the Saxon in 945AD.

That pile of stones,
Heaped over brave King Dunmail's bones
He who had once supreme command
Last King of peaky Cumberland
William Wordsworth, 'The Waggoner'

Two other tributaries of the River Greta, Naddle Beck and Glenderaterra Beck, also have their respective sources high in the fells, the Naddle above Shoulthwaite on Castlerigg Fell and the Glenderaterra on the land between Skiddaw Forest and Mungrisdale Common. Both make for a fascinating walk and it is intriguing that they both face each other on opposite sides of the valley. The Glenderaterra is fast flowing throughout its entire course and there is much evidence of mining in its higher reaches. The Naddle, while busy on the fell side, soon slows as it gets to Dalebottom and winds its way at a leisurely pace, canal like, through boggy farmland.

At one point as it nears the Greta, the Naddle flows directly beneath Castlerigg Stone Circle in its lofty location surrounded by fells and with all its ancient mystery. The circle of 38 stones, with a further 10 in a smaller inner group, is thought to date back to the beginning of the later Neolithic period and was probably built about 3,000BC; although how anyone can come to that conclusion is beyond me.

On the other side of the Greta gorge the Glenderaterra rushes between Lonscale Fell and Blencathra and is joined on the way by the water of Whit Beck as it makes its way off the slopes of Skiddaw and turns sharply to join the Glenderaterra.

All of these little becks as they head towards the Greta have their stories and strong associations with the land and the people. The little but lively and sweet-sounding Whit Beck is no exception. At one point it flows close to Lonscale Farm and can also be heard very clearly when you stand next to a special monument on the spectacularly scenic strip of land, known as the Gale, at the foot of the Skiddaw's purple-brown slopes.

The monument stands in tribute to a family of shepherds, the Hawells, who for many years worked the sides of Skiddaw and other nearby fells from their home at Lonscale Farm. But first let me set the scene by delving deeper into the history of this particular part of Lakeland where, it seems, all streams lead to the Greta and to Keswick.

Shoulthwaite Beck which ultimately becomes the Naddle and a tributary of the Greta. Directly opposite, on the other side of the Greta valley, is the gorge between Lonscale Fell and Blencathra through which flows the Glenderaterra.

Ridge of the Dead

The name Keswick reputedly comes from its cheese making past. It is thought that the name means cheese farm and comes from two Anglian elements 'cese' and 'wic'. I much prefer the argument put forward by former Keswick resident of note, one Canon Hardwicke Drummond Rawnsley (1851 – 1920), Vicar of Crosthwaite, and co-founder of The National Trust, who argued that the name Keswick originates from the time when the Viking chieftains Sweyn, Honig, Ormr, Hundr and Ketel – the forefathers of the Cumbrian dalesmen of today – settled in this part of the world, an ideal place to live with a protective circle of fells, close to life-giving water, and gave their names to their new surroundings; just as the Norse language is to this day related to all manner of places in Lakeland, including, of course, Greta, taken from the Norse 'grjot' and meaning rocky river.

And so it is that the Swinside of today was once the seat or high camp of Sweyn or Svein; Honig was translated to Honig Stadhr, the farm of Honig the Viking, or Honister as it is now known; that Ormathwaite, situated below Skiddaw, is the thwaite or 'clearing in the wood' of Ormr and above which stands Underscar, the caer or camp of Hundr, and so on. Last but not least is Ketel, son of Ormr, who may, after travelling up the River Derwent from the sea, have run his boats ashore at the wyke (or bay) on Derwentwater, giving rise to the name of the early settlement of Ketel's Wyke, the Kelsick and later the Keswick of today? Significantly, perhaps, there is also Kettlewell, near Lodore, not far from the town along the eastern shore of Derwentwater.

I love cheese, especially a particularly flavoursome goat's cheese (best eaten with a dollop of blackcurrant jam) that you can buy these days on Keswick Market on a Thursday or a Saturday, but when it comes to the origins of the naming of a town in one of the most beautiful places on earth, then surely there is no argument when it comes to deciding between cheese making or Ketel, son of Ormr, the Viking adventurer and settler who may have given his name to our town when he and his compatriots arrived here from the far North as peaceful settlers, somewhere between 870 and 950AD.

A fell strongly linked to the burial grounds of the Vikings is Latrigg, previously known in Norse times as Hlad Rigg or the Ridge of the Dead. For a fell of fairly diminutive stature, Latrigg commands amazing views over Derwentwater, Borrowdale, the Vale of Keswick and the River Greta directly below as it curves its way through the woodland like a molten stream in the evening sunlight. Viking cist-vaens or burial cairns were found on Latrigg's heights early in the 19th Century and it is thought that as many as 70 chieftains could have been buried on the fell.

The Hawell Monument on the lower slopes of Skiddaw. Mell Fell is in the centre distance with Clough Head on the right.

The Hawell Monument

It perhaps comes as no surprise to learn that Canon Rawnsley – a great one for building monuments, he was also behind the memorial to the artist Charles Gough on Helvellyn – decided to place a monument to members of the Hawell family, well known Skiddaw shepherds, on the land known as the Gale between the gentle slopes of the back of Latrigg and the steeper full-frontal rise of Jenkin Hill on Skiddaw itself. The Hawells specialised in breeding the hardiest of sheep, the Herdwick, a strain of animal most probably brought to Cumberland by the Norsemen of old (I would tend to discount as being a touch fanciful the theory that Herdwicks came here after swimming safely ashore from a Spanish ship that came to grief off the Cumbrian coast after the defeat of the Armada).

As you stand next to the Hawell Monument there is the distinct sound of Whit Beck streaming off the side of Skiddaw. It runs enthusiastically through a strand of fir trees in the cut in the fell to your right as you look uphill to the heights of Skiddaw and Lonscale Fell and then wends its bubbly and raucous way down from fell to field, past Lonscale Farm where the Hawells worked and lived for many years. From there it joins the Glenderaterra which then races pell mell to the Greta just beyond a beautiful little packhorse bridge over the road linking Wesco with Brundholme. It is a road that was probably an ancient route for travellers making their way to and from Keswick. In fact I think many travellers coming from the direction of Ambleside might have headed through St John's in the Vale towards Threlkeld before heading west towards Keswick and West Cumberland.

The Hawell Monument is made of stone and is in the form of an early British wayside cross, with Scandinavian knot work on the trunk. The Gale is the perfect place for a memorial and as I stand before the monument on a winter's day (December 18, 2011) with snow on the sides of Skiddaw and all the higher fells, it is appropriate that I should hear the sound of a sheep dog barking from the confines of Lonscale Farm, hidden

Part of the text on The Hawell Monument.

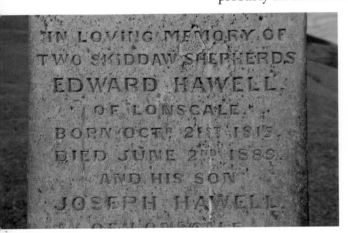

IN LOVING MEMORY OF
TWO SKIDDAW SHEPHERDS
EDWARD HAWELL
OF LONSCALE.
BORN OCT. 21ST 1815.
DIED JUNE 2ND 1889.
AND HIS SON
JOSEPH HAWELL

behind a cluster of trees in the valley below. From the monument, as you look out to the west, there is Grisedale Pike, rising like a pyramid out of the valley, and to its left the knobbled ridge of Causey Pike reminds me of images of the back of the Loch Ness Monster emerging out of water. To the east is mighty Blencathra and beyond that Mell Fell. To the north, clearly, is Skiddaw with people padding up and down its 'motorway' zig-zag path in the snow, while to the south east is the bulwark that is the side of Clough Head and then, beyond that, the rambling extent of the Helvellyn range. A paraglider drifts in the clear blue sky above Clough Head and, as ever, I am left bemoaning the fact that we rarely get blue sky days in the summer when the weather is warm. Deep in the folds of winter I am always seduced by the prospect of summer and warmer days but when it arrives I am invariably disappointed as the warmer air brings with it the low pressure from the west and continual blankets of cloud and rain.

It also occurs to me as I stand there that thousands of people will walk past this monument in the height of summer and many will not even give it a second glance. How many, I wonder, actually take the time and trouble to wander a little off the path to look at the monument and the inscription upon it?

The monument was initially erected in memory of Joseph Hawell and his father Edward, although other Hawell family names were added to the base at a later date.

Joseph Hawell, of Lonscale, was born at Longlands Farm, Uldale, on December 24th, 1854. His father was called Edward and his mother Jane (Walker). Edward was one of five children, John, Jane (who died in childhood) Robert, Joseph and Ann. In 1869 the family moved from Uldale to the secluded farm on Colonel Watson's estate between Lonscale and Saddleback. They were prize-winning breeders of pure Herdwick sheep.

Writer and country lover, Canon Rawnsley knew the family well and wrote: 'The old man (Edward) who had struggled with storm on Skiddaw through his laborious life, failed in health and suffered, as shepherds often do, from terrible rheumatism, and was also troubled with asthma. At last he felt obliged to leave the ingle-nook and take to his bed upstairs. But his love of the shepherd's life was still so strong upon him that a few days before he died he insisted on seeing one of the prize Herdwick rams, and the sons

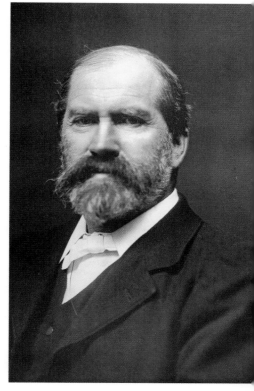

Canon Hardwicke
Drummond Rawnsley.

had a tough job to get it to 'clim' the 'stee' (climb the stairs) and stand in the presence of the dying man. The old man felt death coming upon him shortly after, but he told those who watched they need not trouble to fetch the doctor, as he knew his hour had come, and he was ready to "gang" home.'

Can you imagine the scene and the chaos as the Herdwick tup was carried upstairs, kicking at every step, to fulfil the dying wish of an old shepherd to see such a fine animal one last time?

The son, Joseph Hawell, married Margaret Roberts in 1886 and they had a son, John, and a daughter, Mary Jane. Like his father before him Joseph took a keen interest in politics.

'Of books,' wrote Rawnsley, 'he had not many, but what he had were good and he specially delighted in biographies and history. He never tired of reading of the Spacious Times of Great Elizabeth, the History of Wellington's wars or of Nelson's Exploits. And when the Royal Jubilee and Armada tercentenary came round no stronger hand or more willing heart was found in the whole neighbourhood to build up the huge bonfire on Skiddaw top than Joseph Hawell. As I write I can see him, the perspiration streaming down his honest face, building away with the peats, and handing up the

The small wooden footbridge over the Glenderaterra, a short distance upstream of the point where the beck enters the Greta.

paraffin, bucket by bucket; and hoping, as he told us then, there was not a man in canny Cumberland but would feel the fiery glow of a patriot's heart that night. But he will never help us on Skiddaw top no more . . .

'It is thought that influenza laid its deadly hand on him early in the year 1891, and simultaneously he had some ailment of the gums – toothache he called it. It must have been something more serious. He went to Keswick to see the doctor. The doctor lanced the gum, but the wound took bad ways, and within a day or so the strong man was in bed, weak and delirious. He died on Friday, February 20 (1891). He thought that some strange hands were taking him away by force to another land, and the last words he spoke were these: "No! If I must die, I will at least die an Englishman on English ground!" And so he died.

'On February 23rd, hands tender and strong, the hands of an affectionate brother and true friends, bore the body of a shepherd, dead in his prime – for he was but 36 years of age – down through the cow pasture and over the gurgling Glenderaterra, and so through the silent Brundholme Woods above the wailing Greta away to its rest in English earth beneath the shadow of the old church of St Kentigern in the Crosthwaite valley, within sight of that horned hill of Skiddaw he had loved so well.'

The edition of the *English Lakes Visitor and Keswick Guardian* for Saturday, February 28th, 1891, reported: 'The remains of Mr Joseph Hawell, of Lonscale, were interred at Crosthwaite Church on Monday afternoon with every mark of public respect. In compliance with the wishes of some of the deceased's friends and admirers, the body was brought through Keswick and the tradesmen of the town had put up shutters or drawn blinds. The fixed time for the burial was three o'clock, but the procession was delayed nearly half an hour. The service was conducted wholly by the Rev A.J. Heelis, curate. As soon as the coffin had been removed from the hearse onto the bier, Mr Heelis placed upon it a cross composed of beautiful white flowers. Other friends then reverently brought their tributes, and the lid was entirely covered. Some time elapsed before the whole of the people were seated in the church. Among them were friends from all parts of the district, as well as many Keswick people. It was not surprising that, as he had been such a tower of strength to their party, the Conservatives and members of the Primrose League mustered in great force.'

Foxgloves near the Glenderamackin.

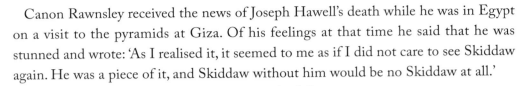

Top: The packhorse bridge over the Glenderaterra at its junction with the Greta.

Below: Skiddaw with Whit Beck running through the forested ghyll on the right. The Hawell Monument is situated on the small hillock of land at the foot of Skiddaw.

Canon Rawnsley received the news of Joseph Hawell's death while he was in Egypt on a visit to the pyramids at Giza. Of his feelings at that time he said that he was stunned and wrote: 'As I realised it, it seemed to me as if I did not care to see Skiddaw again. He was a piece of it, and Skiddaw without him would be no Skiddaw at all.'

Rawnsley wrote the following poem:

March 24, 1891
(In Memoriam)
Joseph Hawell

God has called many following the sheep,
Some to be kings and princes among men
And you He called; and Skiddaw's hollow glen
Mourns for its bravest shepherd fallen asleep;
But we who knew you still your memory keep,
And at the shearing time, beside the pen
Though gone for ever from our mortal ken
Your cheery voice will call us up the steep

For you have climbed the road that leads to heaven,
The simple road of toil and self-denied,
Of duty done to the far wandering flocks
In dewy cold, hot noons, and storm even;
And somewhere He, whose feet among the rocks
For us were red, shall lead us to your side.

H.D. Rawnsley
(Written at the Pyramids, Egypt).

Although Vicar of Crosthwaite, Rawnsley presumably could not officiate or attend Joseph Hawell's funeral and burial at the church because of his travels overseas to Egypt but he visited the family at Lonscale Farm on his return to England.

The Greta . . . a river runs through it

'On reaching home,' he wrote, 'it was with a sad heart that I neared the solitary fell side farm that had been so darkened with loss. There was the same kitchen, the fiddle was on the wall, the bacon flitches (sides of unsliced bacon) hung from the rafter, the stuffed heads of two old favourite shepherd dogs Dainty and Rob looked out from the wall, the gun rested nearby, the medicine horn and lambing bottle were in their places, and the old row of books that the father and he had so often turned to for thought and inspiration, were in their shelf – but there was no Joe!

St John's Beck.

'Robert took me by the hand and bade me sit on the settle, and he would tell me all about it. The poor wife said nothing but just rose quietly and began to spread the table and set tea and when I urged that I would not have her fash herself so or put herself out of the way for me, she urged that it would have been Joe's wish, and I said no more. Then the dogs came in to the room.

" 'Ah,' said Robert, 't' rough un Jess has not forgotten her master yet. She was sair put out o' t' way when my brother lay ill, whined at nights and would not be comforted, and she has only just now, after ten weeks coaxing, consented to follow me when I go to the fell. It's a sair heart I have as I go shepherding now, it's when I'm amang t'sheep I miss him. It comes ower me t'worst when I am looking at t'ewes that we used to talk ower together".'

The Hawells were clearly a strong shepherding family but their interests ranged wider than the world of their farm and both father and son were active politically. In fact when he made speeches on public platforms in support of the Conservative cause Joseph Hawell's opponents would make sheep-like noises in order to try and unsettle this young speaker from a farming and fell side background. Irrespective of politics, the devotion they had to life on the farm and their prized Herdwick sheep was paramount.

"What," once observed the father Edward Hawell, "could more beautify and ornament the noble parks that surround the historic mansions of the squires and peers of England than a few Herdwick rams? Their grey massive heads carried high, set off with their white ears and topping, their large flashing eyes, their solemn twisted horns, their surly noses and strong jaws, their broad projecting breasts and barrel-shaped figures dangling with long broad staples of wool, their solid necks and shoulders crowned with lion-like manes – thus rewarding the shepherd for his 20 years of careful apprenticeship to the trade of Herdwick breeder – their wide gait and short, bristling silver legs and big feet, stamping defiance to all its foes, which is distinctive of that boldness and courage these animals invariably display when fighting like a Spartan."

'Yes,' wrote Rawnsley, 'your Herdwick ram is indeed a fiery creature, as old Hawell well knew. I have seen them fighting and have heard the sound of the shock when the two rams, which have retreated face to face, suddenly rush forward and, springing from the ground, meet head to head and horn to horn.'

I find it intriguing that Hardwicke Drummond Rawnsley's Christian name 'Hardwicke' should be so closely aligned to the Herdwick of the fells in which the Hawell family took such immense pride. The definition of the Christian name Hardwicke is taken from the old English pre-7th Century word 'Heorde' meaning herd or flock and 'wik' in this instance describes a farm or outlying settlement. Apart from any other consideration – and Rawnsley and the Hawells had many other qualities in their respective lives – I cannot help but think that from the outset there would be a natural empathy between the two based solely around the names Hardwicke and Herdwick.

Among Joseph Hawell's belongings was a letter in which he begs of a neighbour the loan of a horse and gear to enable him to bring down on a sledge from Lonscale Crag one of the finest single stones there. He wishes to set it up in some field on the farm, and have his father's name upon it and his father's deeds and prowess as a breeder of Herdwick sheep. The stone would carry a single verse of descriptive poetry beneath, and he feels sure that his friend and neighbour will lend a hand 'to erect a monument to at least one member of the Hawell family whose stainless, honourable, and straight forward life will always be pointed to with pride by his descendants.'

Rawnsley, addressing his late lamented friend, concludes: 'Joseph Hawell, the horses shall yet go, and the sledge shall yet bring its heavy burden to the home farm, and on it shall be engraved two names instead of one, for there are those who honour the son who would so have honoured his sire.'

The Greta . . . a river runs through it

In the July 9th, 1892 edition of the local newspaper *The Lakes Visitor and Keswick Guardian* it was reported as follows: THE HAWELL MEMORIAL - Messrs Bromley Brothers, monumental masons, have completed a most beautiful stone to be placed on Lonscale Fell, just above the Gale. The stone is in the form of an early British wayside cross, with Scandinavian knot work on the trunk and is the design of Mrs Rawnsley. The stone is local and will endure for years to come. The cross stands upon a base of rough-tooled stone with a space worked for the verse contained in the inscription. The inscription proper is cut under the scroll work, and reads: 'In loving memory of two Skiddaw shepherds: Edward Hawell, of Lonscale, Born October 21st, 1815, Died June 2nd 1889. And his son Joseph Hawell, of Lonscale, Born December 24th, 1854, Died February 20th, 1891. Noted breeders of prize Herdwick sheep.

> *'Great shepherd of thy heavenly flock*
> *These men have left our hill*
> *Their feet were on the living rock*
> *Oh, guide and bless them still!*
> *HDR'*

The River Greta with Lonscale Fell and Skiddaw in the background.

The names of John and Robert Walker Hawell (Joseph Hawell's brothers) were later added to the stone. And so it was that Hardwicke Drummond Rawnsley was instrumental, four months after Joseph Hawell's death, in erecting the monument to the Hawells, father and son, that to this day occupies a wonderful location on the promontory of land on the Gale at the foot of Skiddaw's front and with amazing views out towards Keswick, Derwentwater and Bassenthwaite on the one side and Blencathra and the countryside stretching away to the Pennines on the other. And within earshot of Whit Beck as it makes its turbulent way off Skiddaw to the Glenderaterra and the Greta.

River Dwellers

THE HOUSE BENEATH THE BRIDGE

When a river flows through a town, as the Greta streams through Keswick, it also runs inexorably through the life of the town, past, present and future. For those of us who consider ourselves fortunate to have lived virtually on, or right next to, the river for any length of time – and for some this constitutes an entire lifetime spent in a house on the riverbank – then the link is all the stronger and it is true to say that the river has not only flowed through the life of the town and countryside but also through the landscape of our lives.

It is difficult to define the impact of a river on individual lives but you cannot help come to the conclusion that the river is often taken for granted, even by those, like myself, who genuinely appreciate its continual presence. It is only when you pause and ask the question of river dwellers (what does the river really mean in the context of your life?) that they recognise the importance of the river and the part it has played and continues to play in their lives.

Eric Bainbridge, 74, has lived by the River Greta all his life. And for a man with the word bridge in his surname I find it apt that he lives very close to two vastly different bridges. Eric and his family live at The Forge, on the outskirts of Keswick, and are directly beneath the massive road bridge over the River Greta, one of the bridge's giant columns is quite literally in his back garden. Built in 1976 the 'new' bridge, called Greta Bridge (not to be confused with the old bridge of that name at the bottom of the town) was acclaimed 'The Best Civil Engineering Structure of the Century' in 1999. The bridge is nicknamed the 'B-Dum' bridge by some locals because of the sound it makes when lorries and cars pass over the joins at

Facing page: Eric and Kath Bainbridge beneath the Greta Bridge.

Below: The bridge over the Greta at The Forge.

either end where the bridge ends and the road continues. Only a short distance downstream of the 'new' bridge is the old Forge Bridge, a beautiful stone bridge built by the mill owner Jonas Blakey Hardisty in 1817.

Eric Bainbridge came into this world in February 1938 and has lived at The Forge all his life. He was the youngest of three children, Doris, Kathleen and Eric, born to Wilson and Annie Bainbridge. Eric's father, Wilson, was shepherd and farm worker for the Spedding family at nearby Windebrowe, just up the hill from The Forge. The connection with agriculture, helping his dad on the farm all those years ago, obviously left a lasting impression on young Eric and to this day he runs a smallholding, principally sheep, at The Forge and on other land in the area.

A young Eric Bainbridge on his bike at The Forge. Eric and Jackie Newton cycled all the way to Ilkley to see Jackie's Aunt Divina.

Eric was born at No 1, the first property in a row of six small terraced cottages on the right as you enter this tiny hamlet by the River Greta. The Forge was once at the heart of industry in Keswick, firstly with copper smelting in Elizabethan times and then in various forms over the decades, especially in the second half of the 19th Century. Today, signs of its strong industrial past are evident in the shape of the imposing old mill building, at one time a woollen mill, later an electrical works and currently split into flats. The old mill race – once much wider, and now reduced to a small, narrow stream that is dry most of the time – started its life at an old sluice gate next to the Forge weir (where Eric learnt to swim) situated further upstream from the main Forge buildings. The race made its way through a tunnel carved by Elizabethan miners into the rock of a hill and then reappeared on the other side, near an old wooden bungalow (the home for many years of a one-legged character called Willie Wildman) before running down to The Forge and disappearing under the road for a short distance before emerging adjacent to the mill building next to the old stone bridge. A young lad once fell into the millrace when it was high and was swept underground beneath the road, emerging at the other side by the old mill very much the worse for wear. He did, however, survive to tell the tale.

The old stone bridge is an integral part of The Forge and its history and it is probably the case – as it doubtless was with other old bridges in the area – that these stone constructions replaced cruder wooden spans that could have been in place for many years, probably centuries, continually being repaired and renovated before being replaced by the stone versions that stand to this day. At The Forge an old wooden bridge would have provided a link between the south side of the river and what was probably an ancient route from Threlkeld through Brundholme to the north.

On the far side of the bridge is a fine big house called Myrtle Grove, previously the dowager's house for Greta Bank. Male diners from nearby Myrtle Grove apparently used the small house next to the bridge as a place in which to smoke after dinner.

On The Forge side of the bridge, adjacent to the old mill building, and directly across the way from Bridge House, there is a run-off, a sharp sloping bank of layered stones down which the water cascades in times of high water as it returns to the Greta from the millrace. Local anglers Terry ("The Heron") Appleby and Bruce ("Stack") Frampton recall the time when the millrace was used by Keswick Anglers Association to grow young salmon parr. Night time raids by otters put paid to that enterprise and the entire stock was cleaned out; the otters burrowing their way under the netting that had been stretched across the race to protect the fish from predatory herons and the like, but which proved no deterrent to the otters.

Eric Bainbridge and his wife Kathleen have lived for 45 years in the house, Riverside, situated directly beneath the massive road bridge over the Greta gorge. They have raised two boys, James and Mark, but when the road bridge was built in 1976 their home life was up in the air as a mountain of scaffolding sprang up over the Bainbridge family's suddenly diminutive-looking house by the river. The Bainbridges had been in the house for nine years at the time – it was once the home of the manager of the nearby Keswick Electric Light Company – and when the concept and exact location of the bridge was first mooted it was thought that the house would have to be demolished.

As it happened it was decided that the house could stay and, not only that, the Bainbridge family could continue to live there while the bridge was built, quite literally, over their heads. In fact, Eric got a job as a welder working for two years on the new bridge and his commute to work was as easy as stepping out of his house door and

Eric and Kath Bainbridge's house is dwarfed by the gigantic framework of scaffolding used during the construction of the bridge in 1976.
Photograph by B. Greenwood.

River Dwellers

Top: Kath hangs her washing on the line in the shelter of the road bridge over the river.

Bottom: Kath and her children Mark (left) and James with the house and scaffolding for the bridge in the background. Photograph by B. Greenwood.

going straight up a ladder to his place of work. Mind you, it was quite a big ladder, more than 120 ft of ascent. At the height of the operation the bridge used over 300 miles of scaffolding. It was some cuckoo.

The story of the family, the house and the bridge made the national newspapers and there were very impressive black and white photographs of Eric and Kathleen, their children and home dwarfed by the imposing backcloth of a colossus of a bridge covered in scaffolding.

In many of the photographs taken at the time Kathleen has a line of washing – that symbol of domestic bliss – strung out next to the house. The dust and dirt coming down from the bridge construction and associated ground works did not always make for happy washdays. Nowadays the bridge has its benefits. Kathleen's washing can be hung out to dry under the shelter of the bridge when it is raining heavily and lambing time for Eric's 50 or so ewes is also under the protective pillars of the bridge. There were, however, one or two problems with noise levels just after the bridge was completed.

"When it first opened the plates came loose and it used to mek a hell of a clatter when vehicles went ower," recalls Eric. "It was terrible and used to rattle the windows in the house. We got onto our local MP Dale Campbell-Savours and he fettled it up."

Now all you can hear is a gentle 'b-dum' as a vehicle goes over the bridge.

The Bainbridges enjoy their life under the bridge and next to the Greta.

"I love being by the river," says Eric, who has also worked as a miner in the Lakeland fells at Carrock and elsewhere. "In a flood you see all sorts going down and the wildlife round here is plentiful. I like to see dippers on the river – they're wonderful laal things, always on the move – but there doesn't seem to be as many fish now. We've a good following of red squirrels though. They run across Forge Bridge from Forge Brows and Brundholme Woods and we feed them on hazel nuts from the feeder near our back window. They're here first thing in a morning or late afternoon and early evening. We feed birds as well. We've had a good run of bullfinches recently and there was a woodpecker the other day. Nuthatches come here too and are a fantastic bird, one of the best birds there is; they always remind me of cyclists with those swept back helmets."

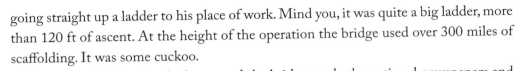

The Greta . . . a river runs through it

"Living by the river is very peaceful," adds Kathleen who is originally from Nottingham. "I love to watch the river. My sister Margaret comes on holiday and says: 'If I had a view like this I would never get anything done.' It's lovely. We look at the red squirrels, herons, dippers and lots of other birds. But we're only conscious of the sound of the river when people point it out to us. When Eric and I look out of our kitchen window we often say to each other while watching the river, the red squirrels and the birds, how privileged we feel to be living here on the river's edge."

At the time of writing, Eric and Kathleen had lived in the house below the road bridge over the Greta gorge for 45 years. The Forge at Low Brigham does not see a lot of the sun, especially in winter when some properties never feel its warming rays at all. Eric recalls The Forge in the days when it was a thriving little community.

"The community has gone with all the older folk dying," he says. "Jimmy and Ida Burgess were in their house for 60-odd years. Edith Burns came into her house when she was two and she was 82 when she died. There were the Vickers, the Gaskells, the Newtons, the Burgesses, the Burns, the Burnyeats and the Rogers. Mrs Rogers would

The community at The Forge. From left to right: Tommy Burns and his daughter Mary, Charlie Forsyth (who was manager of the electric works) Charlie's housekeeper, Mrs Slee, Florence Rogers, Ida Burgess, Jim Burgess and Mary Holbourne.

sit by the weir to collect firewood. She would be there with a swill basket, sitting right on the end of the little wall of the weir and she would fish out bits of wood for the fire with a rake as they floated down from the Bobbin Mill.

"As kids we used to ga up to Low Briery (site of the Bobbin Mill). We used to love it up there. We used to ga through the railway tunnel and would listen to see if the train was coming. You'd put your heed down on the line to see if it was coming and then if you couldn't hear owt you'd ga like hell through the tunnel."

I can recall that there were alcoves cut into the inside of the railway tunnel at regular intervals and if a train came, when we were walking down the line after a fishing trip up the river, we would duck into an alcove until the train went through.

"They only put the alcoves in the tunnel in recent years," says Eric. "They weren't in originally but we never got caught in the tunnel by a train – you could always hear the steam trains but diesels were a bit different. Anyway, we used to go up to Low Briery and there was 'Pop' Mawson up there and 'Bunty' (Marjory) and Muriel Harrison, and Norman Harrison. We used to play up there all the time as kids and used to jump across the millrace. It was a bloody good leap."

The road bridge over The Forge at Keswick also constitutes a massive leap of engineering and I wonder which of the two bridges will better stand the test of time, the old stone Forge bridge, Hardisty's Bridge built in 1817 and still going strong almost 200 years later, or the relatively 'new' concrete road bridge, known as Greta Bridge, built in 1976?

The Forge Gang.
Back row (left to right) Kathleen and Doris Bainbridge, Pat Burnyeat. Front (left to right) Tony Morris, who was an evacuee from London during the war, Malcolm Burnyeat and Jim Burgess.

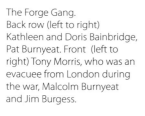

Doris's childhood days at The Forge

Eric Bainbridge's older sister, Doris Price, born in November 1934, now lives on the Latrigg Close housing estate in Keswick – at the end of the Forge Lonning – and she also has very happy memories of her childhood and life at The Forge and playing with children of her generation at nearby Low Briery. A small gang of children, the Bainbridge kids themselves, Doris, Kathleen and Eric and several other local boys and girls, all of varying ages, played together. The Forge, the surrounding countryside, the river and, just upstream from The Forge, the mill at Low Briery, were their playgrounds. It was a childhood paradise where they ran wild and free, although they did have some responsibilities.

"When we cem home from school," says Doris, "we used to have to tek the cows out of the field (where the Greta Bridge now has its giant feet) up to mi dad at Windebrowe for milking. There were usually just the two cows but they could be a handful. If they were that way out they would be charging off the lane and in among aw the nettles.

The Forge Gang, mark 2. Main row (left to right): Pat Burnyeat, Kathleen Bainbridge and her cousin Joan Taylor, Doris and Eric Bainbridge.

River Dwellers

Another job we had to do was weed the cobbled yard at Windebrowe with a knife. There were no weeds then but it's a disgrace now. That's the yard near Dairy Cottage where Tommy Nelson lived. We had to weed all the cobbles and then at night we went into the house – the Irish maids were there then – and we used to give them a hand to churn the butter."

When Doris and her brother and sister and friends were not at school or carrying out odd jobs at home and on the farm at Windebrowe, the world was their own from morning until night, interrupted only by meal times.

"We were always playing on the river," recalls Doris. "We used to swim in the Garden Hole, a big pool just up from The Forge and down from the weir. We'd swim there and by the sluice at the weir. We'd walk across the wooden top of the weir to the island. We called it Pharaoh Island. I don't know how it got that name but we were told that was what it was cawd. And then there was Bluebell Island further up by Low Briery. There were no restrictions on where we went – we just went anywhere.

"We would also play alongside the millrace. I learned to swim at the sluice and then we graduated to swimming at the Garden Hole. Jessie Gaskell was living in Bridge House then, and Audrey Maxwell (nee Nelson – Kenny Nelson's sister, and Doris Price's cousin) fell off this rock at the Garden Hole. It was very slippery and Audrey said 'can you remember the time when I fell in – I slipped off that bloomin' rock and Jessie (Gaskell) dived in and got me out?'

The swimming party. Kathleen Bainbridge and Freda Vickers in the pool above the Forge weir.

"I can remember the Wilkinson family going to the weir on a Sunday afternoon – father Billy (the local cartoonist), his wife Mary and their children Donald, Bill and Jill. Jill was just a laal wee thing then. In the summer we were up there every weekend at the sluice and the weir. Summer was mostly spent in the river. That was our life. When we weren't there we were away up in Brundholme Woods and on Latrigg, sometimes at Horseshoe Crag or Forge Brows. We were always along there. We would collect bluebells and wild flowers by the armful and in the Autumn picked brambles by the bucket full.

"We were always everywhere – up at Audrey and Kenneth's at Windebrowe, at Dairy Cottage. We were up at the Bobbin Mill a lot as well. We used to run up the other side of the river along Forge Brows and come over on t'stones to the Bobbin Mill. Some times we went up the line to the Bobbin Mill to play with Muriel and Bunty and Norman – there wasn't a lot of kids up there, just them three. You (the author) would just be a baby then and when you grew up you and your sister Margaret would be the only kids at Low Briery.

"We were away from ivverybody up there at The Forge and Low Briery. It was our own little world. Nobody knew where The Forge and the Bobbin Mill were in them days . . . there were no signs on the road to say. And when we went to school and said where we lived other kids would say 'where's that?' It was all just up there, ratching about, all together. I thought it was lovely. It was different. Kids today don't do owt do they? They just play on computers. In winter we would sit in, we didn't even have a radio for a lot of years and there was definitely no television. We sat in by the fire and we'd mebbe knit or read books. We used to play games, Ludo and aw that. Monopoly. There wasn't anything laid on . . . well, you didn't want owt laid on. We created our own entertainment. And if it snowed we'd be out in the big field, sledging. Right from the top to the bottom and when you got to the bottom there was the millrace full of icy water – so you used to drop off the sledge before you got to it."

Doris, jokingly, is keen to impress on me how backward we were at Low Briery compared with life at The Forge.

A mixture of facial expressions from (left to right) Doris Bainbridge, her mother Annie, Eric (on Annie's lap) and a shy Kathleen. Inset: Riverside house and free-range poultry.

River Dwellers

From Doris Price's
Forge family album.

Top row (left to right):
The courting couple,
Doris Bainbridge and
Alfie Price on Forge Bridge;
Kathleen Bainbridge and her
sister Doris in the Forge field
with Willie Wildman's wooden
bungalow in the background;
Kathleen and Doris Bainbridge
with (right) Audrey Nelson.

Second row from top (left to
right): Kathleen Bainbridge
and her younger brother Eric
and bike on Forge Bridge;
Sitting at the end of the Forge
Weir are (left to right) Kathleen
Bainbridge, Ann Gaskell and
Freda Vickers.

Third row from top (left to
right): A man, his pipe and his
car. Wilson Bainbridge;
Jim Burgess on the front of the
bike surrounded by (left to
right) Kathleen Bainbridge,
Wilson Bainbridge, and
Ida Burgess; Mike McNichol
and Kathleen Bainbridge.

Bottom (left to right): One of
Wilson Bainbridge's
sheepdogs, the ever-smiling
Glen; "Fluffy", the cat my
grandmother Jane Richardson
gave to a young Doris Price;
Brenda Holbourne, who later
emigrated to Australia, and
Kathleen Bainbridge at the
back of the terraced houses
at The Forge.

"You were really primitive at Low Briery," says Doris, an exponent of a deadpan and dry sense of humour. "You were primitive up there weren't you? You never had nothing – no lights, nothing. You all had oil lamps, but what a fire risk! Everyone up there came down to the garage (opposite Toll Bar Cottage and Calvert Bridge) for paraffin. Quirks had the garage then and it was just a wooden shack and everyone came in from High Briery, The Forge and Low Briery and there was a big drum outside and you had to pump it into your can. And then you lot used to tek your batteries down to Denwoods to get charged up for the radio. Well, we never had a radio for years . . . but you were very primitive up there.

"We didn't have a bath either. We had electric in just so many rooms, one bedroom and the kitchen and the living room. We had some oil lamps but you were far worse off than us. There were three washhouses on the end of the terrace (six houses on the terrace) at The Forge. My mum washed in the middle one on a Monday wid Mary Burns. There was a set pot and fire underneath and a mangle and a dolly tub, and a wooden tub and possers. There were aw sorts of things. And we used the water from the washhouse for a bath. We had no hot water and set bath in them days. It was either a tin bath in front of the fire or standing up in the kitchen sink.

"We didn't have a cooker as such. All the cooking was done on the oven range next to the fire. We had a coal fire going in the living room but the houses were very cold and damp. The side of The Forge where we lived never got the sun until Spring. The sun disappeared in October and cem back in about March. But I've many happy memories of my childhood at The Forge. The best years of your life."

Only a few families lived in the various houses at The Forge but community spirit was strong. One of the more eccentric characters was Robert Wildman, or Willie Wildman as he was known. Goodness only knows what the politically correct and increasingly paranoid 21st Century would have made of him? The information on his background varies. Some people say that he was a batman or served with Brigadier General Wilfred Spedding in World War 1 or, alternatively, was with the Red Cross at the front line and was blown up and badly injured while tending to the wounded. He certainly lost a leg – apparently in the war – and wore a wooden leg as a replacement. One thing is certain. After the horrendous and pointless slaughter of the so-called Great

Willie Wildman and Kathleen Bainbridge. This was at the time that Willie broke his good leg.

War, General Spedding bumped into Wildman on the street in Keswick one day, enquired as to his well being and Wildman told him that he was, to all intents and purposes, homeless. As a result General Spedding provided land for Wildman to build a small wooden bungalow near the rock tunnel and beside the millrace at the head of The Forge. A little wooden bridge over the millrace gave access to the property and its garden. The empty building is still there to this day and was latterly occupied for 40 years by local bus driver, and one time beck watcher (or bailiff) Kevin Connolly and his family. Kevin and his wife Bridget live in a flat in central Keswick and Kevin says that he would love to be back in the little wooden bungalow by the river because he loved his life there. Kevin and Bridget raised two daughters, Sue and Lucy, while living at The Forge.

"We were there for 40 years from 1970," says Bridget, "two years after we were married and we loved it, we were very happy up there. Keswick could be very busy but it was very quiet at The Forge and it was a different world by the river and we had good neighbours in Eric and Kathleen and other people who lived there."

Willie Wildman lived alone in the bungalow for many years. Doris Price remembers him well from her childhood: "He was eccentric. He brought all his coal from the coal yard, pushing it from Keswick in an old Victorian-style, high-sided pram. He also med toffee and would give it to local children. There was no harm in him but sometimes he wouldn't speak for weeks because he was very religious and was with the Lord. When he wasn't with the Lord he'd speak and was normal but he was gaily often with the Lord. Aw the kids in Keswick got to know him and would come up to see him – he med them toffee and gave them religious cards (he also deposited money with Dixons' newsagents in Keswick so that local children could go in and buy books to the value of £1).

"There was ya time that he brok' his other leg, his good leg and he stopped with Jessie and Billy Gaskell at Bridge House and there's a photograph of him in a wheelchair. Their young lads Alf and John, they were devils like. Mr Wildman used to chase us round the bungalow. Well, Alf went the other way and he ran right into him and he knocked him into t' millrace, quite by accident. They'd a hell of a job to git him out."

Young Jill swam the beck at 'Sandy'

The Jill Wilkinson described by Doris Price as a "laal wee thing" as a child is now a little older but only marginally bigger. She lives with her husband, the professorial and likeable Rod Donington-Smith, at the Wilkinson family home, Greta Cottage, Brigham, opposite The Twa Dogs pub. It was at The Twa Dogs where Jill's father, Billy Wilk, the caricaturist, exhibited a lot of his finest work. Many of his superb cartoons are still on the walls of The Twa Dogs and represent a wonderful cross section of local characters from a particular period in Keswick's recent history.

Billy Wilkinson and his wife Mary had three children, Bill, Donald and Jill. And Jill has particularly fond memories of their life at Greta Cottage, backing onto the river itself, and of summer afternoons spent on the river at Town's Field – known as "Townsie" locally – and on the island next to the The Forge weir where people had their time-honoured picnic spots on a Sunday afternoon.

Jill and Rod Donington-Smith at Greta Cottage.

"You have an idea in your mind that the summers then were all sunshine and blue sky and red hot days, but they can't have been," says Jill. "We went up the river on a Sunday afternoon when the sun was shining but we always had the Sunday roast lunch first at midday and poor mother was left to clear and wash up. Dad and Bill and Donald and me would go up to the island and mum would be left to prepare the picnic tea which she would then carry up to The Forge. She'd stand at the end of the weir and yell and somebody would go and help her carry it across the weir on the narrow wooden shelf that stretched across the top of the weir from the sluice gate to the island.

"We always used to sit in the grass on the island at the end of the weir. Our Uncle Stan always used to be on 'his' rock further down from the island. He was an athletic Charles Atlas type figure and I remember him as always being a sort of mahogany colour. He used to lie on his rock all day long. My cousin Bobby and his mum and dad (Jack and Jan Brockbank) always used to picnic on the Brundholme side of the river, opposite the big wall. We just seemed to respect each other's space. It was just something that we did on summer Sundays.

All of a summer's day at the back of the Wilkinson house by the Greta. From the front: Bobby Brockbank, Jill Wilkinson, Bill Wilkinson, Donald Wilkinson and Smut the dog.

"I couldn't swim then. Don and Bill and dad would be swimming and when I think about it now it wasn't very clean, it would be as muddy as anything. You walked in and it looked as though you were wearing wellies made of mud. It wasn't clean but it didn't seem to matter.

"We also used to spend an awful lot of time on the riverbank here at Greta Cottage. We always had a fire going. It wouldn't happen today, but we were left down there with a fire on the riverbank for hours on end and we used to bake tatties. We put them in the fire with their soil on, pushed the tatties into the bottom of the fire and left them all afternoon. Then we'd dig them out of the red-hot ashes and eat them, the black, the muck and the potato and everything and they were absolutely fantastic. We used to pinch dad's rhubarb from the bottom of the garden and boil it up in tins on the fire. We once dug a hole on the riverbank, a deep hole that you could drop into and put tin sheeting on the top of and create a little hidey-hole. The river flooded and filled the hole and our dog, our lovely little dog, the runt of the litter that took fits, had a fit and fell in the hole and drowned. It was very sad. It was called Smut, Billy's dog, a Lakeland terrier.

"I also remember going swimming up at the Sands on Town's Field. People would either go to the big pool at the Sands or the smaller one at the Stones, the top pool in Townsie. I went from our house to the river with my swimming suit on beneath a mac because it was raining. You went to the Sands and you went in the river because it was summer. You got into the river, you had your swim and then you put your mac back on because you were frozen and you ran home to get into your clothes. And you didn't have a bath or a shower or anything like that, you just came back from the river and dried yourself and got straight into your clothes.

"We spent an awful lot of time by the river. We used to go up to the Sands and dig channels down the edges and race sticks."

Jill recalls that she made her first tentative swimming strokes in the shallow water of the millrace at Low Briery on an outing with the landlord of The Twa Dogs, Gerald Hayes and his daughter, Valerie, who also learned to swim in the race.

"When you could swim across the river at the widest part of the Sands you had really made it," Jill added. "You learned to swim there and when I think about it now it was a couple of foot or less of level sand and then it shelved off and went very deep all of a sudden. You could only really swim when you could swim to the other side. Bill would swim with me on my first venture across the river – we would go together – and we went across and I got out on the other bank and I was really proud. He brought me back but before we got to the sandy beach (which gave Sandy its name) he went off swimming on his own. I stood up but it was still too deep and I sank like a stone and came up spluttering. Fortunately he came and hooked me out."

Jill and a friend, Jackie Francis, spent a lot of time on Bluebell Island, opposite the bobbin mill at Low Briery.

"We used to mek dens on the island," Jill recalls. "You never saw another soul. I remember we once left the island for some unknown reason and went up on to Latrigg. It was raining and we were under a big fir tree out of the rain and we had our own little fire on the go. We were warm, it was dry under the fir tree and we had our fire. And the idea of getting up and walking home in the rain didn't have a lot of appeal. So we just sat under our tree and kept the fire going until it got dark. My mam and dad had gone up to the island to find us and we weren't there. I don't know whether dad found us or we just made our own way home eventually but they were really stressed out.

"We spent entire days at the den we made on the island. We'd go up with food to cook on the fire. It's a bit scary really, I don't know if I'd want kids to go off these days and have a fire. Tatties! We lived on tatties," Jill laughs out loud, "and we spent a lot of time paddling around in the river."

Donald Wilkinson recalls that they would also go onto Latrigg and make a corral into which they would attempt to chase Herdwick sheep and, having tired of being shepherds, would race in bogies down the steep hill on Brundholme Road, from the high point just below Horseshoe Crag to Windebrowe. Sometimes their wooden bogies would be tied together nose to tail and they would set off in a convoy; heaven help anyone they met on the road.

Jill remembers that as children they would often go digging for the nuts that could be found in the soil up to a foot down under a tall slender plant that used to grow in the wild and at roadsides. It was called

Bill and Donald Wilkinson by the rock at the foot of Sandy in Town's Field.

a 'Jobby Gernal' and well known 'Jobby Gernal' digger and angler Bobby Brockbank, formerly of Lydias Cottages, Brigham, reveals that these were in fact the pignut, also known as Conopodium majus. The nuts would be dug out with a knife and fingernails and their taste, similar to that of a hazelnut, was well worth the effort and the soil-engrained fingernails. Again, they were not too fussy if the pignuts came with dirt attached for added flavour. Jill recently went on an unsuccessful 'Jobby Gernal' hunt to Town's Field, near to where the stream she calls "Skinny Gutter" runs into the Greta at the head of Forge Lonning and what was recently, until it closed, Castlerigg Engineering works.

Looking back, Jill Wilkinson is dismayed at the way in which people used the river as a dumping ground and thought nothing of it.

"In the old days it was one way of getting rid of your rubbish," she says. "Someone on Lydias Cottages who was having a sort-out threw an old fridge over the back wall of their house into the river, I couldn't believe it. Everybody threw rubbish in the river and that was it."

Brigham in the 1950s / 60s was, not unlike the Forge and Low Briery, a self-contained community in its own right with the Twa Dogs, and its landlord, Gerald Hayes and Brigham School at the heart of the area. Families who lived at Brigham were the

Billy Wilk and grandchild Paul by the Greta.

Bertrams, Brockbanks, Burnyeats, Tysons, Hewers, Cowperthwaites and, of course, the Wilkinsons, to name a few. Billy Wilk Snr and his wife Mary at one time ran a little shop to the front of their house. I remember it well because you could get four Black Jacks for a penny and the gob stoppers were so big it was virtually impossible to manoeuvre them around your mouth; to suck over enthusiastically on a gob stopper from Wilk's shop was to risk death by choking.

The closeness of the river to the little shop had a down side for the business and tested Mary Wilkinson's patience.

"Dad used to go fishing at dinner times when they had the shop which didn't please mum too much because his fishing trips would go on longer than the hour allowed for the midday meal," Jill explained. "Dad was very fond of how the light caught the river. He used to spend a long time watching the heron and the dippers and feeding the ducks. If any kids came here he'd take them down to the river and he had a call for the ducks."

While fishing on the Greta I often came across Billy Wilk when I worked my way downstream from Town's Field to Calvert Bridge at the back of Brigham cottages and houses. Wilk would inevitably pop out for the crack and, if I had one to spare, I would give him a fat brown trout for his breakfast. Always full of conversation Wilk was a great character who loved socialising and was genuinely interested in people, life and wildlife. He was also a past master when it came to telling tall stories.

On one occasion on the riverbank he told me his heron story. This centred on a heron which was having a lot of trouble eating an eel it had caught. Wilk always told the story with a straight face. It was, he said, something he had seen with his very own eyes.

The heron caught the eel and swallowed it whole but the eel had gone right through its body and come out at the other end. The eel swam away, the heron caught and ate it again and the eel escaped in the same way. This was repeated several times before the heron caught the eel and then sat firmly on a rock in the middle of the beck and stayed there to swallow and digest his catch.

And if you believed that, then you would believe owt.

Wilk and my dad Tommy Richardson were great drinking pals for many years and would frequent The Twa Dogs, The Pheasant Inn on Crosthwaite Road and, as night

took over from evening, The Queen's Hotel in Keswick. Many of Wilk's drawings were on display in all three drinking places. Wilk spent many a happy night, supping, talking and telling tall stories to locals and visitors alike and, occasionally, he would burst into song in the front bar of the Queens with Billy Blakeley, a former bobbin mill worker, on the harmonica. Wilk quite literally exploded into a song and the first words were virtually shouted. When Wilk sang you knew it and it was an expression of raw enthusiasm, a passion for life, a pint or three of beer and good company. Once started there was no stopping him.

Wilk's drawings of local characters were taken entirely from memory. He would study his subject in the bar of The Twa Dogs, say, and then retreat across the road to Greta Cottage where he would produce a drawing, show it to one or two people and, if he was happy with it and the response he received, complete the work and either give it to the subject himself or hang it in one of the numerous pubs that were his unofficial and impromptu art galleries. Wilk always drew men, never women. He had discovered, to his cost, that the fairer sex did not appreciate caricatures and much preferred more flattering portrayals.

I love Wilk drawings. Many are hunt related and one of his favourite subjects was the late Blencathra huntsman, Johnnie Richardson. But there were also fishermen, darts players and drinkers, all, without exception, local people and legends in their own lunchtimes. Many were regulars at The Twa Dogs at the time when the aforementioned and unforgettable Gerald Hayes and his wife Anne were the tenants. Gerald had previously worked as a bobbin turner at Low Briery and he and his family lived on the terrace of houses at High Briery before going into The Twa Dogs. Gerald was a real character, a very keen hound trailer, fisherman and sportsman and he features in one of Wilk's cartoons as 'The man wot trains cup winners.' Gerald lost a leg in a motorbike accident but the metal leg he wore as a replacement did not deter him from leading as full a life as possible. He did, however, suffer the indignity of being pulled off his feet after hooking a salmon while fishing at the Yewletts on the River Greta. But there was, apparently, no prouder man in Keswick than Gerald Hayes on the day he took delivery of a brand new car. Gerald would regularly go and sit in his car on The Twa Dogs car park, not drive anywhere (he had not passed his driving test at that stage) but simply to enjoy his new found status as a motorist. His first car was a green Austin Cambridge and he later drove a dark brown Morris Oxford. The cars were specially adjusted for Gerald's artificial leg but he invariably set off in a series of jumps and stop-starts before accelerating alarmingly out of the car park and across Penrith Road.

The Twa Dogs in those days was a gambling den with Gerald at the heart of the operation until a visit from two plainclothes detectives put a stop to that activity.

Gerald was not the only one at The Twa Dogs involved in dubious activities.

Pat Asquith, who lived at Browfoot at the end of the Forge Lonning, recalls that she and other children would remove old bottles from the crates at the back of The Twa Dogs and take them round to the front where Gerald would give them three pence a bottle for 'returning' the empties. They would spend their ill-gotten gains on sweets at Wilk's shop across the road. Gerald was wise to what was going on, but went along with it anyway although he occasionally, by way of recompense, got the children to stack the crates from which they were taking the bottles!

Another local character at that time was little Tommy Burns, a former Bobbin Mill worker, who was only about four foot tall. What he lacked in height he made up for with the amount of beer that he drank; unfortunately he was not of the hollow legs brigade and often came to grief in wending his way home. He lived on the terrace at The Forge with his two daughters, Mary and Edith, and his weekly drunken wobbles along the Forge Lonning usually ended in a hedge from which he had to be rescued by one of his daughters.

A young Pat Asquith, watching and listening from her bedroom window late at night, would see and hear the drama unfold.

Wilk cartoon of Joe Nicholson, darts player at The Twa Dogs. Caricature courtesy of the Wilkinson family.

River Dwellers

"All you could hear for an hour was laal Tommy shouting 'Mary, Mary, will you come and git me out of this dyke. I'm pricklin' like mad and it's hurting. Mary, Mary . . .' Then I would see Mary coming down the lonning and she would say 'come on you silly old bugger, you've been at it again.' And she used to drag him out of the hedge and tek him yam. It happened every weekend."

Gerald Hayes once made the mistake of giving Tommy a lift home when he found him the worse for wear on Penrith Road and, having arrived at The Forge with his passenger, was set upon by one of his daughters for getting her father drunk. As it happened Tommy had not been in The Twa Dogs that particular night but had been down town for his drink.

Many of Wilk's cartoons in The Twa Dogs were accompanied by a one liner such as 'The man wot liked his pop.' Still on show in The Twa Dogs to this day 'The man wot liked his pop' is a particular favourite of mine and is a drawing of the flame-haired Robin Telford, head thrown back and supping a pint. Robin is a great conversationalist and he is also in the habit of stopping and throwing back one last remark by way of a parting shot after you have both wandered off in separate directions. One day on the street in Keswick we had touched on the exorbitant price of drink and as he walked off he had only gone about 10 paces when he suddenly turned and shouted back:

"Hey, Keith . . ."

"What?"

"Yer know what this country needs don't yer?"

"What's that Robin?"

"Cheaper drink and wider pavements!"

There's no answer to that double-edged observation

"THE MAN WOT LIKES HIS POP"

WILK

from the mouth of 'The man wot liked his pop.' Robin lives on Latrigg Close, the housing estate next to The Twa Dogs, and he was in the habit of appearing at the back door of the pub at night with a coal shovel in his hands and carpet slippers on his feet. He had slipped out of his nearby house on the pretext of going to get some coal for the fire, but had popped across to the pub for a quick one. Or two. Hopefully he did not forget to collect a shovel of coal on the return journey.

Another Wilk drawing of which I am fond is that of a character called 'Pom' Boustead, a character who drank at The Pheasant and whose cartoon was hung on the wall of the pub, together, incidentally, with many others including assorted darts players, bikers, horse racers and, showing that Wilk's work has spanned the generations, a picture drawn in the 1930s of Robin Telford's father fishing on the river. The drawing of 'Pom' is a black and white one suggesting it is also of early vintage and the words accompanying it are: 'Another record for The Pheasant. Thirty tops in an hour. Nice work.' This referred to 'Pom' Boustead's liking for small bottles of strong ale and the caricature shows him surrounded by the many bottles and caps he collected on his table during the course of a night's dedicated supping. The barman would not be allowed to remove the bottles until 'Pom' had squeezed out every last drop and got full value for his money. It is a fantastic image of 'Pom' with his prominent nose, overcoat and cap and sturdy hob-nailed, curved boots. Although he lived virtually across the road from The Pheasant 'Pom' would occasionally go home the long way round at dead of night, especially if it was moonlit, and would walk the 10 miles or so around Derwentwater. When he was not in The Pheasant setting new drinking records, 'Pom' was a lengthsman for Cumberland County Council and was also a student of the literature of Charles Dickens. For added interest he also specialised in speaking entirely in rhyme.

"You won't get any knowledge if you don't go to college," was one of his many sayings.

Wilk cartoon of 'Pom' Boustead who set a new drinking record at The Pheasant.
Caricature courtesy of the Wilkinson family.

Autumn colours on the beech trees flanking Sandy pool
and below on the River Greta at Town's Field.

The Greta . . . a river runs through it

When Latrigg Close was a beautiful hayfield

Unlike their father – who would have loved to have received a further education and taken up a full time career in art – both Wilk's sons, Donald and Bill, and daughter Jill went on to study at art college and became artists and teachers, with Jill specialising in ceramics. Bill now lives and works in France while Donald is in Cumbria, in Hadrian's Wall territory at Banks, near Lanercost and frequently returns to his childhood home in Keswick. Over the years Donald has studied and portrayed the River Greta in its different moods.

"I spent hours drawing the river, looking at the colour and the juxtaposition of rocks," he says. "There's a chestnut tree on the far bank at the back of our house and I remember seeing water voles on the other side, washing themselves and sitting in the sun. There was a little stream that comes out on the other side after running under a bridge over the drive to Windebrowe at the top of the wood."

Like his sister Jill, Donald has many happy memories of life at Greta Cottage.

"The river has always been a part of our lives," he says, "and if you had been away for any length of time and you got back late at night the first thing you did in the morning was go down and look at the river at the bottom of the garden. I used to spend a lot of time down there – I always think of the noise of a dipper going up the river and watching it as it swam underwater off a rock looking for food. I used to mess around in Town's Field and I remember finding a dipper's nest just below The Sands among the rocks there. We used to find lampreys in the fast white water above the Sands. They sucked against the rock and would hang on to your fingers. And there was a great spot for minnows there in a little side channel. Dad would always look out of the landing window of the house of a morning and he would invariably say 'The heron's there again.' The heron always stood on the other side of the beck in the morning. The river was an enormous part of dad's life. He took us onto Calvert Bridge and showed us salmon lying in the pool below.

"As a child I found the river quite mysterious in a way, especially some of the really deep pools like the one at Calvert Bridge and the water above Forge Weir. I always think of the Greta as being a green mineral colour. It was pure and then there was the sound, it was always there. If you had people staying over they thought it was raining hard during the night but it was the sound of the river. We usually slept with the windows open and the river was a thread that ran through your life; the stories you heard that were related to the river and the people who lived in Lydias Cottages and the community that was Brigham. As a child you knew everybody who lived there. The railway line ran through and we would put pennies on the line and they would be squashed to twice their size by the train. Latrigg Close (a housing estate built in 1950) used to be a most beautiful hay field before the houses were built.

"I enjoyed being in the river. We played there all the time. Mam and dad once rescued a duckling that was being worried by drakes and they kept it in the bath in the house until it was fit to release. Strangely enough, some time later a mother duck brought a whole brood of little ducks right up to the front of the house. It was the only time this had ever happened and mother said: 'I'm sure that's the duck we looked after.' The

The Greta taken from the railway bridge over the river next to Denton House.

Wilkinson children also carried out their own rescue missions and for them this was to help fledgling jackdaws as they crash-dived into the river below on their maiden flights from nests high in the big wall at The Forge.

"We used to get them out of the river and put them in the long grass on the island," Donald recalls.

Donald also remembers elephants drinking in the River Greta.

"The circus came to town and the elephants went down to the river to drink when the circus trucks and animals came into Keswick along Penrith Road. The elephants would go over the green on the top side of Calvert Bridge and down to the water for a drink."

At that time the circus and the fair usually set up in the field near Joe Clark's farm at Brigham. In other years the circus and a fair were situated near the old stone Greta Bridge at the bottom end of town, on land near what was Ravens Farm. Today, if a circus visits town, it sets up tent in Town's Field, but there are no longer any elephants. Elephants, however, also had another connection with the Greta in that virtually every outsized boulder, such as the ones above Forge Weir and at Low Briery and others in Town's Field, were always known by local kids as 'Jumbo' after the elephant of 19th Century zoo and circus fame.

The River Greta, quite remarkably, also has its own movie history. Donald Wilkinson remembers that the river was used as a location for the making of part of a movie called *Loyal Heart* which starred a sheepdog called 'Fleet' owned by local shepherd Joe Relph. The movie was made in 1946 in glorious black and white and was filmed on location in the Keswick, St John's in the Vale and Threlkeld area. The movie is about a local farmer and his dog wrongly accused of sheep stealing. The dog, "Fleet," and a young friend (son of the accused farmer) resolve the situation in the nick of time and they all live happily ever after.

The film, produced and directed by Oswald Mitchell, was made by The Strand Film Company and the Anglo-American Film Corporation. It starred Harry Welchman and Percy Marmont with Philip Kay as the farmer's son. The film is based on the novel *Beth a Sheepdog* by Ernest Lewis. The acting in the film is pretty ordinary and the dialogue risible – with the actors speaking a polite, stilted version of Cumbrian dialect that emerges as a poor parody of how a local shepherd supposedly talks. Nevertheless it is interesting to see the Cumbrian landscape and farms of the 1940s and the storyline is passable. You can see a full version of the movie on the Internet and the River Greta appears in a scene where "Fleet" the sheepdog is swept away down the fast moving river and is feared drowned. However, it is not the real sheepdog but a dummy on a rope. The scene takes place in the white water at the head of Sandy in Town's Field.

"Joe Relph's dog was a champion sheepdog," says Donald. "Joe was obviously off camera during the shoot but you could see the dog looking at him during filming and wondering 'what the hell's going on here?' We saw what we thought was a dead dog on the riverbank in Town's Field, but it was a stuffed dog attached to a rope."

The Twa Dogs as it used to be. Shepherds meet. Geordie Hutton, of Setmabanning Farm, Threlkeld, Wilson Bainbridge and Joe Relph at an event in Fitz Park.

River Dwellers

The Days of Water Powererd
Mills

Toll Bar Cottage in the days before solar panels
were attached to the slate roof.

The Greta . . . a river runs through it

Toll Bar Cottage and Calvert Bridge

Paul and Eleanor Paxon came to Keswick from Coventry in 1970 and they and their family, Adam, Lizzie and Ben, all born and bred in Keswick, have always considered Toll Bar Cottage, Penrith Road, right next to the beautiful Calvert Bridge, to be their family home. Lizzie now lives and works in Devon, Ben is at nearby Thornthwaite while Adam occupies the cottage with his parents and has a contemporary jewellery-making business in a studio room overlooking the River Greta and the oval-shaped Calvert Bridge pool. It is a workplace to die for and Adam has been keeping a diary of the wildlife and events on the river he has seen from his workshop window (see page 67).

Paul and Eleanor left the Midlands because they wanted to start a new life together elsewhere (the hippy dream - Strawberry Fields for ever) and they thought the Lake District would be a good beginning. Eleanor packed in her job as a teacher, Paul left

Paul and Eleanor Paxon and their son Adam at the water's edge by Toll Bar Cottage with Calvert Bridge in the background.

employment in industry and they headed north, their home a tent and their car a clapped-out Volkswagen Beetle with several million miles on the clock. Forty years later and it seems that Paul Paxon was put on this planet, or so it seems to me, to work on the perpetual improvement and extension of Toll Bar Cottage – the latest additions being 12 solar panels on the roof – while Eleanor, a former Keswick postal worker, was getting fully mobile again after suffering a setback courtesy of a lightning strike while out walking on a Lakeland fell. Both Paul and Eleanor are long-standing (quite literally) volunteers at Keswick's Theatre by the Lake.

Toll Bar Cottage was the site of a former toll gate until 1883 when the turnpike system came to an end. The cottage is situated on the main Penrith Road right opposite Richard and Lynne Cooke's Londis store and filling station. Despite the close proximity of the traffic – the busy main road is only a couple of feet from the walls of the cottage – the Paxons live in relative paradise on the river side of the property, with the river and garden providing a peaceful antidote to all the coming and going and a-toing and a-froing and a-going and a-doing of a 21st Century tourist town and a road that is increasingly thrang with traffic, even at the supposedly quieter times of year. With the road on one side and the calm of the river, the pool and the bridge on the other, life at Toll Bar Cottage must be like experiencing a 21st Century variation of environmental schizophrenia.

"It can be," says Paul. "Some times in the garden you notice the traffic more than you do in the house. If you go back to the days before the A66 by-pass came through, everything came past here and you couldn't be closer to the road if you tried with just a small strip of pavement between the house wall and the road."

Despite the proximity of the traffic, Eleanor would not change her life by the river for the world.

"I can't imagine living anywhere else," she says. "I love living by the river. I find it quite difficult to put into words. I just know that if I ever think about moving away from here my first thought is – 'but what about the river?' Life without being by this river does not bear thinking about. I think I would actually suffer as a consequence. I think we may take the river for granted. I see it every morning but the thought of it not being there – I can't comprehend that really."

When Paul and Eleanor arrived in Keswick in the early Seventies they had very little money, no jobs and were camping at Dalebottom, St John's in the Vale. They started knocking on doors to see if anyone knew of a place available for rent. The farmer's wife at Shoulthwaite Farm said she thought that Toll Bar Cottage in Keswick might be on the market. The Spedding family owned the cottage and the estate's bailiff at Windebrowe, Tommy Nelson, lived at Dairy Cottage; where William Wordsworth and his sister Dorothy lived for a time in the late 18th Century. Tommy was on holiday but his son, Kenny, was down at the nearby Forge and said he would pop up and let Paul and Eleanor see the property.

"We didn't go through the door," explains Paul. "Kenny just opened the window and we stepped right in. Eleanor stepped into the room and said straight away 'I want to live here'."

"It was just the feel of the room," Eleanor added. "I can't explain what it was – it just had a nice feel. My mother grew up in Teddington with the Thames at the bottom of the garden so I had grown up with stories of the river and when we came here and saw this river it was a dream come true."

Today, on warm summer evenings, the Paxons swim in the deep pool below Calvert Bridge.

"As children we were never out of the water," says Adam. "From my studio I see wildlife all day and I'm fascinated by the fact that the river is always different, ever-changing and never still. In as short a span as five minutes you can see many changes. It shows you what the weather's doing further upstream if it becomes coloured or rises quite suddenly without any rain in the immediate vicinity. At other times it has a slate-grey, lime-green quality or a much stronger peaty colour. Then there are the different colour qualities and reflections that you see below the surface of the water.

"When we were children we had mental maps of the river. It was our playground. A childhood friend, Adrian Bacon, said to me the other day that he had been on the river his whole life. He knew the river from a child and from fishing at different points. I wasn't a fisherman but I knew exactly what he meant. I could place my mind anywhere

Fast water where the River Greta narrows at Town's Field.

up and down the river and I still can. I love that. We are pretty well off here for wildlife . . . we have otters, the kingfishers are back again and we get sparrow hawks that flush birds out of the trees overhanging the river, particularly late in the afternoon. There's a heron which fishes in the pool of light created by a street light or the light bouncing off the windows of the nearby timeshare buildings. After they have just stocked the river with trout you'll see it spear fish, 12 attempts 12 fish. You'll see it night after night. The heron is fantastic. I haven't seen salmon in the pool for quite a while but there is something big that jumps late at night. It's got to be the biggest pool on the river."

One of the more unusual occupants of the pool at Calvert Bridge was a goat.

"It was in our early days here and concerned a local character called Malcolm Marley," Paul explained. "I looked out of the window one day and there was a goat in the river and Malcolm on the bridge. The goat was from Greta Bank Farm and had been tethered on the lane to feed on the verges just up from the bridge. Malcolm, who was a little eccentric, had met somebody in Fitz Park and they had been talking about the Vietnam War and he had got rather upset. Anyway he came down the lane and this goat went to head butt him, so he untied it, picked it up, went down to the bridge and tossed it in the river. Fortunately the goat survived."

We have always known the pool simply as Calvert Bridge but I wonder if it has another name?

"Jackie Thompson (who lived at Brigham and worked with my dad Tommy and Ernie Thwaites for the Buttermere Greenslate Company at their yard in the centre of Keswick) used to call it Stand Dub," Paul explains. "They always knew it as Stand Dub as kids. He came out with this tale and I don't know if it was true or not. Anyway, Jackie said to me 'it was called Stand Dub because all the sewage from this point up river used to come down the beck and stand in it. It used to settle in there and that's why it became known as such a good fishing pool.' We always knew when Brigham School was out because kids would be on the bridge with their legs hanging over the parapet and they'd be fishing."

Jackie Thompson, incidentally, also gave the Paxons a gift of cuttings of Virginia Creeper from his nearby house at Brigham and it is this thriving plant that now covers Toll Bar Cottage and the adjacent Calvert Bridge.

The Paxons rented Toll Bar Cottage for £3 a week in 1970 (the deal was sealed on Calvert Bridge a week or so after the impromptu through-a-window site visit with a shake of the hands) and a year later, when they could afford the down payment on a mortgage, the Paxons bought the cottage from the Speddings for the princely sum of £2,250. I dare say it is worth a little more these days.

It has often occurred to me that the sound of a river is very therapeutic and especially so in the quiet of night when sleeping by a river with the window open; as I did during the summer months at Low Briery when we lived in the terraced house by the river and my father worked in the Bobbin Mill. The Paxons also sleep with the windows open at Toll Bar Cottage and they agree that the rhythmic sound of running water over stones is soothing. They do, however, have different feelings about the times when the river is in spate.

Eleanor says that she finds it exciting.

"The power of the river is hypnotic as it races underneath the bridge," she says.

But Paul adds: "You say it's exciting and stimulating, but it tends to worry me. The sheer force of the river is incredible."

Paul recalls that when Adam was a child he knocked on his parents' bedroom door early one morning and said: "Quick! You're going to have to rescue Peter."

Peter was a rabbit and it lived, in the summer, in a hutch on the riverbank.

"I went down there," recalls Paul, "the river was rising fast and I put my foot on the top of the hutch and the thing was about to go. The whole hutch was about to float off down river. I managed to open the hutch door and this rabbit, it was normally not particularly friendly, shot up my arm and clung to my shoulder."

It was not an isolated incident.

Paul: "There was a day many years ago when Adam had a tent on the bank. We were sitting in the kitchen when we

Winter in days gone by could be ferocious. Ice clogs the pool below Calvert Bridge. Picture courtesy of The George Fisher Collection.

heard this rushing sound. I looked out at the apple trees and thought 'it's not windy' and then we realised that it was the river. It was like a bore coming down and I went out and grabbed the tent and the two poles otherwise the whole lot would have gone down the river. If that had happened in the middle of the night, when Adam would have been sleeping in his tent, he may not have been here today. All sorts of things came down the river after that. There had been a cloud burst over Mungrisdale or somewhere up in a tributary."

Paul reckons that they only escaped the serious flooding of 2009 by the skin of their teeth, but Adam believes they were well placed to avoid the flooding, despite being so close to the river.

"I think we are in one of the safest places on the river when it comes to flooding," Adam says. "And that's because we're in the lee of the bridge. It's the bridge that saves us here. There is a greater danger of flooding on the top side."

While Paul still has his reservations about the potential threat from the river in times of flood he still has huge admiration for the beck and its power.

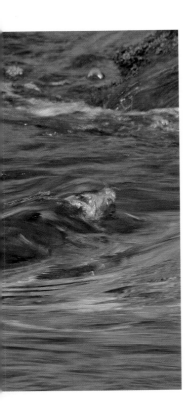

"I really do love the river and find that its power is quite hypnotic," he says. "When it's racing I will spend many an hour awake at night just listening to it. We always sleep with the windows open. And we do tend to think of it as our river. We can get very protective about it."

Do they think the river has improved in recent years in terms of water quality and the presence of wildlife?

"Yes," replies Paul. "The river was devoid of otters as far as we knew. I remember the days when we never saw an otter. Jackie Weightman – who went to Brigham School, just up the way from the cottage – said that before they went to school in a morning they would go down the green on the top side of Calvert Bridge and watch the otters in the river. That was all part of their entertainment."

"There was a long period when we didn't have any otters but now they're back," adds Eleanor. The family also notes that there are fewer fish than there used to be and not as many paddlings of ducks. On the plus side there is a colony of bats under the bridge. On the human front, a relatively new addition is the increased number of canoeists using the river.

"There are loads of canoeists and it is a bit disconcerting when you see an empty canoe drift down," says Adam. "We also now have the dreaded Himalayan balsam (an invasive plant) and invariably we have to pull a bit out of our bank each year."

On the wildlife front, Paul never fails to appreciate the regular flypast of the heron.

"One of my favourite sounds," he explains, "is lying abed in the morning and hearing the heron flying over or under the bridge and saying 'good morning.' He often croaks as he comes by."

Adam: "It's like some form of recognition it's got with going over the bridge."

Still with the heron, Paul adds that when the by-pass and the bridge over The Forge was being built in 1976 he was standing on the old stone bridge at The Forge (Hardisty's Bridge, built in 1817) looking up at the new bridge being erected. At the time it was covered by a mass of scaffolding.

"The heron came up the river and went underneath the old stone bridge," Paul recalls. "But because there was such a mountain of scaffolding surrounding the new bridge he realised he couldn't get over so he sort of banked round. It was only on the third attempt that he went over the stone bridge and then managed to gain enough height to get away over the scaffolding as well."

Herons are not the most graceful of birds in flight, but when it comes to sheer stealth and amazing speed of reaction they are the best fishermen on the Greta. Even more accomplished, dare I say it, than Terry ("The Heron") Appleby who got his nickname because of the time he spends by the beck.

The river also bears gifts and in a high beck in June 2012 it kindly deposited a massive tree trunk on the lower lawn at the back of Toll Bar Cottage. Paul promptly sawed the trunk up and it will keep them in fuel for their wood-burning stove for the winter and beyond.

Brigham.

The Brigham of today is not all that different from the Brigham of days gone by. Calvert Bridge and Toll Bar Cottage are clearly still there, the latter a reminder of the time when England's roads were part of an extensive turnpike network.

The Twa Dogs, flanked by Latrigg Close and Brigham Row, occupies pride of place on the town side of the bend on Penrith Road, opposite Lydias Cottages. The pools and the fast water in Town's Field have not altered significantly – although a massive

River Dwellers

horse chestnut on the far bank of 'Sandy' was washed away in the worst of the recent floods. Trees were planted in Town's Field with great ceremony as saplings many years ago by the children of Brigham School (opened in 1851) and I salute every time I drive past in memory of my dad, also, like me, a pupil at Brigham, and who said he planted one of the trees; although I don't know which one or, indeed, if it is still standing.

The lonning leading to The Forge is probably much the same as it was when a tipsy Tommy Burns staggered home and became entangled in the hedge after a Saturday night out. Across the road from The Twa Dogs, Wilk's shop is no longer there but what was the shop is now part of the cottage where he and his family lived and his daughter Jill and her husband Rod live today. Greta Cottage is easily recognised by a 'rubber' duck sculpted into the roadside hedge. There's also some netting strategically placed over the small pond in Rod and Jill's garden to protect the goldfish from the close attentions of Henry the Heron, as they call him.

Brigham, September 1898.

Adam Paxon's Calvert Bridge Diary

THE OTTER, THE OWL AND A TREE TRUNK

Throughout 2012, Adam Paxon, of Toll Bar Cottage, kept a diary of sightings from the double windows of his studio room overlooking the pool below Calvert Bridge on the River Greta. Highlights were the visits of all manner of wildlife, including an otter, and the aftermath of a flood when the river deposited an entire tree on the family's riverbank garden lawn, a tree that was quickly converted into winter fuel for the cottage. Here are Adam's observations.

January 13, 8.30am: The river is khaki-green and translucent. A heron is fishing the shallows throughout the pool. It is my first sighting of the bird for a while. A pair of goosanders are also fishing, seeking breakfast. Very loud splash late evening, a big fish perhaps?

January 14, 8:30am: Heron flies upstream. River green and translucent, thick and sluggish with cold.

January 15, 10am: River clearer, water level low. This is the seventh day without rain, river running lower and appears colder. Sparkly, sluggish water, lowest level for a while, a lot less khaki in colour and more like glass.

January 16, 7.50am: Heron flies upstream. **8.40am:** Heron returns down river. **9.10am** . . . and back for another look upstream. **10.30am:** A very trim sparrow hawk glides up the river bank into the garden, along the bank and under the rhododendron by the shed at the side of the bridge. Sufficiently deft in its approach it seems to fly in under the chirruping birds' radar. Most stay and carry on hopping around from twig to twig, visiting the feeders. After a couple of minutes the sparrow hawk, not too hungry perhaps, leaves without having made any attempt to catch some late breakfast; just gliding soundlessly along the path through the garden directly under our window. **2.15pm:** The sparrow hawk flies up river swooping under Calvert Bridge and through the trees lining the river.

January 18, 8.10am: The heron flies up river. Darker day, more wind creating ripples on the surface of the pool. Silt clouding the water. **10.10am:** A woodpecker flits about between the large old oak trees on the other side of the river, hammering away for grubs. Not yet visited the garden but may well do so. They have been returning for the past two to three years, often to the same places in the garden and most often bossing the largest nut feeder, sending tits and finches to gossip and twitter in upper branches and nearby shrubs; seemingly aghast.

Yesterday more geese flew over, noisy, sleek and majestically organised. Many groups had flown over previously, perhaps six or eight in the course of a day. Have not seen the kingfisher for a while now and there is scant sign of any fish in the river. This does not seem to stop the mergansers and goosanders though, and they do not seem to be lean so they are obviously getting something. Mallards have been diving every now and then for leftover fallen acorns on the far side of the river.

January 20, Evening: Wind and rain all day, filling the river and colouring the water.

The next morning: 'Tidal' mark of leaves on the bank from the highest point overnight. Tan, caramel-coloured water, completely disguising everything under the surface. Occasional brightness to the south but thick grey clouds to north, land and stone colourful with damp. **10am:** Woodpecker in the far trees, heard but not seen.

January 22, Early morning: Back to cold, glassy, sluggish water. Looks murky before the sun comes up. **8:10am:** A fish leaps near the far bank and a dipper chirrups its way

Adam Paxon at Calvert Bridge pool with the bridge in the background.

up river. The water is a glass green and bedrock and fine stones are visible. Family of crows hanging around during the week. One deftly lifted a lump of bread from mid flow. The reflected light from the nearby timeshare buildings on the opposite bank seems to give the large central rocks in the river a strange radioactive quality.

January 23, 8.10am: Male goosander seen flying and running through the water in pursuit of prey. It is unsuccessful on this occasion.

March 11: Glenderaterra mine walk with Ian Tyler from Keswick Mining Museum. Ian speaks about the processes that have coloured the rocks red. Whenever I have wandered up and down the river these rocks with their distinct colouring have always leapt out at me. There is nowhere else that this particular rock formation occurs along the route of the Greta so all the red rocks must have come from below the mines; rolled down the river by the current and eroded as they travel downstream.

March 18: For the past three days I have walked down to the river under the beech tree at the end of the garden and every day I have found pieces of a heavily pitted tar-like slag, probably relics of copper refining or smelting. The rich industrial heritage of the Greta still tumbles along its bed. I seem to remember finding this same material as a child and recall having my very own museum of the river in which the majority of the exhibits were finds from the river, a child's treasure trove of pieces of pottery, a bottle from Town's Field or an old fishing reel.

For some weeks late at night there have been conspicuous splashing sounds, perhaps a large fish surfacing.

The crows nesting in the tall oaks opposite have white feathers. It is as though paint had been spilled in the nest and each is marked with white.

April 3: Snow has fallen and it is very much colder. The previous week was warm and March was arguably the warmest on record. It included a day when Keswick was the hottest location in the UK.

April 4, 9.50am: Something is causing ripples and stirring the water near the large stones. It is possibly an otter but I cannot be sure.

A piece of heavily-pitted tar-like slag, possibly a relic of copper smelting on the Greta.

April 10: I wonder if the river has been stocked with trout? A heron is fishing in the lamplight just under our window at the near bank. It is a young bird and is easily spooked as I open the window. Later, a larger heron quietly fishes the near shallows. Arching and stabbing its prey, moving a little then freezing, levering itself into position and plunging into the water to its left. It takes six fish in the 30 minutes that I watch.

April 12, 2.40pm: A sparrow hawk zooms down river. **7.17pm:** Two female and three male mergansers are trawling the pool, engaged in a feeding frenzy. In two groups the mergansers fly through the water – quite literally 'flying' underwater – harrowing the fish. They are quick and cause quite a commotion as they chase the fish to the edge where one may be rewarded. At times like this I have seen the heron get in on the act. Positioning himself on the bank and hoping the hunting pack will shoo fish in his direction. The mergansers are not pleased and try to chase the heron away.

April 24, 11:38am: A 12 inch eel snakes its way through the shallows along the bed of the pool.

April 28: The first ducklings I have seen on the river this year, a mother with 10-12.

April 29, 4.16pm: As the sun gets higher in the sky at this time of year it shines much more brightly into the pool at midday. When the river is clear of silt the entire riverbed is visible. An eel roams the sunlit depths. But where have the large boulders gone? The three largest ones we used to sit on when we swam in the river as children are nowhere to be seen. As children we had to be careful not to collide with them while swimming

The drawing entitled 'Pink River' by Carry Akroyd (www.carryakroyd.co.uk). The image of the heron flying up stream with the road on the heights in the background reminded me very much of the Greta and our resident herons.

but they were good for diving off. Now they have gone – washed away by a flood presumably – and all that remains is the smooth, flowing bedrock meeting the shallow bank of sand.

In the warmer weather our cat 'Monkey' (a silver-spotted Egyptian Mau) spends much of his time outside. He roams around at night and when not dozing in semi-shade during the day will hunt voles and mice in the reeds along the riverbank or in the garden walls. He only returns when he's hungry, much as the three of us did as children. He will also hide in the reeds hoping to surprise a passing duck. Unfortunately, he has presented himself at breakfast with a clump of duckling feathers in his claws.

June 5, 9.31am: A pair of mergansers hunting the pool. It has been mostly Goosanders this year. **9.09 pm:** A mother and two young mergansers explore the pool.

June 8, 2.15pm: A junior dipper is being fed on the opposite bank under a low overhanging branch.

June 11, 8.33am: Two large ducklings and their mother preen themselves on rocks.

June 22, 9.30pm: The river has been rising all day after heavy rainfall. The swollen river surges under the bridge and almost covers the bank in the garden. **11pm:** The water is now covering the bank and roaring through the arch of the bridge.

The brown molten water carries with it great limbs and branches, and a number of entire trees, large and small, sail past. Some branches are seemingly in harmony with the flow while others clatter and scrape along, turning over and over and exposing shattered stubs where branches have been severed off.

June 23, middle of the night: The river has been in spate all night. Rocks and boulders can occasionally be heard tumbling and rolling along. Sometimes it appears that a rock has become trapped, unable to move on and the sound of its restricted movement is heightened before it is dislodged and rolls on down the river. **8.52am:** I see an otter moving through the floodwaters towards the far bank. It is gliding effortlessly through the powerful flow of the water, manoeuvring its way upstream, foraging and diving along the bank as it goes. **10am:** One of the trees carried along by the flood has been deposited half on half off the riverbank just under our window. It rocks gently in the wash from the river and is not entirely free of the water. **2pm:** The river is still covering most of the bank, splashing over the surface of the raised patio next to the bridge.

Planters and pots from the patio have been moved out of harm's way and the cast iron table and chairs are roped together in a corral and lashed to a tree. **6pm:** As the flood waters recede they leave the big long tree high and dry on our riverbank. **6.48pm:** The otter is again to be seen swimming beneath the far bank. This time it swims strongly across the current to explore the near bank under our window.

It is only 20 or so feet away from my partner Shadi and I as we watch it diving and re-surfacing several times before finally emerging under the bridge on the far side. From here it moves gracefully into the main stream and glides effortlessly down the river and over the rapids before diving out of sight.

July 9: The rhododendron on the bank is beginning to bloom. Crows are almost demanding food on the balcony of a timeshare building just downriver. The crown of our riverbank garden / lawn has been given a fresh coating of silt and small stones during the flood. The grass will grow through and the bank will absorb the sand. But the water's edge, raked by the flood, will take time to recover.

July 11: Dad begins chain-sawing the tree into sections so that it can be split into logs for winter fuel.

July 12: The tree is now in logs ready to be dried for the fire and all that remains is a great dune of sawdust, the root ball and six feet or so of the trunk for the river to dispose of the next time there is a flood. In the meantime it will become home for all manner of grubs and insects and perhaps a fishing perch for the kingfisher. **2.14pm:** The sun shines directly onto the pool which is a rich caramel colour, darker where it is deeper in the middle and golden as it thins towards the edge.

July 15, 1pm: A red squirrel dashes along the handrail (what we call The Squirrel Express Way) of the path along the opposite bank. In the dappled light it bounds onto the path and away downriver.

August 13, 1.06pm: A mink, glossy dark brown, a native of America and descendant of escapees from UK fur farms, scurries furtively along the far side of the bank and under the bridge. It scuttles along in search of food, darting here and there to explore, then enters the river and swims away upstream.

August 14, 11pm: I am trying out a new flashlight when the beam catches the eyes of a creature under the arch of the bridge on the far bank. A mink, perhaps the same one I had seen the day before, emerges from a grassy knoll and slips into the water and out of sight.

August 15, 9.40am: The mink is again to be seen on the opposite bank. It crosses the river to our side and forages beneath the bank. It slinks away after another fleeting visit.

In summary: As autumn approaches the bats, present all summer and which live under the arch of the bridge, continue their evening forays; dark moving shadows flitting this way and that, honing in on insects in the night air. They will feed over the pool for hours but on other occasions are not to be seen and must be feeding elsewhere. Sometimes the sparrow hawk is making a last sweep as the bats begin to appear. The bats do not want to be airborne when the sparrow hawk is about. This is the time that the heron is making his way back up the river as well. In the Autumn, with the reduction in the foliage on the trees, the pool and its immediate area have different sounds and our vision is more far reaching. The Virginia creeper on the bridge turns a deep burgundy colour and eventually the leaves start to fall and float down the river. Acorns are dropping from the oaks on the far bank and the ducks are feeding among them as they drop like small bombs from the branches above. Most splash harmlessly into the water but occasionally there will be a direct hit on the head of a duck.

We are increasingly aware of owls hooting in the night and on one famous occasion there is an owl in a tree on the opposite bank and an otter in the pool. I am convinced that they are communicating with each other as the owl's hoot is followed by the reply of the otter.

As winter approaches all of this reinforces the feeling that the river is fundamentally important to me. It is hypnotic and has a soothing, calming effect. It is fantastic to be able to see what I see every day from my studio window. The river is always different, no two days are alike and I feel privileged to be in a position where I can, if I am here, look out at the river, the pool and the bridge all the days of the year. It is amazing what you can see in one relatively small place, a place where nothing remains the same.

BRIDGES
CALVERT BRIDGE AND WILD BROWN TROUT

Calvert Bridge is a lovely old stone bridge that slopes gently downhill from left to right as you look at it from the side facing the town. The bridge, most probably built in 1804 – 1805, looks at its best in the Autumn when its westerly wall, overlooking the deep, long, oval pool below, is covered with the rich burgundy leaves of Virginia creeper, a plant that has as big a hold on the adjacent Toll Bar Cottage as it does on the bridge itself.

Calvert Bridge is to me the most appealing of the four venerable stone structures over the Greta, including the one at the bottom of the town that bears the name of the river, Greta Bridge, and then, a little further upstream from Calvert Bridge, the Forge Bridge – or Hardisty's Bridge as it was known in the days when mills lined the river – and, higher still up the beck, Threlkeld Bridge. It is under the twin arches of the latter that the Glenderamackin and St John's Beck, at one time known as The Bure, merge to form the Greta below the old Keswick to Penrith road at the foot of Lambs Brow.

All the bridges, with the possible exception of Calvert Bridge, may have started out as simple wooden structures, renovated and improved over the centuries until the existing structures were made of stone. The stone bridges have certainly stood the test of time and have demonstrated over the years that they can withstand the most powerful of flooding and all the debris and broken-down trees that are flung at them by raging spate water. Greta Bridge was certainly under immense pressure during the floods of 2009, but it came through unscathed despite temporary closure amid initial fears that its foundations may have been irretrievably damaged.

Threlkeld Bridge (once known as New Bridge) Greta Bridge and a third structure, the original wooden version of the Forge Bridge (although there was also probably another early wooden bridge in what is now Town's Field) are the oldest on the river, and are indicated by parallel lines drawn through the river on maps dating back to 1576.

While each bridge is beautiful and distinctive in its own way Calvert Bridge, probably the youngest of the bridges, remains my personal favourite because it is the one with which I relate most strongly through distinct childhood memories of fishing trips.

Facing page:
Calvert Bridge

It was here, on the jagged slate parapet of the bridge top, that we leant over as kids to cast our nylon lines into the pool below.

The dub at Calvert Bridge was well known for its plump brown trout and catching them from the heights of the bridge involved a fair amount of skulduggery as we attempted to fool the fish. Our bait was a small piece of doughy bread moulded to and entirely covering a tiny barbed hook, usually size 16; the bigger the number the smaller the hook. Around this miniscule piece of dough we would plaster by way of further disguise a veritable gob stopper-sized ball of soft and pulpy bread that had been chewed to mush in our mouths. The continual chewing of bread is not one of life's pleasanter tasks and leaves your mouth feeling as dry and caked as the inner workings of a lime pit on a baking-hot summer's day.

Once it had been thoroughly chewed, mushed and applied to the hook, the entire caboodle, I cannot recall whether or not we used a small piece of lead-shot higher up the line to give the bait depth, was dropped into the water some 30 or so feet below as we clung precariously to our uncomfortable perches on top of the bridge wall. Our carbon fibre rods stretched out and down over the river and the brown trout some 40 or so feet below.

As soon as the ball of bread hit the water it would begin to break up. Darting trout would accelerate the process by dashing in at speed, nose butting the larger ball of bread as it slowly sank and smashing off pieces which they would then devour. As the feeding frenzy intensified as many as 30 fish would be attacking the big ball of bread and the scene below would be a mass of fast moving trout, here, there and everywhere as the bread rapidly disintegrated under the onslaught. It was not unlike watching a shark attack in miniature. Within seconds the bread had gone and only one small piece would be seen sinking slowly to the bed of the river where it would remain untouched.

And that piece, without fail, was the piece of dough that contained your hook. After each failed effort another young angler would try his luck as we took it in turns to attempt to catch a trout by this method . . . little wonder the trout beneath Calvert Bridge were so big and fat; they benefited from a perpetual food chain raided from the bread bins of housewives on Windebrowe Avenue and Latrigg Close, the two council housing estates in the immediate vicinity of the bridge and where most of us young anglers lived and from which we would emerge with rods and wellies (and bread) at all times of day and night.

How the trout knew which piece of bread hid the hook was a mystery. Perhaps they could see or feel the nylon line? Perhaps the line with the hook attached sank less slowly? Were the trout such experts at this game of life and death that they knew instinctively which tiny ball of doughy bread was suspicious? That they recognised one piece of dough might spell their doom, while the rest was safe to eat, once it had been broken away from the main ball of mush, was beyond doubt. The bait containing the hook nearly always remained untouched while the rest disappeared in double quick time. The same thing happened all too often for it to be mere coincidence.

But occasionally, and only occasionally mind you, a careless, greedy, less river-wise, or short-sighted trout got it wrong and you would feel the tension through your finger on the line of a fish taking the bait. You would quickly strike, hooking the fish and, after a short but spirited fight, haul the catch, rod bent double over the bridge, out of the water and up and away towards the parapet. Once it was hauled over the rampart of the bridge the fish dropped onto the path where it flapped and bounced and thrashed before being grasped with both hands and knocked on the head. The trout was admired for its size and sleekness and gleaming, beautifully speckled flanks, all the more attractive while still wet from the river. It was then consigned to the dark of the fishing bag and, ultimately, the frying pan and breakfast.

Simply hooking a fish did not always guarantee its capture. Sometimes the tiny size 16 hook failed to hold and a trout could be half way up the bridge wall when fish and hook parted company and the trout would plummet back with a splash into the water, doubtless wondering to itself 'what on earth was that all about?' and from then on in become increasingly wary of tiny pieces of dough that did not look quite right.

We would spend hours after school, over weekends and during school holidays, on Calvert Bridge shredding our legs and arms on the rough and sharp slabs of the parapet, the slate on top having been laid in such a way, upright and pointy, to presumably deter lads like us from clambering onto the bridge wall and, perhaps, falling into the river below. As it was we almost bled to death as a result of cuts and grazes we suffered from the stones.

Bridges

We would fish in all weathers in the river – rain was not an issue then – and Calvert Bridge was one of our regular ports of call. The top side of the bridge, where in times of flood the water backed up against the side of the stone wall, was always a good place for fishing for brown trout. The bait then, in the high muddy brown water, was worm. The trout had retreated out of the fast main current and were feeding on any morsels that were washed their way in the quiet eddy created as the water circled back on itself in the lee of the bridge. Worm fishing was a completely different art to that of fishing with bread from the parapet of the bridge.

The main baits we used were worm in a flood, bread at any time when the river was clear, a very occasional foray with cheese, which was not strictly legal, salmon roe (very illegal) and minnow, the latter being deadly and a sure fire means of catching the biggest of trout, or the large-headed cannibals as we called them because of their tendency to eat their own species or salmon fry.

Floating bread was all the rage for a time when we discovered that trout would rise to the surface to take in pieces of bread thrown from the rear of houses that backed onto the river, such as those at Brigham and at The Forge, upstream from Calvert Bridge. A piece of dry bread, hook attached and cast out into the head of a pool and allowed to float down stream to the waiting trout, was a deadly bait and the fish seemed oblivious to the trap. They certainly showed none of the guile or suspicion of the trout in the pool beneath Calvert Bridge.

I must confess to the fact that, as lads bored of fishing towards the end of one long summer's day, we once resorted to catching ducks with floating bread. I think it may have happened accidentally at first – a duck was too quick for its own good – but we soon realised, once the novelty had worn off, that it was not a pastime we were eager to repeat . . . although the ducks were a doddle to hook, if not to actually catch and release. It all seemed to fly, quite literally, in the face of the tradition of fishing and merited the anger of the little old ladies who caught us in the act.

The Calvert connection

As lads on Calvert Bridge we were oblivious to the history of the bridge and its surroundings, to the fact that a turnpike was once situated next to Toll Bar Cottage at the Penrith road end of the bridge, and that at one time the area was heavily industrialised, especially further upstream (at The Forge and Low Briery) and downstream from the bridge (opposite the Millfield) with mills and water wheels along the banks of the river. There may have been as many as 49 water wheels on the river and at one time there were no fewer than 27 mills powered by the river and mill races. An Ordnance Survey map for the mid 1860s clearly shows the extent of the mills and the races and sluices that were in place along the river from Low Briery and The Forge to below Greta Bridge, and the intriguing street formations and old yards of 19th Century Keswick. This all helps to build a picture of what the town was really like, especially from the mid 1860s to the early 1900s (see also The History Files at the end of the book).

We were also ignorant of the fact that the name of the bridge came from the Calvert family who lived at Greta Bank (Brundholme Country Houses at the time of writing) and that William Calvert built the bridge in 1804 – 1805 shortly after the house, Greta Bank, next to the old Windy Brow farmhouses, was constructed. Previous to Calvert Bridge and the Forge Bridge being built there was probably also an older wooden bridge, giving access across the river from Town's Field. That bridge may have been in the location of the big wide pool we call "Sandy" and in which we used to swim as children. The wooden bridge apparently led on to a path which went right in front of the windows at Greta Bank and on to a route that led from old Windy Brow to Applethwaite. There is every indication among the undergrowth and trees directly below Greta Bank that a path may indeed have descended to "Sandy." That bridge was clearly a somewhat ramshackle affair and once it degenerated was never rebuilt or repaired. It was clearly to the advantage of the proprietor of the Greta Bank estate that people should use Calvert Bridge because of the greater privacy it afforded the fine home at Greta Bank which still stands, an impressive mansion, creamy-white and substantial under the slopes of Latrigg.

Bridges

William Calvert was an intriguing character, a military man and also an innovator and entrepreneur who endeavoured – unsuccessfully as it happens – to grow oats on the higher reaches of Latrigg or, as he put it, "to carry the plough much nearer heaven than was ever dreamed of a few years ago."

The name Calvert in this area appears to go back to the 16th Century when German copper miners came to Cumberland. The Germans who came over bore such names as Heckstetter, Calvert, Ritseler, Moser, Puphbarger, Clocker, Colysinge, Stanger, Hedgler, Flowterer, Slaygll, Beyrnparker, Prowker, Lipmawer, Hound, Sanninger, Torver, Norspalmer, Tempp, Tiffler, Tibler, Cayrus, Beck, Zinogle and Yearle. They intermarried with Keswick women and one of the marriages in the Crosthwaite parish register is that of 'Hanre Moser, Duchman, and Elizabeth Clark of Newlands, November 23rd, 1567.'

In the late 18th Century Windy Brow was the home of the German coppersmith Hans Rosie and his descendants – their name being anglicised to Raisley – and Windy Brow was later owned by the Calverts. William Calvert's father was Raisley Calvert (Raisley also being the Christian name of one of his two sons) steward to the Duke of Norfolk and who cared for the duke's estates at Greystoke. There is a plaque in his memory in St Kentigern's Church, Mungrisdale. The family moved from the Threlkeld area to Wharton Hall, Greystoke, where two more children (in addition to William) were born, Raisley Jnr in 1873 and Anne in 1775. William himself had been born in 1770 and was baptised at Threlkeld Parish Church on July 5th, 1770.

William went to school at Hawkshead where, significantly as it later transpired, he made friends with one William Wordsworth, of Cockermouth. The boys came from similar backgrounds in that Wordsworth's father was an agent for Sir John Lowther, the Earl of Lonsdale. After school William Calvert joined the Duke of Norfolk's Regiment of the Militia (then known as the 12th Regiment of Foot). The father, Raisley Calvert Snr, died in 1791 and William and his younger brother, Raisley, inherited his fortune. Young Raisley Calvert, tragically, did not live long enough to enjoy his inheritance.

It was through his older brother that Raisley Calvert Jnr got to know William Wordsworth. William Calvert and Wordsworth toured the West Country together in July 1793. The two Williams spent time in the Isle of Wight where they looked on as the English fleet prepared for war against France. Eventually Calvert returned to Keswick on horseback while Wordsworth set off on foot to walk across Salisbury Plain. Later in 1793 the aspiring poet visited William and his brother Raisley at their family farm at Windy Brow, developed a few years later into Greta Bank. The following April William and his sister Dorothy were reunited – they had been separated in childhood since 1778 through the death of parents – when William Calvert invited them to stay in the farmhouse at Windy Brow. Brother and sister travelled by coach to Kendal then walked the 18 miles to Grasmere and a further 15 miles to Keswick.

William Calvert was away with his regiment when William and Dorothy stayed with his tenants at the Windy Brow farmhouse, Dairy Cottage. They lived there for about six weeks. Soon afterwards, Dorothy, who was 22 when at Windy Brow, wrote a letter to a friend, Jane Pollard: "You cannot perceive anything more delightful than the situation

Bridges

of this house. It stands upon the top of a very steep bank, which rises in a direction nearly perpendicular from a dashing stream (the Greta) below. From the window of the room where I write, I have a prospect of the road winding along the opposite banks of the river, of a part of the lake of Keswick and the town, and towering above the town a woody steep (Walla Crag) of a very considerable height, whose summit is a long range of silver rocks. This is the view from the house; a hundred yards above it is impossible to describe the grandeur. There is a natural terrace along the side of the mountain, which shelters Windy Brow, whence we command a view of the whole vale of Keswick (the Vale of Elysium, as Mr Gray calls it). This vale is terminated at one end by a huge pile of grand mountains, in whose lap the lovely lake of Derwent is placed; at the other end by the lake of Bassenthwaite, on one side of which Skiddaw towers sublime and on the other a range of mountains, not of equal size, but of much grandeur; and the middle of the vale is of beautiful cultivated grounds, interspersed with cottages, and watered by a winding stream (the Derwent) which runs between the lakes of Derwentwater and Bassenthwaite.

"I have never been more delighted with the manners of any people than the family under whose roof I am at present. They are the most honest, cleanly, sensible people I ever saw in their rank of life and I think I may safely affirm, happier than anybody I know. They are contented with a supply of the bare necessaries of life, are active and industrious and declare with simple frankness unmixed with ostentation, that they prefer their cottage at Windy Brow to any of the showy edifices in the neighbourhood, and they believe that there is not to be found in the whole of the vale a happier family than they are. They are fond of reading, and reason not indifferently on what they read.

"We have a neat parlour to ourselves, which Mr Calvert has fitted up for his own use, and the lodging rooms are very comfortable. Till my brother gets some employment he will lodge here. Mr Calvert is not now at Windy Brow, as you will suppose. We please ourselves in calculating from our present expenses for how very small a sum we could live. We find our own food. Our breakfast and supper are of milk, and our dinner chiefly of potatoes and we drink no tea."

While at Windy Brow, Dorothy received a letter from an aunt, Mrs Crackenthorpe, of Penrith, who urged her not to prolong her stay and criticised Dorothy for her life

The Greta . . . a river runs through it

style. This was at a time when young ladies were frowned upon if they disported themselves in any way as to suggest a life of questionable morals, impropriety or vulnerability. The accusatory tone of Mrs Crackenthorpe's letter and her interfering (she was an unpopular figure in the Penrith area) is given short shrift by the much younger woman. Dorothy, clearly an individual of some character and not one to kowtow to the observations of a more elderly and pompous relative, tells her aunt, in the nicest possible way, and with the use of some diplomatic and carefully constructed language, to mind her own business.

Dorothy takes up arms with the words " . . . I am much obliged to you for the frankness with which you have expressed your sentiments upon my conduct and am at the same time extremely sorry that you should think it so severely to be condemned. As you have not sufficiently developed the reasons of your censure, I have endeavoured to discover them; and I confess no other possible objections against my continuing here (at Windy Brow) a few weeks longer suggest themselves, except the expense, and that you may suppose me to be in an unprotected situation.

"As to the former of these objections I reply that I drink no tea, that my supper and breakfast are of bread and milk, and my dinner chiefly of potatoes from choice. In answer to the second of these suggestions, namely that I may be supposed to be in an unprotected situation, I affirm that I consider the character and virtues of my brother as a sufficient protection; and besides I am convinced that there is no place in the world in which a good and virtuous young woman would be more likely to continue good and virtuous than under the roof of these honest, worthy, uncorrupted people: so that any guardianship beyond theirs I should think altogether unnecessary.

"I cannot pass unnoticed that part of your letter in which you speak of my 'rambling about the country on foot.' So far from considering this a matter of condemnation, I rather thought it would have given my friends pleasure to hear that I had courage to make use of the strength with which nature has endowed me, when it not only procured me infinitely more pleasure than I should have received from sitting in a post chaise, but was also the means of saving me at least thirty shillings.

"In mentioning the inducements which I have to stay at Windy Brow for a few weeks longer, it would be unnecessary to speak of the beauty of the country, or the pleasantness

of the season. To these are added the society of several of my brother's friends, from whom I have received the most friendly attentions, and above all the society of my brother. I am now 22 years of age and such have been the circumstances of my life that I may be said to have enjoyed his company only for a very few months. An opportunity now presents itself of obtaining this satisfaction, an opportunity which I could not see pass from me without unspeakable pain. Besides I not only derive much pleasure but much improvement from my brother's society . . ."

On receiving this letter from Dorothy Wordsworth, I imagine that Mrs Crackenthorpe's reaction would be along the lines that her niece would meet with a sad end sooner or later if she continued with her reckless behaviour. 'You mark my words. Harrumph . . !'

Dorothy and her brother would clearly get to know Raisley Calvert Jnr well during their stay in 1794. Later that year, after brother and sister had left Windy Brow, William Wordsworth returned to find that Raisley was seriously ill with tuberculosis. William Calvert was away with his regiment in Northumberland and Wordsworth suggested that he might accompany Raisley on a visit to Portugal to improve his health. The journey was aborted after they had travelled only as far as the Robin Hood Inn, Penrith. Wordsworth nursed Raisley at Windy Brow until his premature death in January 1795. In his will, Raisley Calvert left William Wordsworth £900 and this enabled the young writer to pursue his life as a poet. The bequest of Raisley Calvert to Wordsworth is to this day synonymous with altruism and generosity and the name Calvert was used, to this end, in providing the title for the national organisation The Calvert Trust which provides adventure holidays for the disabled throughout the UK. The Calvert Trust Riding Centre, part of the Lake District branch of the organisation, is quite literally across the road from the old Windy Brow farmhouse where Dorothy and William Wordsworth stayed at what turned out to be a crossroads in their creative lives.

Just as Raisley Calvert did not forget Wordsworth in his will, nor did the poet forget his benefactor.

"I should have been," Wordsworth recalled, "forced by necessity into one of the professions, had not a friend left me £900. This bequest was from a young man with whom, though I call him friend, I had but little connection and the act was done entirely

Facing page:
The Forge Bridge, also known as Hardisty's bridge.

Bridges

from a confidence on his part that I had power and attainments which might be of use to mankind."

Wordsworth wrote the following sonnet in memory of Raisley Calvert:

> *Calvert! it must not be unheard by them*
> *Who may respect my name, that I to thee*
> *Owed many years of early liberty.*
> *This care was thine when sickness did condemn*
> *Thy youth to hopeless wasting, root and stem —*
> *That I, if frugal and severe, might stray*
> *Where'er I liked; and finally array*
> *My temples with the Muse's diadem.*
> *Hence, if in freedom I have loved the truth,*
> *If there be aught of pure, or good, or great,*
> *In my past verse, or shall be in the lays*
> *Of higher mood, which now I meditate —*
> *It gladdens me, O worthy, short-lived Youth!*
> *To think how much of this will be thy praise.*

Threlkeld Bridge, also known as New Bridge. This picture is from the Clough Head side of the bridge and shows the Glenderamackin going underneath one of the twin arches.

Growing oats on Latrigg

The story of the river, Calvert Bridge and the Calvert family does not end there.

William Calvert was also linked to other Lakes poets, including Samuel Taylor Coleridge. When Coleridge, his wife Sara and their son Hartley came to live in Keswick in 1800 they stayed with the Calverts before moving into Greta Hall. William had retired from the militia by this time and was building the country house at Windy Brow which became known as Greta Bank (not to be confused with the nearby Greta Bank Farm). It was also around this time that he built the bridge that was to carry his family name forever and a day. *The Cumberland Pacquet* newspaper of April 1804 carried an advertisement in which John Banks, probably of Banks and Co, pencil makers, of Keswick, invited tenders for building a bridge at the site. The Greenwich Hospital Estates, as Lord of Manor, gave permission for the bridge to be constructed. As noted by William Green in his *Tourists New Guide* of 1819 John Banks and William Calvert were joint owners of the bridge. They allowed the bridge to be used by people on foot or horseback en route for Skiddaw. Calvert also, at about this time, created a zig-zag footpath up Latrigg.

Wordsworth (by then happily ensconced with his sister Dorothy in Dove Cottage, Grasmere) Coleridge and Robert Southey (the latter and his family joined Coleridge and his family at Greta Hall in 1803) were all friends of William Calvert and must have used the bridge frequently when visiting him at Greta Bank as well as in their walks through the countryside. The late Michael Davies-Shiel, of Windermere, who carried out meticulous research work on the subject of the mills and bridges on the River Greta wrote: "It seems reasonable that the bridge for which tenders were invited in 1804 is – allowing for repairs – the one that stands today."

It was William Calvert's intention to build a laboratory at Greta Bank and he suggested that Wordsworth and his sister Dorothy should come and live with him at the mansion; Coleridge, Wordsworth and Calvert could then study chemistry together. Coleridge was certainly enthused by the plan and wrote to Humphry Davy (the British chemist and inventor) in Bristol asking for advice on the setting up of a laboratory. But the plan failed to materialise and Wordsworth did not come to live in Keswick, although

Bridges

he and his sister Dorothy were regular visitors from their Dove Cottage home (December 1799 – May 1808) over the Raise (Dunmail) in Grasmere.

Undaunted, William Calvert continued to take a keen interest in science and invented a water clock and an instrument for measuring the height of mountains by triangulation. He was clearly a talented individual but at least one of his schemes did not meet with the success that his undoubted enterprise and initiative warranted.

Roy Ellis, of Keswick, who has written a paper specifically on William Calvert (1770 – 1829) relates the story of William Calvert's interest in new methods of farming.

"In 1805," Roy writes, "John Christian Curwen, of Workington Hall, had founded the Workington Agricultural Society. The Society encouraged improved farming practices. Curwen had a model farm at Workington where he experimented with drainage and irrigation, developed root crops, reared better breeds of cattle and sheep and tried out chemical and bone manures. William won several prizes for his sheep and became a Vice President of the Keswick District of the Society.

"In 1811, at the height of the Napoleonic Wars, grain prices were exceptionally high and farmers were looking for more land on which to grow crops. William decided to plough 60 acres on the summit of Latrigg (the site of an ancient Norse burial ground) at a height of 350 metres above sea level. He built a new road up the fell side from Greta Bank in order to get his plough to the top, and planted oats. In his President's address to the Workington Agricultural Society Curwen said: 'Mr Calvert has given a most spirited example in the improvement of his allotment of Skiddaw. I must heartily wish success may attend this undertaking as it will have a powerful effect in producing further mountain enclosures.'

"In his address the following year he added: 'Mr Calvert's oats, on Latrigg, are looking well,' but he doubted that tillage at that height was advisable and suggested that pasture would be more profitable. He added 'I already see the disposition to carry the plough much nearer to heaven than was ever dreamed of a few years ago.' Unfortunately the experiment was a failure. The oats failed to ripen due to the altitude and William lost a lot of money."

Still, nothing ventured nothing gained . . .

The Greta . . . a river runs through it

Never do today what you can do tomorrow

To continue the family history of the Calverts, William Calvert married Mary Mitchinson on June 2nd, 1801 at St Mary's Church in Carlisle. The Duke of Norfolk was one of the witnesses. Mrs Calvert was 'a clever housewife' but she was 'blessed with an ingenious husband,' whose motto was 'never do today what you can do tomorrow.' Mrs Calvert was clearly a strong character and Canon Hardwicke Drummond Rawnsley, Vicar of Crosthwaite, Keswick, wrote of her: "Those who have looked upon the pretty little pencil drawing of her, in her quaint scuttle bonnet, or half hat, half bonnet, will see at once what a remarkable face Mrs William Calvert must have had. And those who have been permitted to peep into the family house-keeping account she kept, will see that while her husband was a man of ideas, a man of fine intellectual sympathies, whose bane was procrastination, and whose motto was 'never do today what you can do tomorrow,' Mrs. Calvert was practical, methodical, and capable of being as good or better a steward of the Duke of Norfolk's estates than ever Calvert could have been. Accomplished too was Mrs Calvert, to judge by her beautiful pencil sketches of her husband's face that remain to us; and as for kindness, let Southey's letters attest how thoughtful for her friends she was, and how careful for the welfare of other households, even down to seeing that they were supplied with such cats as 'The Zombi,' or 'Othello,' to keep down the mice."

The couple had four children, John Mitchinson, (born 1802), Raisley (1803), Mary (1804) and William (1810). William the Snr regularly attended St Kentigern's Church where his children were all baptised. Throughout this time the Calverts, the Coleridges and the Southeys were friends and, apparently, 'the Greta Hall children and the Windybrowyites were inseparable.' Of the Calvert children it is recorded that John was "a very human, lovable, good, and nimble man — the laughing blue eyes of him, the clear cheery soul of him, still redolent of the fresh Northern breezes and transparent mountain streams."

Sheep dipping at Greta Bridge. Picture courtesy of the George Fisher Collection.

And little Mary Calvert grew up the girlfriend of Sara Coleridge and Edith May Southey, and remembered with pride helping Edith to make and put the wreath of laurel on her father's head when he returned to Greta Hall in 1813 as Poet Laureate. This Mary Calvert, wedded in August, 1824, to Joshua Stanger (descendants of 16th Century German copper miners reunited through marriage) "heard the poet Southey make his delightful speech at the wedding breakfast; while, for all that her brother John's blue eyes laughed so merrily, her bridesmaids were sad, and Sara Coleridge's dark eyes grew dewy, and Dora Wordsworth's grey eyes softened and filled with mist. She left her girlhood's friends and was parted from the valley of her love for 19 years. Yet her heart was with this home of her youth; and she returned the year that Southey died and in the house whose entrance from the main road is not a bowshot from Shelley's old lodging on Chestnut Hill, she dwelt for 47 years. That home, high-lifted with finest prospect of the Keswick Vale of any known hereabout, with sound of falling water at her door, and yew-tree shade above her roof, to remind her of the old farm house of Fieldside which it supplanted, saw gathered within its hospitable walls the fading circle of friends that made Lakeland famous. Thither came the Southey children, thither the Coleridges, and the Wordsworths. On its walls were the tokens of that fair friendship, in pictures of the poets and their belongings. In its bookshelves the writings of the honoured Lakeland School, and hidden away in secret drawers, the cherished albums filled with scraps, and letters, and verse of the famous guests and friends.

"How many times," continued Rawnsley, "did one leave Shelley's cottage and Chestnut Hill, and pass up the road towards Ambleside for one hundred paces and enter the park-like meadow-land made glorious with the rich background of Latrigg larch and the purple of Blencathra's hazel bowers, and look from Fieldside's lawn of sun and shade down the steep cleft thro' which the Greta flows, hurrying to Brundholme's overhanging wood?"

Mary Calvert was buried at St Kentigern's Church on February 10, 1890 (she was 87) and with her the memories of the Lakes poets, including those of Shelley and his visits to her childhood home at Greta Bank.

It was November 1811 when the poet Percy Bysshe Shelley, only 19, came to stay in Keswick with his bride, Harriet, aged 17, and her older sister, Eliza Westbrook.

William Calvert invited Shelley to Greta Bank, lent him linen, persuaded his landlord (of the cottage at Chestnut Hill) to lower his rent and introduced Shelley to Robert Southey. Shelley did not take to Keswick and was highly critical of the town and its people; even to the point of saying that local factory workers, whom he described as debauched, were guilty of drowning their illegitimate children in the River Greta.

In January 1812 Shelley was attacked by robbers at his front door and soon afterwards decided to leave Keswick for Ireland. His last week in the town was spent with the Calverts at Greta Bank.

A painting entitled 'Windy Brow, on the River Greta' and dated 1795. It is a watercolour (246 x 349mm) by Joseph Wilkinson (1764 – 1831).
I believe that this beautiful old painting must have been painted from a viewpoint down river of Town's Field and that the low bridge (just visible bottom right leading to the footpath) could well be an old bridge no longer there and which was superceded by Calvert Bridge (built in 1804 further downstream) and the Forge Bridge (built in 1817 further upstream).
The painting is reproduced courtesy of The Wordsworth Trust, Jerwood Centre, Dove Cottage, Grasmere.

The Windy Brow seat

Finally, the Calvert family friendship with the Lakes poets also left another legacy in the vicinity of Windy Brow, one that, unfortunately, cannot be detected today but which is recalled in the words and thoughts of William Wordsworth, his sister Dorothy and Samuel Taylor Coleridge.

In her Journals Dorothy Wordsworth records on one occasion that she walked to Keswick, setting off at Grasmere at 5 minutes past 10 and arriving at half past two.

She further recalls in her journal for the Saturday morning of August 9th, 1800: "I walked with Coleridge in the Windy Brow woods."

And then on Wednesday, 13th of August there is the simple entry: "Made the Windy Brow seat."

This is thought to be a direct reference to the fact that William and Dorothy Wordsworth had, in 1794 when they stayed at Dairy Cottage, Windy Brow, constructed a turf seat in the woods at Windy Brow on a steep bank overlooking the River Greta, and that in 1800 she presumably made some repairs to the seat. The Wordsworths, and later Coleridge, were in the habit of making woodland resting places out of stones, dirt,

Looking upstream to the Greta Bridge from the old stone Forge Bridge.

and then covering the seat with turf, moss and flowers. The seats were in various places over the surrounding countryside and were used as meeting and resting places where they would admire the view, reflect, write or converse.

Both Wordsworth and Coleridge are reputed to have written poems about the Windy Brow seat which presumably overlooked the Greta. Wordsworth's was called 'Inscription for a Seat by a Pathway side Ascending to Windy Brow' while Coleridge's paraded under the title 'Inscription for a Seat by the Road Side Half-way up a steep hill Facing South' (1800). From the titles of the poems I believe that the seat may have been half way up and just to one side of the little road that still leads from Forge Bridge to Windy Brow and emerges to join Brundholme Road near Dairy Cottage where the Wordsworths stayed. There is a suggestion that there was a collaborative element to both pieces of writing or that they may have been one and the same. The one that has been attributed to Coleridge (but which may well have been written in part or whole by Wordsworth) was first published in *The Morning Post* of October 21, 1800 (Coleridge's birthday) and was reprinted in the *Lake Herald* of November 2nd, 1806. It was published under the signature 'Ventifrons' – this being dog-Latin for Windy Brow. It reads:

A view from the heights of the Greta Bridge looking down on The Forge and Forge Bridge.

INSCRIPTION FOR A SEAT BY THE ROAD SIDE
HALF-WAY UP
A STEEP HILL FACING SOUTH
Thou who in youthful vigour rich, and light
With youthful thoughts dost need no rest! O thou,
To whom alike the valley and the hill
Present a path of ease! Should e'er thine eye
Glance on this sod, and this rude tablet, stop!
'Tis a rude spot, yet here, with thankful hearts,
The foot-worn soldier and his family
Have rested, wife and babe, and boy, perchance
Some eight years old or less, and scantly fed,
Garbed like his father, and already bound

Bridges

The River Greta with
Blencathra in the background.

To his poor father's trade. Or think of him
Who, laden with his implements of toil,
Returns at night to some far distant home,
And having plodded on through rain and mire
With limbs o'er laboured, weak from feverish heat,
And chafed and fretted by December blasts,
Here pauses, thankful he hath reached so far,
And 'mid the sheltering warmth of these bleak trees
Finds restoration—or reflect on those
Who in the spring to meet the warmer sun
Crawl up this steep hill-side, that needlessly
Bends double their weak frames, already bowed
By age or malady, and when, at last,
They gain this wished-for turf, this seat of sods,
Repose—and, well-admonished, ponder here
On final rest. And if a serious thought
Should come uncalled—how soon thy motions high,
Thy balmy spirits and thy fervid blood
Must change to feeble, withered, cold and dry,
Cherish the wholesome sadness! And where'er
The tide of Life impel thee, O be prompt
To make thy present strength the staff of all,
Their staff and resting-place—so shalt thou give
To Youth the sweetest joy that Youth can know;
And for thy future self thou shalt provide
Through every change of various life, a seat,
Not built by hands, on which thy inner part,
Imperishable, many a grievous hour,
Or bleak or sultry may repose—yea, sleep
The sleep of Death, and dream of blissful worlds,
Then wake in Heaven, and find the dream all true.

The Greta . . . a river runs through it

Wordsworth also wrote a poem, written in 1833, and devoted entirely to the River Greta. The poem indicates that he thought very highly of this four mile stretch of water:

TO THE RIVER GRETA, NEAR KESWICK

GRETA, what fearful listening! When huge stones
Rumble along thy bed, block after block:
Or, whirling with reiterated shock,
Combat, while darkness aggravates the groans:
But if thou (like Cocytus from the moans
Heard on this rueful margin) thence wert named
The mourner, thy true nature was defamed,
And the habitual murmur that atones
For thy worst rage, forgotten. Oft as Spring
Decks, on thy sinuous banks, her thousand thrones,
Seats of glad instinct and love's carolling,
The concert, for the happy, then may vie
With liveliest peals of birth-day harmony:
To a grieved heart, the notes are benisons.

So there we have it. Calvert Bridge stands as proud and as solid today as when it was built in the early 1800s. It is remarkable how an old stone bridge over the River Greta and the name which is attached to that bridge can bring to mind such a wealth of far reaching information, most of which is contained within a relatively small area of Keswick stretching from Greta Bank to the bridge itself which still quietly dominates the landscape near Toll Bar Cottage on Penrith Road.

In the September 20th, 1889 edition of *The Lakes Visitor and Keswick Guardian* I came across a letter to the newspaper which was written by a correspondent describing himself as 'an old Keswickian, writing from Sydney, New South Wales.' The correspondent noted: "Before the late poet laureate, Mr Southey, died, I had frequently been on foot and on horseback to the top of Latrigg by way of Calvert Bridge (which was haunted in those days) passing three road ends (also a haunted place)."

Personally, I have never been aware or felt aware of any ghosts in or around the vicinity of Calvert Bridge, although the area probably has a dark past in that I have heard stories of people deciding to end their days by throwing themselves off the bridge into the river below. It has also been suggested that an old oak tree just up the lane – where Brundholme road snakes towards Keswick – was once used as a hanging tree.

Be that as it may.

In the Keswick of the early years of the 21st Century, Paul and Eleanor Paxon's (see chapter on River Dwellers) Toll Bar Cottage next to the bridge has a series of modern solar panels on its slate roof to generate electricity. It amuses me that directly opposite where the old turnpike once stood next to the cottage and where the farmers would invariably grumble at having to pay a toll to take cattle to market, there is now a modern day filling station and store. The service station is visited each and every day by thousands of cars and their drivers as they head in and out of the busy tourist town that is modern day Keswick; a town where, not all that long ago, horses and carriages were the usual form of transport.

The Keswick of today is a town not all that far removed from the days of the turnpike and the mills, provided you look carefully and are aware of the historical landmarks.

Greta Bridge. A watercolour by Lucy Gipps whose father was the Rev Henry Gipps, Vicar at Crosthwaite from 1855 to 1878.
The painting is reproduced courtesy of Keswick Museum and Art Gallery.

Two hundred or so years later, I can still make a strong connection with the early years of the 19th Century. Much of old Keswick is still to be seen today and it is not difficult to imagine day-to-day scenes from the Keswick of yesteryear; even though the life style of the town has changed significantly, every other retail outlet is an outdoor store, the cars have been evicted, quite rightly, from the Market Square, the streets are packed with holidaymakers and hiking boots and approach shoes have replaced clogs as the essential footwear of choice.

It is fascinating to consider all this, but for this Keswick lad, and many like me, Calvert Bridge will always remind us of the many hours we spent in the dream-like days of our Huckleberry Finn childhood, clinging precariously to the bridge's jagged slate parapet and trying our best to catch wild brown trout with bait that consisted of a big soggy ball of well-chewed bread.

And the only care we had in the whole wide world was who amongst us would catch the biggest fish; if, that is, we succeeded in catching a fish at all.

Threlkeld Bridge with the rivers Glenderamackin (left) and St John's Beck joining under the twin arches of the bridge to form the River Greta.

'The bridge hangs gracefully over the river'

The following extract from Thomas West's *Guide to the Lakes* (1779) casts an interesting light on the River Greta and its tributaries, the Glenderaterra, Glenderamackin and St John's Beck and describes Threlkeld Bridge as New Bridge. It also makes reference to one of the viewing points, or stations, as follows: 'The point for viewing this uncommon scene, is directly above the bridge, which hangs gracefully over the river ...'

It reads: 'Another select station for a morning view, is on Latrig, a soft green hill that interposes between the town and Skiddaw. The ascent is by Monk's-hall, leaving Ormathwaite on the left, and following the mountain road about due east till you approach the gate in the stone-wall inclosure; then slant the hill to the right, looking towards Keswick, till you gain the brow of the hill, which exhibits a fine terrace of verdant turf, as smooth as velvet. Below you, rolls the Greta, and, in its course, visits the town before it joins the Derwent, where it issues from the lake, and then their united streams are seen meandering through the vale till they meet the floods of Bassenthwaite, under the verdant skirts of Wythop brows ...

'Proceed, as soon as you can till you arrive at the brink of a green precipice; there you will be entertained with the noise of the rapid Greta (roaring through a craggy channel) that, in a run of two miles, exhibits an uncommon appearance, forming twelve or more of the finest bends and serpentine curves that ever fancy pencilled. The point for viewing

The beautiful St John's Beck at a point near Bridge End Farm where a packhorse bridge sits in front of the road bridge beyond.

this uncommon scene, is directly above the bridge, which hangs gracefully over the river. The town of Keswick appears nowhere to greater advantage than from this station. Helvellyn, in front, overlooks a vast range of varied hills, whose rocky sides are rent with many fissures, the paths of so many rills and roaring cataracts, that echo through the vales, and swell the general torrent. To the east, Cross-fell is discerned like a cloud of blue mist, hanging over the horizon. In the middle space, Mell-fell, a green pyramidal hill, is a singular figure. The eye wandering over Castle-rigg will discover the druid temple on the southern side of the Penrith road.

'Return to the path that leads down the ridge of the hill to the east, and, arrived at the gate that opens into a cross road, descend to the right, along the precipitous bank of a brawling brook, Glenderaterra-beck, that is heard tumbling from the mountains, and concealed by the woods that hang on its steep banks. In the course of the descent, remark Threlkeld-pike, browned with storms, and rent by a dreadful wedge-like rock, that tends to the centre. There are many pastoral cots, and rural seats, scattered round the cultivated skirts of this side of the mountains of Skiddaw and Saddleback, sweetly placed and picturesque. The northern side is less hospitable, being more precipitous, and much concealed in shade.

From the bridge, the road leads to Threlkeld, and falls into the Penrith road, four miles from Keswick. The last mentioned brook, Glenderaterra, divides Skiddaw from Saddleback, called here Threlkeld-fell. From the front of Mr. Wren's house, the eye will be delighted with the vale of St. John, sweetly spread out in rural beauty between two ridges of hills, Lothwaite and Naddle-fells, which, in appearance, join together just behind the Castle-rocks. These, in the centre point of view, have the shew of magnificent ruins. A river is seen on both sides of the vale, lengthening its course in meanders, till it meets Threlkeld-water, or Glenderamackin-beck, at New-bridge, where it takes the name of Greeta. This picture is improved at the brow of the hill, on the western side of the house. Here the Greeta is seen from the bridge, running under the hill where you stand, and on the right, coming forth in a fine deep-channelled stream, between steep wooded banks. In a field on the left, near the second mile-post, stands conspicuous, the above-mentioned wide circus of rude stones; the awful monument of the barbarous superstition which enslaved the minds of ancient times.'

Castlerigg Stone Circle.

Industry
THE DAYS OF WATER POWERED MILLS

chapter four

A walk today along the lower reaches of the River Greta, down bank from Low Briery, through The Forge and the town to the old Greta Bridge, provides many clues to the river's strong industrial past. Victorian mill-style buildings, small clusters of old housing in outlying locations and a scattering of broken down weirs, sluice gates and disued mill races, are the most obvious indications of former industry linked to the water-power of the river.

Yet very few people, from their casual observations, would have any real inkling of the extent to which the flow and force of the river was at one time utilised for industrial purposes, especially between the years 1700 to the early part of the 20th Century but also in Elizabethan times at The Forge and at Brigham when mining was paramount and there were smelting works beside the river. In the Victorian era industry lined up along its banks and lead waste was flushed into the river from mines on Blencathra, the toxic pollution wiping out fish and aquatic life for miles downstream. The town had little or no sewage system and the river was nothing more than an open sewer, a dumping ground for all manner of household rubbish and waste. Cleansed occasionally by heavy rain and spate water it would not, even at the best of times, be particularly pleasant.

Rivers have a certain aroma, almost an earthy smell, but in its industrial heyday, when Keswick did not have a flattering public health record, in terms of housing or sanitation, the Greta would probably reek to high heaven; especially in the vicinity of the tannery on the riverside near what is now the silver bridge and Riverside Lodge.

Apart from those notable occasions in recent years – January 2005 and November 2009 – when it was transformed into a raging torrent causing flood and destruction, the River Greta of today is in the main a relatively peaceful stream. The quality of the water is much improved from the days of industry and waste and as it gently meanders through the picturesque countryside of its upper reaches, especially where it has cut its way over the centuries through Brundholme Woods, it is exceptionally beautiful.

Facing page: The old sluice gate leading into the millrace at Low Briery on the outskirts of Keswick. Water from the race provided the power for the Bobbin Mill.

Below: The remains of the wooden supports at the head of the weir leading to the sluice at Low Briery.

Further down stream the landscape changes to the more urban, but in many respects the river is no less scenic where it reaches the town and flows parallel to Penrith Road and alongside the green, cultivated and leisurely acres of Fitz Park with its rich variety of trees, gardens, paths and open spaces, before performing a big S and coming back on itself towards Greta Bridge at the foot of the town. The river reaches its nadir at the rather unromantically named Cement Point, the no-turning-back pool, often frequented by opportunist lake pike, at the junction where the Greta merges with the River Derwent as it flows out of Derwentwater on its journey from the Borrowdale fells to the sea. It is at this point that you often get an interesting contrast in colour between muddy or peaty water flowing out of the Greta in times of spate and, parallel to it, the much cleaner bottle-green water of the Derwent as it leaves the lake.

These days the outward character of the river and its immediate surrounds in the area of the town has been much changed by the installation of multi-million pound flood defences. In today's tourist town with its legions of coffee houses, cafes, pubs, restaurants, gift shops and outdoor / leisure wear outlets, clustered on or around the Moot Hall and its open-plan, motors-free paved area in the town centre, you cannot also fail to notice the flood defences along the river side . . . substantial slate-covered walls, a large section of the one at High Hill being topped with reinforced glass, easier on the eye than a much bigger wall and through which people can continue to enjoy the view of the river and the fells; although it is a little bizarre to see a reflection in the glass of traffic lines and cars running straight down the Greta's central current and the rooftops of the

The sluice gate at The Forge.

houses on the other side of the road sitting on the flanks of Skiddaw and Latrigg.

Meanwhile, the wall created opposite the Upper Fitz Park is of Hadrian proportions when viewed from the park side of the river; nor is it easy to look over the wall into the river from the Penrith Road side of the Greta. I always enjoyed leaning over the old wall and railings to watch a trout rise to take a fly and to admire the easy grace with which it rose quickly to the surface and then glided back to its original position, holding its place in the stream and poised to rise again; ever alert for the opportunity of food, its mouth and jaw gaping white at intervals against the backcloth of the

The Greta . . . a river runs through it

river bed. This gentle, rhythmic, effortless and at times lightning-quick movement of the wild trout is supreme and far better, in its way, than anything you will ever see at the Royal Ballet.

The general appearance of the river today as it runs through Keswick and beneath Greta Bridge must be a significant improvement on the days when the town's former industrial needs – at a time when tourism was in its relative infancy – influenced the way in which the river was used and, in many ways, abused.

Sluice gate at Low Briery.

While there have been many changes to the environs of the Greta over the years the river is oblivious to them all. Unlike the town, which sleeps, the river is constantly on the move. It flows on regardless, taking the most direct route possible from the mountains to the sea, irrespective of the ways in which it has evolved and been influenced by the machinations of Man and the changing life and rhythm of the town. In 1864, for example, when the Cockermouth-Keswick-Penrith railway (the CKP) was built, the course of the river was physically altered in the upper reaches, at a place known to anglers as The Pigfields (just above Low Briery) to avoid the railway company having to construct two additional and costly bridges over the river.

It is at this point that I ought perhaps to confess to being a living example of Keswick's industrial past, a veritable fossil indeed, in that I spent my childhood from years one to 11 in a terraced mill house, one of three in the row, on the site of a working Bobbin Mill at Low Briery. Not only that I also, in my spotless youth, worked for several years at the Cumberland Pencil Company pencil factory by Greta Bridge.

It seemed a natural progression to go from making pencils to becoming a writer.

The pencil factory, sadly, is no more. Or at least it is no longer in Keswick, other than having a tourist presence in the town in the shape of its museum which, while small, still stands out with its multi-coloured signage and banners against the backcloth of the disused mill building.

The writing was arguably on the wall for the pencil factory after the Lake District Planning Board, in its wisdom, or lack of it, decided in 1999 not to approve a £5m

Industry

Scenes around Greta Bridge.
Top: The old pencil works with
Greta Hall to the top right and
Latrigg behind.

Below: The weir and pencil
works on the low side of the
bridge.

Looking at these original OS maps for the Keswick to Threlkeld area, charted 1860 – 1864, helps enormously in creating a picture of what the town was like in terms of the many yards, streets and mills there were and how far the centre of population had extended into the countryside; very little then compared with today. It is fascinating to trace the course of the river and its adjacent railway line and the point at which the natural route of the river was physically altered, in the early 1860s, by the railway builders so that fewer bridges over the river needed to be constructed (follow the course of the dots in the central current to see the line of the original flow). It is also interesting to note the number of weirs and the positions of their adjacent millraces; traces of these are still to be seen.

The maps, the first OS maps for the area, are works of art and paint a fantastic picture, the river appearing as a light blue wash, buildings in maroon and roads in cream set against the black and off-white of the remainder.

The maps are reproduced courtesy of the Cumbria Archives Centre, Lady Gillford's House, Carlisle.

The time traveller

It is intriguing to look back on Keswick's industrial past and to envisage life as it was in the mid to late 19th Century when the town's development as a place of industry and mills was arguably at its peak before the scenic appeal of the Lake District and an influx of many thousands of visitors changed dramatically the feel and commercial direction of the town.

Looking at the original Ordnance Survey maps for the Keswick to Threlkeld area charted 1860 – 1864 (see fold out) helps enormously in creating a picture of what the town was like in terms of the many yards, streets and mills there were and how far the centre of population had extended into the countryside; very little then compared with today. It is fascinating to look now at those original OS maps of the town and area and to trace the course of the river and its adjacent railway line. The maps, the first OS maps for the area, are works of art and paint a fantastic picture, the river appearing as a light blue wash, buildings in maroon and roads in cream set against the black and off-white of the remainder. A much more rudimentary Tithe map of the 1840s is equally intriguing in showing the original course of the river in the days before the arrival of the railway.

Add to the overall picture a wealth of other material – gleaned primarily from the pages of the then local newspaper *The Lakes Visitor and Keswick Guardian* – and it becomes much easier to draw on your mental imagery and get a genuine feel of what the town was really like in years gone by. So much so that where ever I now look in the town and by the river I get snapshots of mid 19th Century Keswick. It's good to live in the early years of the 21st Century and to also, at the same time, have the ability to 'live' in the same location two centuries previously. Time travel is more readily available than you might think; you should give it a try.

My research into Keswick's industrial past and specifically that of the water-powered mills (1700s – 1960) has been helped enormously by the work of Mike Davies-Shiel, of Windermere, who, sadly, died before the results of his endeavours could see the light of day. Keswick Historical Society, based in the town's Museum and Art Gallery, kindly provided me with the documentation on Mike's work.

The workforce involved in the mills probably amounted to a minimum of 500 adults and there would have been many more outworkers and suppliers, carters and the like, to keep the mills going. The railway, when it arrived in 1864, boosted some production lines, particularly bobbins and pencils, but had a negative impact on the large wool carding mills and all of those, except one, had closed by 1876 as they changed over to the more commercially rewarding trades of pencil and bobbin making.

The textile mills made threads of many types for the haberdashery trade, sending out tons of ribbons, tapes, plaids, shawls, linings, braces, moleskins, jeans, waistcoatings, nun's lace, cuffs, cap-springs, braid, caps, girdles, worsteds, buckrams, cloakings, beeding, gimps, shirtings, hair nets, neck ties, busks, aprons, sagathies, orleans, ginghams, linens, cambrics, tassels, boot laces, darmly cotton, hooks, eyelets, bodkins, needles, round cane, whalebone, belts, lute strings . . . to mention a few! Some mills specialised in blankets, duffels and warm woollen clothing while others sent their threads to larger firms in Yorkshire and Lancashire.

In the early years it would appear that 19 of the 27 water-powered mills were engaged in the textile trade, these being 10 woollen, one cotton, three flax, four fulling and one dye mill. By the late 19th Century and in the early 20th Century, 21 of the mills were

This colourful picture of an angler fishing the fast flowing water below Forge Bridge also shows the full scale of the old cotton mill with is tower. It is entitled 'Mill at The Forge, River Greta' and is the work of E.N. Grayson.
Painting reproduced courtesy of the Keswick Museum and Art Gallery.

involved in the timber trades, namely 11 pencil, seven bobbin, two sawmills and a single Cedarwood mill.

Of the 27 water-powered mills all had converted to electric power except one (Low Briery Bobbin Mill) by the end of World War II. A total of 14 of the mills were still in operation in 1939 and 11 in 1961. The last working mill, as stated previously, was the Cumberland Pencil Mill at Southey Hill near Greta Bridge.

Referring specifically to The Forge on the outskirts of town this was originally a location for Elizabethan smelting works. Copper ore said to contain silver was discovered in Cumberland and in May 1565 the Queen granted a warrant to bring in a small army of foreign workers. The first contingent of German miners, 20 in number, came to Keswick in September of the same year and many more followed. The Company of Royal Mines worked the mines and the ore was brought from Newlands 'to beyond (what is now) Calvert Bridge by the Greta river, and the smelting mills were put down at a place still called The Forge. The mill race, which we speak of as the Hammer Hole, cut with wedges and big hammers in the same way as levels were driven in the mines at Newlands, may still be seen.' A weir was built across the Greta – the same one that has now virtually been washed away by flooding – and the water was brought to the smelting works through a tunnel (still in existence) cut into the rock of an adjacent hill and leading to the mill race; the latter more or less dried up now except in times of high water. It has been stated that the smelting works at The Forge were destroyed by Cromwell's soldiers during the Civil War but Mike Davies-Shiel contended: "The forces of Oliver Cromwell did not halt the business of mining and smelting around Keswick. Indeed, they continued to finance and run all the establishments, except one – and that had closed of its own choosing just prior to the start of the Civil War. The carry-over may still be seen at mills in Brigham and in the many German or Austrian surnames that are today accepted as being traditional Lakeland family names, such as Banks, Dixon, Jenkinson, Parker . . ."

This watercolour of a mill on the River Greta is dated September 21st, 1898 but I believe the mill in question is much older. The mill in question is called Wren's Mill and was situated close to where there is now a row of riverside cottages on Penrith Road, opposite the entrance to Wordsworth Street. Painting reproduced courtesy of the Keswick Museum and Art Gallery.

The foreign workers certainly made quite an impression when it came to harnessing the power of the river to make light work of what had previously been back-breaking toil, although there was still plenty of opportunity for the latter. William Camden, historian (circa 1586) stated: "Keswick is at this day much inhabited by minerall men, who have heere their smelting house by Derwentside, which with his forcible streame (the Greta) and their ingenious inventions serveth them in notable steede for easie bellowes workes, hammer workes, forge workes, and sawing of boords, not without admiration of such as behold it."

After this early industrial foray allied to mining The Forge may have lain relatively dormant until industry returned to the site and a cotton mill was built there, on the south bank of the Greta, most likely in the 1790s. The mill had several storeys, had a distinguishing bell turret and, apparently, resembled the early carding mill at Millbeck which was working by 1796. The Forge cotton mill belonged, in 1819, to Messrs Blakey and Hardisty and Mr Hardisty's home was Myrtle Grove, situated on the Latrigg side of the river at The Forge. Hardisty had dye houses on the site, as well as the cotton works, and these were under the management of John Dover.

There were connections between the industry at The Forge and the Dover family's woollen mills at Millbeck, and the quickest route between the two places was via the Forge Bridge (built by Hardisty in 1817). The Tithe map for the early 1840s shows that Dover and Co had a fulling mill at the Forge.

By the mid 19th Century The Forge had become a busy industrial centre. Besides the fulling mill, the Tithe map shows a dye house and yard, a pencil mill housed in the old cotton mill and a workshop and mill that may well have been another pencil mill. There was also a missionary room at The Forge and monthly services were still held there in the 20th Century. The brewery at Brow Foot – at the end of the Forge Lonning – is shown on the 1860s OS map. Keswick's first electricity supply was being generated on the site of the old cotton mill by the end of the century.

The writing on the wall tells the story. The mill was situated opposite Lower Fitz Park.

My kingdom for a bobbin

Just a little further upstream from The Forge, Low Briery was also generating a lot of activity with woollens made there from 1826 – 1900s and pencils and bobbins from 1837 – 1961. My father, Thomas Henry Richardson, went to Low Briery as a four year old in 1915 with his father Harold and his mother Jane (nee Robinson) and four sisters, Florence Emma, Henrietta May, Marjory and Violet Annie. The family moved to Low Briery from Field Head Farm, Mungrisdale, where Harold was a farm labourer. From what I can gather my grandfather – who died before I was born – farmed at Low Briery (there was a farm attached to the mill) and may also have worked with horses at the mill. After leaving Brigham School at the age of 14 my father served his apprenticeship as a bobbin turner at Low Briery and worked there for 34 years until its closure. At one time the mill employed up to 120 and had its own railway platform on the Cockermouth-Keswick-Penrith line for the use of workers.

Hard woods such as ash, birch, beech, sycamore, lime, alder, chestnut and teak were used in the manufacture of bobbins because they did not warp. The wood went through as many as 40 different processes before a bobbin was produced. Bobbins were made in all shapes and sizes. The larger bobbins were used for electrical wiring, the wire in £1 and the charming old 10-shilling notes (of which I have fond memories on childhood birthdays when they were occasionally tucked into greetings cards) or for carpets. Others were used for weft threads in the Irish linen trade and smaller bobbins were used for silk or cotton and in the woollen industry.

The painting is entitled 'Cotton Mill, near Keswick on the River Greta'. It is the work of Joseph Wilkinson (1764 – 1831) and is a watercolour 246 x 349mm. The cotton mill in the background is the one at The Forge. I believe the work was painted from a situation on the far bank of the river at Town's Field, possibly at the foot of the pool we now know as 'Stoney'.
Picture courtesy of the Wordsworth Trust, The Jerwood Centre, Dove Cottage, Grasmere.

My father recalled that in his day the wage for a time-served bobbin turner was £3 1s 6d for a 48 hour week and that the bobbin mill was the first in the Keswick area to work a five day week.

"On the Friday night you'd all line up at the offices," he said, "and you all had a number, they shouted your number out and you got your pay in a laal tin box."

He also remembered that at one time there was a textile mill at Low Briery and it specialised in making intricate bottom edgings for waistcoats.

"They used to call it Fancy Bottom down there (at Low Briery)," he said, "but it was the bobbin mill that really brought work to Keswick. When it was at its height there would be 40,000,000 bobbins garn out ivvery year."

Bobbin making was the final industry at Low Briery when the mill was closed and sold. It is now a holiday village and the main mill building, where bobbins were turned on lathes, the space buzzed with machinery and overhead belts, and the air was thick with sawdust, now houses a small leisure area including a heated splash pool for children.

The giant wooden cranes, which would carry the trunks of trees as if they were

This drawing of the River Greta was created by William Green (1760 – 1823) of Ambleside and was published by him in 1809. It is described as a soft ground etching and is 330 x 440mm. The identity of the building on the right is unknown but I am confident that it is situated off what is now Penrith Road opposite its junction with Wordsworth Street. Looking up the river I am sure that the boulder on the left bank is still there, roughly opposite the site of the old swing bridge near Millfield.
Picture courtesy of the Wordsworth Trust,
The Jerwood Centre,
Dove Cottage, Grasmere.

matchsticks, have long disappeared from the landscaped area surrounding what once was a working mill and farm. And the terraced houses where we lived, with their outside toilets, are now modern holiday homes at the heart of the static caravan site cum holiday village.

My father, when asked if he had any regrets about the mill's closure and the changed nature of the site, replied: "Oh dear, no. Ivverything's got to mek progress. That's the way of the world."

The same is true of the town and the wider Lake District. Keswick, set in one of the most beautiful locations on planet earth, and at one time a place of industry with mills of several different persuasions flanking its river, now relies almost entirely on the hundreds of thousands of visitors that its very special environment attracts each year. The tourists sustain its livelihood and its way of life in a constantly changing world; a world in which Keswick – once known for its pencil making – is now promoted as The Outdoor Capital of the UK.

Childhood
AND THE MILL

For the best part of 10 years of my young life, from year one to year 11, the River Greta flowed within a few paces of the back door and steps of our house at Low Briery, at that time a working bobbin mill and farm on the fringe of Keswick, situated in the valley of the river at the bottom of a lane leading from the old Penrith Road. In fact my first recollection in life is of sitting in a pram at the top of Bobbin Mill Lonning, as we called it, while my mother Emmeline, Emmy for short, bless her, talked for what seemed an eternity to another woman while I quietly seethed with impatience in the confines of my pram. I am not entirely sure whether or not I was wearing a dummy at the time but had I had words to express myself they would have been along the lines of "For goodness sake . . . I want to go home. Are you going to stand there yakking (talking) all day!"

Mini childhood tantrums apart, I am sure that the close proximity of the river and the fact that it was an ever present in my formative years had a beneficial – although some might say differently – effect on my nature. I believe that living in a house with the constant and almost subliminal sound of running water over pebbles and stones close by, has a very positive impact on the soul. Even during sleep I am sure that the soothing sound of the river washes womb-like over the brain and that it is all to the good.

The house where I live today on the Windebrowe Avenue housing estate in Keswick, and have lived, off and on but more on, since we left Low Briery when I was 11, is a few hundred yards from the River Greta. I still hanker to be by the river and take every opportunity to walk by the Greta, through the countryside of Brundholme Woods to Threlkeld or the more urban environment of Fitz Park in the centre of town. The river provides therapy and solace in dealing with life's less positive elements and can be a source of quiet inspiration when thinking through ideas. When ever I have the good fortune to stay in a place away from home that is close to a running stream it immediately takes me back to Low Briery and the River Greta.

I am drawn to water and especially to rivers, but also to the sea, and am convinced that this is entirely due to the many happy years I spent as a youngster by the river.

Facing page:
Looking down on Longtown Field and the River Greta, above Low Briery and the old Bobbin Mill, from the footpath through Brundholme Woods. Note the railway bridge in the background. This is the same bridge that is the subject of a beautiful painting of a steam train, the river and two walkers later in this chapter. Longtown Field was a significant play area in my childhood.

Above: The author aged six is pictured on the left of this photograph together with his cousin Alan and sister Margaret and two toddlers who must have been passing at the time and looking for a photo opportunity. Sadly I have no idea who they are.

Low Briery itself was an unusual combination. Located on the outskirts of Keswick it was principally a bobbin mill with a farm and a row of three terraced houses and other outbuildings. I remember, only too well, a big round iron water tank, near the farm, and in which, to my horror, a farmhand drowned an unwanted litter of kittens, tied in a sack. It was the one dark deed that I can vividly recall from my days (1951 – 1961) at the bobbin mill and farm and gave me my first lesson that for some unfortunate creatures life can be cruel and short-lived.

On a happier note there was a farm sheepdog, Jet, which I befriended and – in the absence of other boys and girls my own age at the mill – I spent as much time as I could with Jet. I was fond of Jet and he was fond of the fact that I was in the habit of feeding him cow cake. My idea of bliss at that early stage in my life was probably sitting in the sun on a wall at the back of our house overlooking the River Greta, eating my favourite sweets and reading a Davy Crockett (King of the Wild Frontier) comic with Jet at my side, my pal crunching happily on the cow cake I had 'borrowed' from the farm store next to my gran's house.

Buildings at Low Briery. My grandmother Jane Richardson and Aunty Marjorie lived in the cottage left of centre.

The Bobbin Mill was a big adventure playground that I had all to myself and in which I ran riot, although not in a destructive way; it was just that my imagination and my legs – I remember making a vow to myself one day that I would never, ever, stop running – were working overtime. Low Briery is now a holiday village complete with caravans and chalets and while the main mill building is still there the part of it where my dad worked on the lathes is now a mini leisure centre, complete with a small pool and play area for children.

As a small child you always envisage a place as being far bigger than it is in reality and when you revisit years later, and at a height of 6 foot two, you have some difficulty in relating the past with the present because everything looks so much smaller.

The Greta . . . a river runs through it

The house where we lived – the middle one of three in the terrace backing onto the river – is still there but the properties are much improved; in our day there were no bathrooms and just a very basic row of outside hole-in-the-wood toilets. The farm cottage, where my grandmother lived on the other side of the mill to our terraced house, no longer has the wonderful black, cast iron range on which she cooked, using the small ovens either side of the fire and various metal platforms that swung out over the flames. In those early days we did not have electricity and relied on candles and oil lamps for lighting. As Doris Price recalled with amusement in an earlier chapter we were all fairly primitive at Low Briery in comparison with the small community at The Forge where they were more advanced and had their very own electrical company. Unfortunately for them, The Forge dwellers, tucked away in their valley down by the river, only rarely if ever saw the sun in winter while we fared better at Low Briery.

The brick-built bobbin mill at Low Briery was an active, noisy and dusty place, a factory in the middle of the countryside and situated down by the river. Inside the mill there was a mass of whirring machinery and overhead belts, all generated by water from the mill race which drew on the River Greta via a sluice gate at the end of the weir about 100 yards or so upstream. My father, Tommy, who worked in the mill, came to Low Briery when he was four years old after being born at Fieldhead Farm, Troutbeck (near Mungrisdale). In his spare time at the mill he would make green heart fly rods on the lathes. He also introduced me to fly-fishing on the Greta and I can remember being entranced by the vivid colours of the trout he caught on the fly one Sunday afternoon from a fast-flowing pool just above the weir. I also took up fishing as a small boy and was not immediately successful. Night lines baited with worm and left in the beck to the back of the house seemed only to attract eels which curled and writhed, snake-like, around your arm as you tried to remove the hook. The first brown trout I caught, in the low side of the millrace, was so small I had to put it on a saucer in order to make it look bigger as I paraded it proudly through the various houses at Low Briery.

Technically speaking you had to have a licence from the River Board to fish for trout but I made do with a permit from the Bobbin Mill office, a slip of paper that gave me permission to fish on Low Briery water. The man who gave me the permit told me that if I succeeded in catching a trout then I ought to put salt on its tail, pop it back in the water and then catch it once more; it would taste better that way. Naturally, I believed him but did not take his advice.

The mill had wooden outbuildings full of row upon row of racks of open sided shelf-like constructions, stretching to the roof, and bearing wood of all shapes and sizes. Dusty-floored alleyways separated the shelves and I was like Tarzan in his jungle, swinging from 'tree to tree' between the racks containing the strips of wood destined for the mill and a future as bobbins, big and small. At its peak Low Briery produced 40 million bobbins a year, about half of the world textile industry's demand. The bobbins were mainly used for cotton but also had their uses for silk, Irish linen and the wire that was once used in old pound notes (see chapter 4 on mills for more information).

Massive wooden cranes on circular concrete blocks looked down on the mill, like gigantic herons scanning the water for minnows; or swinging across the landscape of this little piece of industry in the countryside like those long-legged aliens from HG Wells' classic *War of the Worlds*.

High Briery on the old Keswick to Penrith road. The cottages were demolished to make way for the A66.

The cranes were used to haul tree trunks around and as if that and the mill was not enough activity for one relatively small vale near the river, the old Penrith-Keswick-Cockermouth railway line ran past the mill and trains would call at the single Low Briery platform to drop off and collect workers at the start and end of the working day. In those days a footbridge over the railway and a path up the fields connected Low Briery to the solitary line of terraced houses, High Briery, situated on the old main road at the top of the hill. The High Briery houses were later demolished to make way for the A66. In my childhood, the railway trains were steam as opposed to the diesels that came later. I used to stand on the footbridge over the railway when the steam train came through and close my eyes before being blanketed in the billowing white smoke as the train passed beneath the bridge. I emerged coughing and spluttering with my face, hair and clothing covered in little black smudges.

Nowadays there is a display board near the old platform and on it is a large photograph, probably taken in the 1930s, of all the mill workers at that time, plus information about the mill and its products. While we can peer in on their world through this image – my grandfather Harold may be standing on the far right with one of the horses he worked with – I wonder what they would make of 21st Century England if only they could look out of the display and information board at the thousands of walkers, runners and cyclists who every year use the old Keswick to Threlkeld railway line as a path?

Looking back on my time as a boy at Low Briery it occurs to me that had the mill not closed in 1961 I would probably have ended up following in my father's footsteps and would have worked there; an apprentice bobbin maker. In reality the entire working environment of the bobbin mill and, for that matter the nearby railway line, was a death trap for an adventurous small boy with little appreciation of life's hazards (although I was told not to go onto the railway line) and I was lucky to survive the following: crushing when digging a hole under a woodpile which promptly fell on me (dad came to my rescue); drowning when I slipped off a rock into a deep pool in the river while trout fishing, I somehow scrambled back onto the bank, drenched from head to foot – I could not swim at the time; a blow to the head when I was hit by a works wagon while

Mill workers at the Low Briery Bobbin Mill.

riding my three wheeler bike, pretending that I was The Lone Ranger complete with cowboy hat and six guns with explosive caps. On that occasion I escaped with a gash to the head after colliding with the rear of the lorry.

To limit my chances of an early death from drowning, I had my first swimming lessons in the safety of the shallow and enclosed water in the millrace before progressing to the river above the weir. My dad taught me to swim the breaststroke and supported me gently with the palm of his hand under my chest as I moved my arms and legs frantically in the water like a frog. As my confidence grew he moved his hand away without me knowing and I was swimming of my own accord; until, that is, I realised my support system was no longer there, panic set in and I started to flap, swallow water and sink until dad's hand returned to lift me up once more.

Amazingly I returned the favour when I took my dad, by then in his late seventies, on holiday to Madeira, the first time he had been abroad and the first time he had flown. I persuaded him one evening to join me in a dip in the pool of the hotel where we stayed; a hotel, incidentally, where he soon had the lunchtime, poolside bar staff conversant with the ethics of the Cumbrian (Keswick branch) 'pensioners' half.' The object was to leave a little beer in the bottom of a pint glass, ask for a half pint and if they had anything about them the barman would invariably fill it to the top! Dad had not swum since those early days at the bobbin mill where he would swim and bathe in the deep pool above the weir – he always took a bar of soap as well as a towel on a swimming trip. Now in the autumn of his life here he was in another pool in a distant land, light years from those days at Low Briery, and was not entirely sure if he could remember how to swim. I kitted him out in a pair of my swimming shorts (far removed from the itchy, woollen, maroon-coloured dookers of my childhood) and he proved that his self doubt was entirely justified by launching into a somewhat frenzied breaststroke

This is a superbly rich and colourful painting of a steam train on the railway bridge over the River Greta, just above Low Briery and the Bobbin Mill weir. Longtown field is situated on the far side of the bridge. Artist unknown.

and promptly going under. In a complete role reversal of what had happened all those years ago in the millrace at Low Briery I now found myself supporting my dad with my hand as he learned to swim all over again. He soon got the hang of it.

After our evening meal in the hotel in Funchal we would usually make our way across the road to a bar that doubled as a grocer's store. I mention this because the people there treated the elderly, and in this instance my dad, with the utmost regard and courtesy, bordering on adulation. If only people in all countries showed the same respect the world might be a better place.

The millrace where I had my first swimming lesson was also the scene each autumn for a rather unusual Atlantic salmon rescue mission. I would help a mill worker, Jackie Bertram, who was also a keen rod and line angler, to free the salmon that were caught, like minnows in a trap, in the millrace. Jack, a big, pipe-smoking circumference of a man who, if I remember correctly, wore dark blue overalls tied round with a leather belt, Wellington boots clamped to his feet and a cloth cap atop his head, would stop the flow of water into the race by shutting off the sluice at the weir. He would then wade into the increasingly shallow water and the cloying mud of the race, catch the salmon and throw them up to me on the bank. I would gather a fish in my arms or grasp it as best I could with both hands on the slippery tail, and hurry across the narrow field separating the race from the river, the fish gasping and thrashing in my hands. On reaching the beck I would lower the salmon into the river where it would thrash out powerfully and dart towards the deeper water and, eventually, hopefully make its way back to the sea from whence it came. The life cycle of the salmon is amazing, especially that part where the fully grown salmon leave their far north feeding grounds and follow the moon, the stars, the scent of the water and heaven only knows what else, to make their way out of the sea and into the mouth of the same river in which they were spawned. And then to fight their way to the higher reaches of that river to spawn, sometimes on the self-same gravel beds where they were given life.

Without a helping hand from Jackie Bertram and myself in a supporting role, all the salmon that had become trapped in the millrace – unable to make their way out after entering with the flow of water on the raising of the sluice gate – would have died. As it was some of them, after their 'flight' across the field in my arms, may have made their way safely back to the sea and future generations of their offspring are probably still running the river to this day; although, sadly, in vastly reduced numbers. But that's another story.

The Bobbin Mill and Low Briery and the Greta were clearly the landscape of my childhood. The twisting lane leading to the mill from the old Penrith Road was beautiful by day, with first primroses and then yellow and orange poppies along its banks and the occasional feast of small, bright red, wild strawberries at the height of summer. At night, however, it became a living nightmare, a dark place and a 'killing' ground for all manner of evil hidden among the trees as my childhood imagination got the better of me.

The lane was about a quarter of a mile long and it was the central section, where trees towered over it, that set my heart racing. It could all have been avoided but the family of a pal, Jeff Parker, who lived in a house near the top of the lonning, had a black and white television. I was so entranced by the miracle of TV (we only had a wireless, Wilfred Pickles and 'Listen with Mother' at the Bobbin Mill) that I can recall staring at the test card during the day in the vain hope that something might happen. Black Beauty was serialised on Sunday evenings in winter and it was essential viewing. Unfortunately the clocks had gone back and the light outside Jeff's house at Eleventrees

Bluebells in a wood next to the River Greta.

was fading fast as the drama unfolded on the small screen. By the time that week's instalment ended at about 6pm and I had to make my way home the night was already blacker than Black Beauty and my nerves were on edge at the prospect of going down the Bobbin Mill Lonning, all alone in the dark.

The shapes and movement of branches and trees, stirred by the breeze, or the sudden light snap of a twig or, heaven forbid, the sound of something shuffling around in the undergrowth, would terrify me. I did have options when faced by the unknown or the legions of the undead. Option one was to pretend to be brave, to stride out purposefully and to whistle a carefree tune. Option two was to leg it, as fast as my short-trousered legs would carry me, helter-skelter all the way down the lonning until the solitary night light on the side of the mill came into view and I knew, once I saw it, that I was almost safe.

Safe, in truth, was how I felt about my childhood world at Low Briery. I believed in Father Christmas, that if you broke a vase or a mirror you got seven years bad luck, and I was sheltered away in a world of my own with the woods and the river close by, plenty of opportunities for wild imagination and adventure. And despite the closeness of the mill, the railway and the river and all that they provided, either real or imaginary, I was largely oblivious to the dangers they posed. I have vague recollections of a protracted illness that confined me to bed with a poisoned arm for a large part of a primary school year but other than that – and the minor incidents I related earlier on my narrow escapes from death by crushing, drowning and beheading – nothing really fazed me. The outside world of Brigham Primary School and a scary headmaster with an irrational scream and shout temper and a worrying tendency to use the cane as punishment for minor offences, presented much more of a threat to peace of mind.

Marigold.

But in the safe environs of Low Briery, the surrounding countryside and the mill's resident little community – only a handful of families, Richardsons, Tysons, Bertrams and Coates lived there – the opportunities for fun were endless. In my mind's eye the summers were a big blue sky across which the sun rose, arced and set without fear of interruption from cloud. Flies became permanently attached to strips of sticky paper hanging from the kitchen and living room ceilings. I fished for trout or swam in the River Greta, and with my sister Margaret collected swathes of bluebells or Marguerites from the woods and banks, or captured, and later released, ladybirds in jam jars from a field at the top of the lonning. Marigolds, a personal favourite, grew strong, yellow and purposefully at the water margins of the river or in boggy ground elsewhere. The wild strawberries were at their most succulent but frustratingly small on the railway embankment or the bank at the side of the lonning.

In the summer there were the occasional family holidays to seaside resorts like Blackpool and Morecambe and I was sometimes packed-off on the bus to Aunty Lilly and Uncle Bas's home in Shirley, near deepest Solihull, for a childhood holiday with a difference in the Midlands and where I missed the sight and sound of the river. My play area there was a back lane that reeked in high summer of rotten fruit from an adjacent grocery store. It somehow did not quite match the appeal of my home by the Greta. I remember being put on the bus in Keswick and setting out on this epic journey all alone. When I got off at Birmingham and sat waiting in the bus station my small brown suitcase stayed on the bus and Uncle Basil had to pursue it virtually all the way to London in his car to retrieve my belongings and, more importantly, my £3 spending money for the holiday. My Uncle Basil was not pleased.

At Christmas we had family gatherings at Low Briery with parties held at different houses on the main days of Christmas Eve, Christmas Day, Boxing Day and New Year's Eve. A cold spread of ham, pickles, turkey, stuffing, bread covered with Cumberland rum butter, and cakes, sherry-laced trifles, cups of tea and then alcoholic drinks for the men and women and pop for the kids was usually followed by a game of cards. On one occasion I was persuaded to sing a song and was so self-conscious and shy that I only agreed to do so as long as I could stand out of sight behind a curtain. I reckon I had a good voice and inherited it from my mother who used to sing at Keswick's Methodist Chapel on Southey Street. But the traditional in-house entertainment after we ate was the card game, Newmarket, played on a table in front of the fire. The card game was big on excitement and, after a quiet beginning, the excitement mounted and to win the final hand of the night with a mountain of coins at stake was wonderful. I did win that final hand occasionally and I guess it was fixed for me to do so. Either way I'm not complaining. The card games lasted until about midnight with the heat of the fire almost unbearable and the room heavy with cigarette smoke; smoking was all the rage then and I was attracted to the supremely white untipped cigarettes in their gleaming silver cases and the way in which a smoker would tap the cigarette end against the case, just so, before striking a match and lighting up. I had to make do with a pack of white, sugar-flavoured cigarettes with their little red tips to represent the burning tobacco.

The dangers of smoking were not fully appreciated in those days, but in some other respects healthy eating was light years ahead. Spring brought new life and to cleanse the blood of the heavy diet of meat eaten during the winter months it was traditional to use new green shoots for the Cumberland Herb Pudding that had a very distinctive flavour.

My grandmother Jane Richardson (nee Robinson) was the eldest of eight children born to Robert and Mary Ann Robinson (nee Walker), of Helton, near Penrith. Jane herself was born at Cookelty, Underskiddaw, a house situated on the Keswick to Bassenthwaite road near the turn off to Millbeck. I have a faded picture in my mind of my grandmother stooping over in a field at Low Briery to pick the Bistort that is the key ingredient in the dish, that and the tops of young nettles. My gran made the best Cumberland herb pudding in the world, of that I am sure. We ate it as a vegetable dish to accompany the Sunday roast. These days I find the taste so exquisite that I would probably eat it on its own although it would be tempting to have it for lunch with roast beef, roast potatoes and Yorkshire puddings and recreate those far off days when gran made herb puddings in the springtime for the Sunday tables of our respective households at Low Briery.

When the mill closed we eventually moved into Keswick and my dad worked as a stonemason in the town and later at Honister while my mam worked in the old laundry and then in the canteen at Keswick School.

The link with the mill was not immediately broken because long after its closure my grandmother Jane and her daughter, my Aunty Marjorie, continued to live at Low Briery, although it must have been strange for them at first with only largely themselves for company after the mill fell silent. Despite this considerable change, moving home after the closure of the mill, we were never far from the River Greta and it continued to flow through my life. It still does to this day some 60 years later; a mere drop in the life span of the river and in the context of time.

And when I ask myself the same question I have asked of other river dwellers in the writing of this book (what does the river really mean in the context of your life?) the answer can be summed up in one word. Everything.

We are all made largely of water and we all rely on water. The rain that falls on the mountains fills the streams and rivers and lakes and flows to the sea before returning to descend on the land and to fill the rivers once again. Not a single drop of water is lost along the way in this amazing cycle, a continual and never ending circle that embraces birth, life, death and renewal. Is it pure coincidence that the lines of a river on the land are so very much like the veins that run through the human body or through the fabric of something as fragile as the leaf of a tree? I think not.

We pollute water at our peril.

Wild swimming at Town's Field

Stony, the pool on the River Greta, at Town's Field, was always my place of choice for a swim when I was a lad. Sandy, the large pool with its own beach at the bottom end of the field, tended to get murky and dirty and you were never quite sure what hidden dangers, a rusty old tin or broken bottle, might wait in the deeper water where it suddenly dropped off out of your depth and where sticks and other debris tended to accumulate. Stony, on the other hand, was crystal clear and shallower with a colourful bed and a big boulder smack dab in the middle on which to clamber and leap.

But would Stony still hold the same pleasures for a sixty year old revisiting the swimming haunt of his boyhood?

It was the early afternoon of May 25th, 2012 when I visited Stony and the sky was blue and the sun was hot. Unfortunately the water was cold but I soon acclimatised, so much so that at one point, when the sun was hidden by a cloud, it was warmer in than out. I swam up and down the pool several times, on and under the water, before hauling myself out on a rock at the foot of the pool and sunbathing. This was ecstasy and the only place to be in the heat of the afternoon.

The pool did not appear to hold much in the way of fish life. A lonely salmon fry and a small trout were the only visible results of my underwater forays although I later saw a shoal of minnows at the water's edge on Sandy. Small clouds of insects were blown across the surface of the river, carried this way and that on the whim of the breeze. On the banks the greenery was lush among the trees and lower lying foliage as a couple of cabbage whites fluttered by.

In the stretch of river below my sunbathing spot on the rock the water moved more quickly past the sticky-out stones as it gathered impetus on its journey to a much bigger pool fifty or so yards below, the middle dub on Townsie and the one with a great big Jumbo rock at its side, one of three such rocks in Town's Field alone. It was here that Val Corbett managed to get her superb, all action image, of local children swimming in the river leaping from the top of Jumbo and using an old inner tube to float down the beck.

The sun bakes me as I lie on the rock in Stony, one foot dangling in the cool of the

Previous pages:
Wild swimming in the River Greta. The youngsters pictured here in this amazing composition are having fun in the middle pool in Town's Field, Keswick.

The Greta . . . a river runs through it

river. I relish the heat of the sun as the water dries on my body and enjoy the sight and sound of the river as well as that distinctive, almost earthy aroma of the beck.

I return to the water and alternate between swimming and exploring the pool and basking on the rock. After a while I decide to venture downstream, swim through the middle dub past Jumbo and then enter the narrow, fast, white water rapid that leads directly into Sandy. It is exhilarating and fun and the force of the water – even though the river is low – is surprising and I am tossed around by the current.

I swim into Sandy and take my life in my hands by deciding to risk a shallow dive off the big rock on the far side of the river. I swim across the pool to the beach, proof positive that I can, indeed, swim (see River Dwellers chapter and Jill Wilk's observations on swimming at Sandy).

Wild swimming such as this in Town's Field is most definitely one of life's great pleasures. And it does not matter one iota whether you are six . . . or have reached the double-edged state in life that is sixty going on six.

Greta Hall

YOUNG SARA COLERIDGE FELL INTO THE RIVER

chapter six

This drawing created in the early years of the 19th Century by a young Dora Wordsworth – daughter of the poet William – shows Greta Hall, Keswick, home of Lakes poets, with the River Greta running past below. The sketch also shows a rather unusual wooden bridge, a somewhat flimsy affair stretching across the river and emerging out of buildings on the left bank to open land on the far side. The entire construction, sloping from left to right, is supported by cross beams at its half way point and there are wooden hand rails, parallel to each other, to prevent people from falling into the water and to assist their passage over the river.

There is every indication to suggest that this may be the type of wooden bridge over the Greta which was at the centre of a dramatic incident involving the river and the poets Samuel Taylor Coleridge and Robert Southey and their families during their residence at the distinctive Greta Hall, high on a hill overlooking the town and surrounding countryside. The incident involved Sara Coleridge, fourth and youngest child and only daughter of STC and Robert Southey's niece, Sarah Fricker. In the incident young Sara had a narrow escape from serious injury and possibly drowning but was, not surprisingly, traumatised by the event.

Facing page: Wild garlic by the River Greta below Greta Hall and a favourite walking place for the poet Robert Southey.

The River Greta with Greta Hall in the background and a rickety looking wooden bridge over the river, possibly the one from which Sara Coleridge fell into the river when she was two. The pencil drawing, 82 x 120mm, is the work of Dora Wordsworth (1804 – 1847) daughter of the poet William. Picture courtesy of the Wordsworth Trust, The Jerwood Centre, Dove Cottage, Grasmere.

Greta Hall

Sara was born at Greta Hall on December 22nd, 1802. At the time of her birth her father was only 29 years of age but already struggling, despite his relative youth, with the various maladies, physical and mental, that were exacerbated by his growing reliance on laudanum. Sara's brother Hartley was six and Derwent was four at the time of the incident (a brother Berkeley had died a baby in 1798). STC described Hartley as "a strange, strange boy, exquisitely wild, an utter visionary, like the moon among the thin clouds he moves in a circle of light of his own making. He alone is a light of his own, of all human beings I never saw one so utterly naked of self. Hartley is all Health and extacy (Coleridge's spelling) – he is a spirit dancing on an aspen leaf – unwearied in joy, from morning to night indefatigably joyous . . ."

And in correspondence relating to the birth of Derwent on September 14th, 1800, STC wrote to Humphry Davy in Bristol, postmarked Keswick, October 13th: "My wife and children are well – the baby was dying some weeks ago so the good people would have it baptized – his name is Derwent Coleridge – so called from the River. For fronting our house the Greta runs into the Derwent – had it been a girl, the name should have been Greta. By the bye, Greta, or rather Grieta, is exactly the Cocytus of the Greeks - the word literally rendered in modern English is 'The Loud Lamenter' – to Griet in the Cumbrian dialect signifying to roar aloud for grief or pain, and it does roar with a vengeance."

And the poet described his daughter Sara as: "My meek little Sara, a remarkably interesting baby, with the finest possible skin and large blue eyes; and she smiles as if she were basking in a sunshine, as mild as moonlight, of her own quiet happiness."

In the month of June 1805, Sara, only a toddler of two and a half years at the time, somehow tumbled through the wooden railings of a bridge over the Greta – possibly the bridge in the drawing or one very similar – and fell a considerable height into the water. A young lad who was working at his father's nearby forge came to her rescue.

When she was nearing the end of her days Sara Coleridge reflected on this traumatic incident in her early life and the effect that it had upon her constitution. In September 1851, eight months before her death, Sara Coleridge turned back the years to her childhood at Greta Hall and wrote: "Of this first stage of my life, of course, I have no remembrance; but something happened to me, when I was two years old, which was so

The Greta . . . a river runs through it

striking as to leave an indelible trace on my memory. I fancy I can even now recall, though it may be but the echo or reflection of past remembrances, my coming dripping up the Forge field, after having fallen into the river, between the rails of the high wooden bridge that crossed the Greta, which flowed behind the Greta Hall hill.

"The maid had my baby cousin Edith, sixteen months younger than I, in her arms; I was rushing away from Derwent, who was fond of playing the elder brother on the strength of his last two years seniority, when he was trying in some way to control me, and in my hurry I slipped from the bridge into the current. Luckily for me young Richardson was still at work in his father's forge. He doffed his cap and rescued me from the water. I had fallen from a considerable height, but the strong current of the Greta received me safely. I remember nothing of this adventure but the walk home through the field. I was put between blankets on my return to the house; but my constitution had received a shock, and I became tender and delicate, having before been a thriving child."

It was noted that the trauma of Sara having fallen into the River Greta "helped to change her to the delicate creature, whose large blue eyes would look up timidly from under her lace border and mufflings of muslin."

The river incident was also referred to by Dorothy Wordsworth in correspondence from Dove Cottage, Grasmere on June 11th, 1805, to Lady Beaumont, Grosvenor Square, London: "We expect Mrs C (Sarah Coleridge) at the end of this week – she is to bring the little darling Sara with her, who has by the mercy of God escaped from an accident that you will shudder to hear of. She slipped from the servant who was playing

This pencil and watercolour is entitled Fields, River and Greta Hall and is the work of William Westall. The artwork, 93 x 156mm, is dated pre 1850. Picture courtesy of the Wordsworth Trust, The Jerwood Centre, Dove Cottage, Grasmere.

Greta Hall

with her near the Forge at the bottom of the field, ran upon a wooden bridge which I believe has been built since you were at Keswick and fell into the Greta – the Bridge is very high above the stream and the water was low – it is almost miraculous that she was not dashed to pieces. A man from the Forge went a considerable way down the river and took her out. She was put to bed immediately and soon recovered, but she has never been perfectly well since. Mrs C hopes however that the change of air will entirely restore her. What a shock, for her poor father, if after his sorrowful voyage, he had heard tidings of her death too!"

The 'sorrowful voyage' was Coleridge's journey home from travels to Sicily and Malta and a direct reference to the death at sea of William Wordsworth and Dorothy Wordsworth's brother John, commander of 'The Earl of Abergavenny' shipwrecked off Portland in February 1805 with the loss of 260 lives.

In fact, an earlier part of Dorothy's correspondence (related above) was: "We conclude now, that he (Coleridge) will be at Malta when the tidings of my Brother's death and the loss of the Abergavenny reach that place; and we have no doubt that he will come by the first Ship afterwards."

Writing in general of her early life at Greta Hall, Sara Coleridge described her childhood home as " . . . dear Greta Hall, where I was born and where I resided till my marriage, at twenty six years of age, in September 1829 (on marrying she went to live in London). It was built on a hill, on one side of the town of Keswick, having a large nursery garden in front. The gate at the end of this garden opened upon the end of the town. A few steps further was the bridge over the Greta. At the back of Greta Hall was an orchard of not very productive apple trees and plum trees. Below this is a wood stretched down to the riverside. A rough path ran along the bottom of the wood, and led on the one hand (the Skiddaw side of the vale) to the Carding Mill Field, which the river near by surrounded; on the other hand, the path led below the Forge Field, onto the Forge. Oh, that rough path beside the Greta! How much of my childhood, of my girlhood, of my youth, was spent there!"

It is worth explaining that the Forge referred to here is not The Forge at the other end of Keswick beyond Brigham, and a scene of much industrial activity at one time, but a forge nearer to the heart of the town itself and only a short distance from Greta Hall, most probably beyond a field now occupied by the Greta Hamlet housing complex.

Later Sara refers to her bedroom at Greta Hall and writes: ". . . that dear bedroom where I lay down, in joy or in sorrow, nightly for so many years of comparative health and happiness, whence I used to hear the river flowing, and sometimes the forge hammer in the distance at the end of the field; but seldom other sounds in the night, save of stray animals."

And in a quote from 1849 she says: "I'm pleased to hear of primitive river bathing. It reminds me of my Greta Hall days."

Sara also recalled her "thoughts of the hills and lakes, and still more of the rivers and streamlets, my dear beloved Greta rushing over the stones by the Carding Mill field, or sweeping past swollen with rains; and all the lovely flowers, specially the yellow globe flower, which fringe the banks or lurk in the woods or crowd and cluster in the open glades . . ."

The name Greta is irrevocably linked, through lending its name to Greta Hall, to some of England's most famous poets and the river, in turn, clearly played an important part in the lives of the Lakes poets, their respective families and numerous visitors to Greta Hall. In the early 1800s the pleasing sound of the river would not suffer from the distraction, as it does today, of cars and lorries thundering along the A66 or streaming back and forth, like ants on the move, through the streets of the town. The sound of the river, whether in raging spate or the more cheery and restful burbling over rocks during periods of lower water, is something that could be fully appreciated in pre-motorised days and from the open windows of houses during the day or, perhaps more especially, at night. The clip-clop of horses' hooves and the gentle, gritty churn of carriage wheels on the surface of roads, such as they were, would complement the soothing sound of the water.

To fully appreciate the sound of the river I would suggest that you venture out at dead of night, when traffic is virtually non-existent, and listen to the river. And I mean *listen* to the river, the "perpetual voice of the Vale" as Coleridge described it. You will be amazed at the sweet sound that it makes and how the noise of the river is turned up to a perfectly acceptable full volume when the world is asleep and the car ignitions and sirens and the various clarion calls of the day are temporarily and blessedly

Greta Hall

Robert Southey (1774 – 1843).

switched-off. That the river was important to Coleridge and Southey and their respective families during their residence at Greta Hall (a flighty Coleridge did not linger long but a more steadfast Southey remained there until his death in 1843) is evident in their various correspondence. Although, having said that, William Wordsworth, a frequent visitor to Greta Hall, was the only one of The Big Three to write a poem directly about the river (see Calvert Bridge chapter on page 97).

Coleridge and his family were the first to arrive at Greta Hall in July 1800, and were joined there by Robert Southey and his entourage on September 7th, 1803.

"I write to you from the Leads of Greta Hall, a Tenement in the possession of S.T. Coleridge Esq, Gentleman-poet and Philosopher in a mist," STC wrote to a friend, Samuel Purkiss, from Greta Hall, Keswick, in a letter dated July 29th, 1800 (a few days after his arrival there). "This Greta Hall is a House on a small eminence a furlong from Keswick, in the County of Cumberland. Yes, my dear sir! Here I am – with Skiddaw at my back – on my right hand the Bassenthwaite water, with its majestic case of mountains, all of simplest outline. Looking slant, direct over the feather of this infamous Pen, I see the sun setting – My God! what a scene! Right before me is the great Camp of single Mountains – each in shape resembles a Giant's tent! and to the left, but closer to it than the Bassenthwaite Water to my right, is the lake of Keswick, with its islands and white sails, and glossy lights of Evening, crowned with green meadows; but the three remaining sides are encircled by the most fantastic mountains that ever earthquake made in sport; as fantastic as if Nature had laughed herself into convulsion, in which they were made. Close behind me at the foot of Skiddaw, flows the Greta. I hear its murmuring distinctly – then it curves round almost in a semi circle, and is now catching the purple lights of the scattered clouds above it directly before me."

And in observing his son Hartley he wrote: "I hear his voice at this moment distinctly; he is below in the garden, shouting to some foxgloves and fern, which he has transplanted, and telling them what he will do for them if they grow like good boys! This afternoon I sent him naked into a shallow of the river Greta; he trembled with the novelty, yet you cannot conceive his raptures . . . Some time ago I watched Hartley under the trees, down by the river – the birds singing so sweetly above him and he was evidently lost in thought."

The Greta . . . a river runs through it

A few months later and his passion for his new home and surroundings had clearly not abated. If anything he appears to be even more thrilled and enthusiastic, writing in a letter to Josiah Wedgewood on November 1st: "Every thing I promised myself in this country has answered far beyond my expectation. The room in which I write commands six distinct Landscapes — the two Lakes, the Vale, River, & mountains, & mists, & Clouds, & Sunshine make endless combinations, as if heaven & Earth were for ever talking to each other. Often when in a deep Study I have walked to the window & remained there looking without seeing, all at once the Lake of Keswick & the fantastic Mountains of Borrowdale at the head of it have entered into my mind with a suddenness, as if I had been snatched out of Cheapside & placed for the first time on the spot where I stood. And that is a delightful Feeling — these Fits & Trances of Novelty received from a long known Object. The river Greta flows behind our house, roaring like an untamed Son of the Hills, then winds round, & glides away in the front — so that we live in a peninsula. But besides this ethereal Eye-feeding, we have very substantial Conveniences. We are close to the town, where we have a respectable & neighbourly acquaintance and a sensible & truly excellent medical man. Our Garden is part of a large nursery Garden which is the same to us & as private as if the whole had been our own, & thus too we have delightful walks without passing our garden gate."

Coleridge created a little sketch in which he placed Greta Hall in the context of the S curve of the river with the use of the capital letter B and lower case r to indicate what was what. "r r r is the river," he wrote, "and B my house." The line drawn across the top of the S presumably indicates the old Greta Bridge. I am unsure what the other solitary straight line might signify.

The reference to the "medical man" is significant in that initial correspondence. Samuel Taylor Coleridge was something of a wild child. He struggled as a result of the mental scars inflicted by the brutality of life at boarding school where he was regularly beaten by a sadistic master, his generally unhappy marriage during his time at Greta Hall, financial problems, illness (stress induced?) an inability to settle down to regular work and, in short, accept his lot in life and its many positives. These facets of his life tempted him to increasingly seek solace and relief from his physical and mental ills through the

Samuel Taylor Coleridge's sketch of the curve of the River Greta and the placement of Greta Hall.

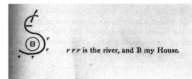

r r r is the river, and **B** my House.

Greta Hall

bottom of a glass containing opium in the form of laudanum – taken with brandy – and the appropriately called Kendal Black Drop, a mixture stronger than laudanum. As a result of his addiction he was at times a most wretched soul in torment, unable to sleep and plagued by nightmares and demons. As the years passed he increasingly distanced himself from Greta Hall and his family there.

His correspondence from Greta Hall at the time when his condition, mental and physical, appears to be unravelling, is illuminating and makes fascinating reading. While addiction, pain and suffering are not to be laughed at, I am afraid that I found amusement in his constant references in correspondence to his physical and mental state. It was almost as if Coleridge was inventing an increasingly bizarre range of complaints and the levels of his pain and anguish were hitting new heights with every passing letter. His letters continually harp on about his state of body and mind. What the recipients actually felt when reading all this – were breakfast tables continually intrigued by conversations along the lines of "guess what Coleridge has gone down with now?" – is anyone's guess. But this ongoing litany of medical complaints must have inspired genuine sympathy or considerable entertainment, and quite possibly both.

Shortly after his arrival at Greta Hall in 1800 Coleridge wrote: " . . . till now I have been grievously indisposed – now I am enjoying the Godlikeness of the Place in which I am settled, with the voluptuous and joy-trembling nerves of convalescence."

Unfortunately this period of relative calm and recovery by the River Greta was not to last.

He was soon suffering from "two blood red eyes that would do credit to massacre itself . . . they are so blood red that I should make a very good personification of murder." He was also "carried off by six large boils which appeared behind my ear down to my shoulder and harass me almost beyond endurance. . . ."

And he added for good measure: "For the last month I have been tumbling on through sands and swamps of Evil & bodily grievance... I had leeches repeatedly applied to my Temples."

He then goes down with yet another painful and, in one respect, embarrassing malady. On Tuesday night, January 7th, 1801 he wrote to a friend and benefactor Thomas Poole: "I write, alas, from my bed, to which I have been confined for almost the whole of the last three weeks with rheumatic fever – which has now left me I trust – but the pain has fixed itself in my hip and in consequence, as I believe, of the torture I have sustained in that part and the general feverous state of my body, my left testicle has swollen to more than three times its natural size, so that I can only lie on my back, and am now sitting wide astraddle on this wearisome bed. O me, my dear fellow! The notion of a Soul is a comfortable one to a poor fellow who is beginning to be ashamed of his Body. For the last four months I have not had a fortnight of continuous health. Bad eyes, swollen eyelids, Boils behind my ears and heaven knows what..."

There was further lurid information on the issue of the swollen testicle: "... my left testicle swelled, without pain indeed, but distressing from its weight; from a foolish shamefacedness almost peculiar to Englishmen I did not show it to our doctor till last Tuesday night. On examination it appeared that a fluid had collected between the Epitidymus and the body of the testicle. Fomentations and fumugations of vinegar having no effect I applied sal ammoniac dissolved in ferjuice and to considerable purpose; but the smart was followed by such a frantic and intolerable Torment which the Damned Suffer in hell. In all the parts thro' which the spermatic chord passes I have dull and obtuse pains – and on removing the suspensory Bandage the sense of weight is terrible."

The swollen testicle was followed by what Coleridge described as "irregular or retrocedent gout, no doubt in part due to the use of the brandy and laudanum which they had rendered necessary."

He was also suffering from a dry husky cough and profuse sweats at night. In short he does not present a picture of health and there is every indication that he has become a slave to opium.

"I have had a frightful seizure of the cholera morbus or bilious colic," he wrote on

Greta Hall

September 27th, 1801, "but the danger is past and I am assured that I will be much improved in my general health by the violent discharges."

On the contrary. On October 21, 1801 – the day after his 29th birthday – he wrote that he was suffering from bowel complaints and sickness and vomiting and added, on a slightly more optimistic note, "my knee is quite gone down and the frosty air has greatly improved my general health. But a fit of rain, or a fit of grief, undoes in three hours what three weeks has been doing. I am a crazy, crazy machine!"

The cogs of the crazy machine were again stopped in their tracks by a humble thorn.

"I had a thorn run into my leg, some inch and a half from the ankle close by the tendo Achilles," he wrote. "I have reason to believe that it has broke in – an incision has been made to no purpose but the wound keeps open and a suppuration is forming and when formed it may bring forth the corker. I have suffered great agony, I am more than lame for I cannot without torture move my leg from a super horizontal position. Whether I exaggerate illness or no remains to be proved."

The influenza he contracted seemed only too real. On May 17th, 1803, he wrote: "I arrived at Keswick on Good Friday and with the influenza which I caught off an old man in the mail . . . It was influenza which showed itself in the form of rheumatic fever – crippling my loins – but distinguished from it by immediate prostration of strength, confusion of intellect on any attempt to exert it, a tearing cough with constant

Southey's study at Greta Hall. Painting reproduced courtesy of the Keswick Museum and Art Gallery.

expectoration and clammy honey-dew sweats on awaking from my short sleeps. . ."

Tuesday, March 20th, 1804: "I have been seriously, alarmingly ill – a diarrhoea of incessant fury for 10 hours." Thankfully, unlike the story of the swollen testicle, he spares us the finer detail.

Concentrating on Samuel Taylor Coleridge's catalogue of various ailments tends to detract from his quality as a thinker and writer, the poet who wrote such wonderful pieces as Kubla Khan:

> *In Xanadu did Kubla Khan*
> *A stately pleasure-dome decree:*
> *Where Alph, the sacred river, ran*
> *Through caverns measureless to man*
> *Down to a sunless sea . . .*

And there were clearly many times – including his memorable nine day walking tour of the Lake District in August 1802 (detailed in the late great Alan Hankinson's book *Coleridge Walks the Fells: A Lakeland journey retraced*) – when he must have been in more robust health and recorded the first known rock climb (Broad Stand). On occasions such as these his multifarious illnesses and complaints clearly retreated into the background and did not overwhelm him to the extent that he could not undertake any physical exertion or derive any pleasure from his surroundings (one imagines that a swollen testicle can be somewhat inhibitive and potentially obscure the view). The letters from Greta Hall also contain flashes of keen observation on the colour and appearance of the river at different times of day and night.

On October 19th, 1801, he wrote: "On the Greta over the bridge by Mr Edmondson's father in law, the ashes, their leaves of that light yellow which Autumn gives them, cast a reflection on the river like a painter's sunshine."

August 10th, 1802: "I saw such a sight as I never before saw. Beyond Bassenthwaite at the end of the view was a sky of bright yellow-green; but over that and extending all over Bassenthwaite and almost to Keswick church a cloud-sky of the deepest most fiery orange. Bassenthwaite Lake looked like a lake of blood-red wine – and the River Greta, in all its winding before our house and the upper part of Keswick lake, were fiery red – even as I once saw the Thames when the huge Albion Mills were burning amid the

Greta Hall

shouts of an exulting mob – but with one foot upon Walla Crag, and the other foot exactly upon Calvert's house at Windy Brow, was one great rainbow, red and all red, entirely formed by the clouds."

October 1803: "Thursday morning, 40 minutes past one o'clock. A perfect calm. Now and then a breeze shakes the heads of the two poplars (and disturbs) the murmur of the moonlight Greta, that in almost a direct line from the moon to me is all silver – motion and wrinkle and light – and under the arch of the bridge a wave ever and anon leaps up in light."

Friday, October 28th, 1803: "Noon. Walked with Southey up the Greta, to the Theatre of Wood, with the cowl of green field on its top, opposite the Sopha of Sods – for the last time / unless the woodmen let their leaves come out next spring before they begin their devastation."

I think that he may be referring here to the view from Brundholme Woods down across the river and onto what we know as Longtown Field where the field and massive U bend of the river, just beyond Low Briery, are overlooked by woodland rising towards Latrigg. This particular 'Sopha of Sods' – the poets doubtless built more than one in

The walk through Brundholme Woods. This path looks down on Longtown Field.

the area – could be where the path through the wood from Keswick in the direction of Threlkeld splits into two, one going down a series of steep wooden steps towards the river and the other cutting across and into the wood at a higher level. This junction would seem a natural place to create a sofa or viewing platform from which to survey the scene below. The place here catches the sun, commands wonderful views of the field and river below and is decked with rich moss and turf, ideal for making a natural seat in the land from which to admire the scene. Nowhere else that I know of on the Greta more fits the title 'Theatre of Wood,' and the stage would be Longtown Field itself, with the curving line of the river a natural barrier between the auditorium of the woods and the field.

Saturday morning. October 29th, 1803: "Three o'clock. The Moon hangs high over Greta and the bridge, on the first step of her descent and three hours at least from the mountain behind which she is to sink: nearly full – not a cloud in heaven, the sky deep sable blue, the stars many and white in the height of the sky, but above, around and beneath the Moon, not a star; she is starless . . .

"Yet there is no gleam, much less silver whiteness on the Lake. Simply it is easily seen and even the Greta, stretching straight in an oblique line underneath is not silver-bright, or anywhere near brilliant, but rather the gleam of some baser composition imitating silver, it is a grey brightness like the colour of an ash grove in keenest December moonlight. The mountains are dark, low, all compact together, quiet, silent, asleep – the white houses are bright throughout the vale and the evergreens in the garden. The only sound is the murmur of the Greta, perpetual voice of the Vale."

Wednesday morning, 20 minutes past two o'clock. November 2nd, 1803: "The voice of the Greta and the cock-crowing. The voice seems to grow, like a flower on or about the water beyond the bridge, while the cock crowing is nowhere in particular, it is at any place I imagine and do not distinctly see. A most remarkable sky! The moon, now waned to a perfect ostrich's egg, hangs over our house almost – only so much beyond it, garden-ward, that I can see it, holding my head out of the smaller study window. The sky is covered with whitish and dingy cloudage, thin dingiest scud close under the moon and one side of it moving, all else moveless; but there are two great breaks of blue sky . . . The water leaden white, even as the grey gleam of water in latest twilight. Now thinning,

Greta Hall

Southey's study at Greta Hall. Through the window is Walla Crag.
Painting reproduced courtesy of the Keswick Museum and Art Gallery.

the break over the house is narrowed into a rude circle and on the edge of its circumference one very bright star – see! Already the white mass, thinning at its edge, fights with its brilliance – see! It has bedimmed it, and now it is gone and the moon is gone. The cock-crowing too has ceased. The Greta sounds on, for ever. But I hear only the ticking of my watch, in the pen-place of my writing desk, and the far lower voice of quiet change, of destruction doing its work by little and little."

Wednesday night, November 9th, 1803: "Forty five minutes past six. The town with lighted windows and noise of the clogged passengers in the streets – sound of the unseen river – mountains scarcely perceivable except by eyes long used to them and supported by the images of memory. . . I went to the window, to empty my urine pot, and wondered at the simple grandeur of the view. 1. Darkness and only not undistinguishableness; 2. The grey-blue steely glimmer of the Greta and the lake; 3. The black yet form-preserving mountains; 4. The sky, moon-whitened there, cloud-blackened here – and yet with all its gloominess and sullenness forming a contract with the simplicity of the landscape beneath."

'The Loud Lamenter'

Just as Samuel Taylor Coleridge eventually, and by degrees, drifted away from the domesticity of Greta Hall (he died in Highgate, London, on July 25, 1834, aged 62) Robert Southey, who had a dog called Dapper (I thought you ought to know that), became very much a part of the fabric of Keswick and of Greta Hall, and was as solid and dependable as a rock. Over the next 40 years Greta Hall became known simply as 'Southey's House.' But his life was not without its travails. He and his wife Edith lost four of their eight children. Edith, who suffered from physical and mental illness, was particularly affected by the death of her daughter Isabel in 1826 and had a complete collapse in 1834. She was taken to The Retreat, the pioneering, Quaker-run asylum in York, where she was diagnosed as of 'unsound mind' and treated with 'purgatives, remedies, and leeches.' She was released in 1835 'as admitted,' that is, uncured and incurable. Edith spent her final years at Greta Hall, where she was cared for by Southey and their daughters Bertha and Kate. Southey described her death, in 1837, as a release from "a pitiable state of existence."

Robert Southey came to Greta Hall – where Coleridge and his family were already in situ – on September 7th, 1803. Southey lived there until his death on March 21st, 1843 and is buried in the churchyard at St Kentigern's Church, Crosthwaite. Famous visitors during Southey's lifetime at the hall included Percy Bysshe Shelley, William Hazlitt, Sir Walter Scott and his son in law John Gibson Lockhart, James Hogg (the Ettrick shepherd) William and Dorothy Wordsworth, of course, and Thomas de Quincey, to name a few.

Just like Coleridge, Southey was enraptured by the place in his early days at Keswick and in a letter (to John King) from Greta Hall dated September 28th, 1803 wrote: "What a country is this Land of the Lakes, for a man who loves mountains as though he were a true-born Swiss! I would try to give you the situation of this house if I could find words enough for the combination of beautiful sights in the panorama which it commands. One of its good effects on me will be to force me often to long walks. We propose setting out for a three days ramble as soon as my eyes and Coleridge's flying gout will let us be tolerably comfortable.

Greta Hall

Brundholme Woods with the River Greta.

"Tell Charles to ship me off six dozen of port by a Liverpool vessel, directed here by way of Whitehaven. It will be forwarded as regularly as by a wagon. And in the hamper or box let him put in a quarter of a pound if half a pound of the crystallised lemon juice which you use, for no lemon are to be had here, and Edith is so fond of vegetable acids that I am sure they do her good."

In a letter (to Charles Danvers Esq) from Greta Hall, Keswick, October 1803 he wrote: "Today I have been tracking the river Greta, which, instead of a Great A, ought to have been called Great S; but its name hath a good and most apt meaning, 'The Loud Lamenter.' It is a lovely stream. I have often forded such among the mountains of the Algarve, and lingered to look at them with wistful eye – if I may so express myself, with a feeling that it was the only time I was ever to behold the scene before me, so beautiful! That feeling has often risen in me when gazing upon the permanent things of nature which I am beholding but for a time."

And he added: "I once thought of a ballad wherein the personage was to be a little old man who had the power of extending any part of his body to any length. If I had that gift myself I would crane my neck over the three hundred miles between the Greta and the Avon and look in at your window."

Letter (to John King) November 19th, 1803: "Coleridge is now in bed with the lumbago. Never was a poor fellow so tormented with such pantomime complaints. His disorders are perpetually shifting, and he is never a week together without some one or other. He is arranging materials for what, if it be made, will be a most valuable work under the title 'Consolation and Comforts' which will be the very essential oil of metaphysics, fragrant as otto of roses, and useful as wheat, rice, port wine, or any other necessary of human life."

Letter (to CW Williams Wyn MP) November 24th, 1803: "I shall turn to those of sound, which always affect me very much and, having dwelt on them, add: 'A blind man would have loved that lovely spot.' Your Dee, certes, is a most lovely river between Llangollen and Corwen – there where it rolls over amber-coloured rocks. But the finest

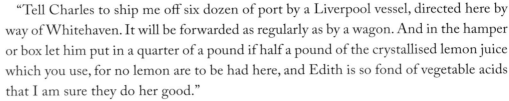

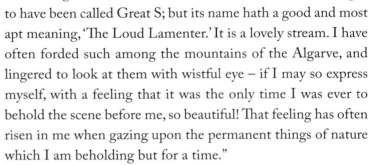

The Greta . . . a river runs through it

scenery we saw in Wales was before Llanrust, in that wild valley where the river so often rested in dark dead pools; what the Spaniards call the remansos of the river. Oh, I could show you such a mountain river here in our Greta – 'The Loud lamenter' which is the plain English of the Norse name! (by the bye gritar is the Portuguese word to lament aloud) – and such a famous bridge over which Peter Elmsley could no sooner pass, with his load of flesh and blood, than the heaviest can get over the razor-edged leading to paradise over Hell."

Letter (to Miss Barker) dated April 18th, 1804: "We have fine things enough from the windows, but to get at them a long way and not a pleasant one. In one direction I can shorten the disagreeable, in a way which would not be quite so convenient for you – by doffing shoe and stocking, and fording the Greta at the bottom of the orchard. By good fortune the finest river scenery lies within two miles of the house and not a tourist has ever heard of it. You will delight in the Greta and curse the Bishop of Llandaff for cutting down its woods." (The Bishop of Llandaff was responsible for the estates in the vicinity and there appears to have been some controversy over his approach to forestry).

Letter (to Charles Danvers Esq, Bristol) May 13th, 1806, on the subject of leaving London to travel to Keswick: "I put myself in the Carlisle mail on Saturday evening and arrived safe and sound yesterday afternoon. The noise of the coach is still in my ears, and my solids seem to be jellified by so much shaking; but I am quite well, thank God, and heartily happy to feel myself at home by my own fireside and once more in my Cumberland costume. London never agreed with me so ill. I caught a severe cold and cough, and felt my breathing much affected by that cursed composition of smoke, dust, smuts, human breath, and marsh vapour, which passes for an atmosphere in the metropolis.

Saddleback (Blencathra) and the River Greta. The engraving is taken from Daniel and Samuel Lyson's Britania Depicta, published in London by T. Cadell and W Davies in 1815. The engraving, 197 x 548mm, is the work of Joseph Farington (1747 – 1821), based on the work of W. Woolnoth.
Picture courtesy of the Wordsworth Trust, The Jerwood Centre, Dove Cottage, Grasmere.

"No letters from Coleridge of a later date than August. We hear of him by several quarters; he was at Rome in the beginning of February, much noticed there, and going to spend a few weeks in the country on his visit. This is the news from Englishmen

Greta Hall

The remains of the weir beneath Greta Hall.

who saw him there. It is not to be supposed that letters should regularly arrive from other persons, and all his be lost. Wordsworth thinks he has delayed writing till he finds it painful to think of it. Meantime we daily expect to hear of his return. I am more angry at this silence than I choose to express because I have no doubt whatever that the reason we receive no letters is that he writes none; when he comes he will probably tell a different story and it will be proper to admit his excuse without believing it."

Here, clearly, were the grumblings of family discontent – Coleridge's wife Sarah was the sister of Southey's wife Edith (the sisters having the maiden name of Fricker) – at Coleridge's continual absences from the family home. But life went on without him. Southey became a father figure for two families as he continued to fall deeply in love with the Lake District, Greta Hall and his immediate surroundings, not least, the sight and sound of the River Greta. He would spend many hours on the banks of the river beyond the orchard down the steeply wooded slope at the back of Greta Hall. The little wood that stretched down to the Greta is still there, in spring and early summer bedecked in the rich green leaves and white flowering heads of wild garlic that are profuse along the river bank. It was here by the Greta, adjacent to the rough path referred to by Sara Coleridge, who played there as a child, that Southey would occupy a covered seat where he would read or think. Or, doubtless, simply sit and do nothing, relax and look at the river and listen to its melodic sound as it ran over stones and moved inexorably past en route to its rendezvous with the Derwent and its journey to the sea.

The scenery upon the river, wrote Southey, in his Colloquies, "where it passes under the woody side of Latrigg, is of the finest and most remberable kind - ambiguo lapsu refluitique, occurrensque sibi ventures aspicit undas." The lines in Latin are by Ovid in Metamorphoses VIII II 163-164 where he describes the River Meander – "it flows and flows back in an uncertain course, and confronting itself sees the approach of its own waves."

And of Greta Hall he wrote: "Nothing in England can be more beautiful than the site of this house. Had this country but the sky of Portugal, it would leave me nothing to wish for . . ." I am sure that many people who experience the Cumbrian climate, and especially its grey, damp summers, year in year out would echo those sentiments entirely. Southey's life at Greta Hall would tend to follow a set routine. Canon Hardwicke

The Greta . . . a river runs through it

Drummond Rawnsley, an invaluable and colourful recorder of events of the day, wrote: "Southey might have been seen any day in the 40 years he dwelt at Greta Hall, in black coat and corduroy trousers, strolling out before breakfast, or sitting at his desk in his study till two; then, after dinner, with black or black-blue peaked cap, and fawn coloured, all-round coat, not swallow lappeted, very neatly dressed — 'Never seed him wi' a button off in my life,' an old man once said to me — starting for his constitutional, at a three mile walking pace, with book in hand, and clogs on his feet. The children sometimes with him, borne on 'their noble jackass,' sometimes with servants, bairns and all bound for a picnic on the lake; sometimes pestling away at blackcurrants for blackcurrant wine; sometimes building, all the household of them, the bridge of stepping stones across the Greta, which Southey commenced in 1809, and which was constantly needing a little repair. But back again would Southey come to tea and talk in the great library at six, and there, after the London paper was read, the lamps were lit, he wrote his letters, for he generally made a point of replying to his correspondents on the same day. Such letters! So full of humour and of his own best thoughts; I do not wonder Wordsworth thought that, in them, was Southey's best and deepest expression of himself.

"His favourite walks were the terrace road under Applethwaite, Latrigg, Skiddaw Dodd, Causey Pike, Newlands, and Newlands Beck, whereto, when Tom Southey was at Emerald Bank, he oft-time resorted, and, plunging in the pools, disported himself like any river god. Brundholme Woods above the Greta too was a well-loved walk with him . . . to the Druid Circle would he go, but Walla Crag and Watendlath had special charms for him. Yet, perhaps his favourite round of all was through the Great Wood, up Cat Ghyll, between Falcon Crag and Walla Crag, and so home by Rakefoot and the Moor, or by Spring's Farm."

Throughout all this there is a tremendous sense of order and enjoyment of life. But of all the accounts of the various escapades on which he and his family and friends set out from Greta Hall the most memorable is that in the year 1815 when, following a suggestion from Robert Southey himself, Poet Laureate, bonfires were lit on Skiddaw to celebrate victory over Napoleon at the Battle of Waterloo.

In a letter to his brother Harry, who was a doctor, Southey wrote from Keswick, August 23rd, 1815: "Monday, the 21st of August, was not a more remarkable day in

Greta Hall

your life than it was in that of my neighbour Skiddaw, who is a much older personage. The weather served for our bonfire, and never, I believe, was such an assemblage upon such a spot. To my utter astonishment, Lord Sunderlin rode up, and Lady S, who had endeavoured to dissuade me from going as a thing too dangerous, joined the walking party. Wordsworth, with his wife, sister, and eldest boy, came over on purpose. James Boswell arrived that morning at the Sunderlins (Derwent Bank). Edith, the Senhora (Miss Barker, author, painter and close friend of Robert Southey, she lived at Greta Lodge, next to Greta Hall and was known as 'The Senhora') Edith May, and Herbert were my convoy, with our three maid-servants, some of our neighbours, some adventurous Lakers, and Messrs Rag, Tag, and Bobtail, made up the rest of the assembly.

"We roasted beef and boiled plum-puddings there, sung 'God save the King' round the most furious body of flaming tar-barrels that I ever saw; drank a huge wooden bowl of punch; fired cannon at every health three times three, and rolled large blazing balls of tow and turpentine down the steep side of the mountain. The effect was grand beyond imagination. We formed a huge circle round the most intense light, and behind us was an immeasurable arch of the most intense darkness, for our bonfire fairly put out the moon.

Skiddaw by J.B. Pyne.
Painting reproduced courtesy of the Keswick Museum and Art Gallery.

"The only mishap which occurred will make a famous anecdote in the life of a great poet, if James Boswell, after the example of his father, keepeth a diary of the sayings of remarkable men. When we were craving for the punch, a cry went forth that the kettle had been knocked over, with all the boiling water! Colonel Barker, as Boswell named the Senhora, from her having had the command on this occasion, immediately instituted a strict inquiry to discover the culprit, from a suspicion that it might have been done in mischief, water, as you know, being a commodity not easily replaced on the summit of Skiddaw.

"The persons about the fire declared it was one of the gentlemen – they did not know his name; but he had a red cloak on and they pointed him out in the circle. The red cloak (a maroon one of Edith's) identified him; Wordsworth had

got hold of it, and was equipped like a Spanish Don – by no means the worst figure in the company. He had committed this fatal faux pas, and thought to slink off undiscovered. But as soon as, in my inquiries concerning the punch, I learnt his guilt from the Senhora, I went round to all our party, and communicated the discovery, and getting them about him, I punished him by singing a parody, which they all joined in: 'Twas you that kicked the kettle down! 'twas you, Sir, you!'

"The consequences were that we took all the cold water upon the summit to supply our loss. Our myrmidons and Messrs Rag and Co. had, therefore, none for their grog; they necessarily drank the rum pure; and you, who are physician to the Middlesex Hospital, are doubtless acquainted with the manner in which alcohol acts upon the nervous system.

"All our torches were lit at once by this mad company, and our way down the hill was marked by a track of fire, from flambeaux dropping the pitch, tarred ropes &c. One fellow was so drunk that his companions placed him upon a horse, with his face to the tail, to bring him down, themselves being just sober enough to guide and hold him on. Down, however, we all got safely by midnight; and nobody, from the old Lord of seventy-seven, to my son Herbert, is the worse for the toil of the day, though we were eight hours from the time we set out till we reached home."

Newspaper reports of the time provided the additional information that the atmosphere was dusky but free of mists, that the bonfires on Skiddaw could be seen for miles around, as far away as Broughton in Lancashire, and that the toasts were to "the health of the Prince Regent, the Duke of Wellington, and Prince Blucher, drunk three times over an immense bowl of punch-royal, each of the toasts being announced to the world below by the discharge of cannon and God save the King, and Rule Britannia, were sung in full chorus, accompanied by a band of music . . . and they quitted the summit of the mountain at ten o'clock, descending by torch-light, and reached Keswick about midnight, where the festivities closed with fireworks and the ascent of a balloon, on which were inscribed the words 'Wellington and Waterloo'."

Greta Hall

The Greta Hall of the 21st Century

I visited Greta Hall for a Theatre by the Lake 'Words by the Water' literature festival event in March 2012 on a day when I was in the latter stages of a debilitating bout of man flu. It occurred to me that Coleridge might be taking his revenge for my taking the rise out of his oft-mentioned fragile physical and mental condition. After walking a mile from my house to the hall I made my way inside, after picking a route through the hens, cockerels and ducks in the garden. No sooner had I sat down inside than I broke out in a heavy sweat, of the cold, damp, back of the shirt-clinging variety. I was also feeling a little disengaged and light-headed. I was clearly badly in need of a few glasses of laudanum and it occurred to me that it would be good if the present occupants of Greta Hall might dispense a little Kendal Black Drop to restore me or finish me off, one or t'other. No such luck. As it was they had lit welcoming log fires in every room and provided cakes, coffee and tea, none of which I could readily appreciate because of my condition. However, I did enjoy listening to the poetry of Coleridge and Southey being read aloud (in Southey's study) in Greta Hall with its lovely old rooms and fireplaces 200 or so years after these two great but very different writers had sat down to write in this most literary of riverside establishments; my sincere apologies to any of those present who subsequently went down with a virus.

Greta Hall as it is today.

One of the fireplaces in Greta Hall is particularly noteworthy with its elaborate woodcarvings of four Lewis chess pieces. Southey's wife, Edith, apparently designed the fireplace and the wood came from a ship used to build the original St Andrew's Church in Borrowdale; the church was consecrated in 1687 and was subsequently rebuilt and enlarged in stone.

The life of Greta Hall today bears uncanny comparison with the days when first Coleridge and then Southey and their assorted family, children, houseguests and various entourages occupied this wonderful house high above the River Greta. The Greta Hall of the early years of the 21st Century – just like its 19th Century predecessor – is a busy, energetic, thriving, artistic, avant-garde, lively, inviting and most positively never dull place to be. Its maize-like rooms – a tour is to invite confusion and end up at your starting point without being entirely sure how you got there – are full of warmth and exude colour, hospitality and modernity while at the same time never losing their vivid and all-embracing sense of history.

I love it. The whole place is a celebration of life.

When the Southeys arrived at Greta Hall in 1803 they were childless (having just lost their daughter) but there were the three Coleridge children aged seven, three and one. In 1829 when the house was left in the sole occupation of the Southeys, seven more children had been born to them. By a bizarre coincidence today's occupants of Greta Hall, Jeronime and Scott, also have seven children and the gardens and outbuildings are home to legions of ducks and chickens and cockerels as well as rabbits, guinea pigs, the dog, Millie, the cat, Na and, in the spring, a few orphan lambs from a local farm.

While the children born to Robert and Edith Southey had conventional names, the Southeys were not averse to giving their animals, and especially the cats, very exotic and unusual titles. Jeronime and Scott appear to have extended that tradition to their children. In order

Aquella with a bunch of wild garlic flowers.

Greta Hall

of appearance on Planet Earth they are Akasha (20) the twins Zael and Sol (18), Zenon (16), Khem (10) Neha-nami (7) and Aquella (5). The youngest was the first child to be born in Greta Hall since Southey's last child was born there and was actually born in Southey's bedroom, the room in which the poet died on March 21, 1843. Aquella, a lively little soul, is not hesitant in offering up the information to visitors that "Southey died on the bed and I was born on the floor."

It is clear that Jeronime and Scott love their house on the hill overlooking Keswick with its amazing views all round the district. Their feelings of enthusiasm for the house are not dissimilar to those expressed by Coleridge and Southey in correspondence in the early 1800s, shortly after they had first arrived at Greta Hall.

"The house gets the sun all day and the sun moves round the house until it sets over Grisedale Pike," says Scott, originally from Glasgow and who is not about to exchange his fast-talking Scots accent for Cumbrian dialect. "There was an amazing sunset the other night where the sun went down beyond the mountains but then reflected back onto the clouds and there was a wonderful purple, fiery orange on the surface of the lake and the rivers. Whenever you walk up the stairs you will find yourself stopping and taking in the scenery. From every window there's a view. You must come up on the roof with me one evening and watch the sun go down."

Scott and Jeronime with three of their seven children, Sol, Aquella, Neha-nami and the dog Millie by the River Greta below Greta Hall.

It is an offer I cannot resist. As it happened it did not quite go according to plan. We ventured onto the rooftop late one afternoon in the aftermath of a thunderstorm and spent a laudanum-free few minutes admiring the view and speculating on how much the vista of the more immediate vicinity and Keswick would have changed over the last 200 years or so. In the distance the mist drifted up the mountain slopes framing Borrowdale and Derwentwater as the sun made a half-hearted attempt to pierce the grey. The sun's feeble efforts were a marginal improvement on my less than lish attempts to squeeze my frame through the skylight window that gives access to the roof from which Coleridge and Southey would have admired the self-same scene, day and night.

"When you get a full moon it's stunning," Scott adds. "As the moon comes up it shines through the windows of Southey's study where the original crown glass has a lot of defects and the shadows and patterns are reflected onto the back wall of his study. It creates the most beautiful moonlit effect."

Scott and Jeronime were living and working in Hong Kong when they bought Greta Hall on the recommendation of Jeronime's brother, Ben Palmer, who lives in Cockermouth. Scott and Jeronime were working in the Far East as a children's entertainer and a teacher, respectively. Jeronime now supports the design and technology department at Keswick School while Scott travels to Hong Kong from time to time to pursue his career in entertainment. The house was actually bought by them in 1998 but it was not until 2004 that the family moved to Keswick and Greta Hall.

Scott was infatuated from the outset and his passion has never waned.

"It's a very happy house," he says. "A lot of people say it's a lovely house with amazing energy; which is nice because that's how I feel about it. I have always felt very welcome and have a good connection with the house. Our offer was accepted before we had actually seen it because we were in Hong Kong at the time and when it was accepted I got on a plane and came back to look at it. There's a wild video of me going round the house saying 'oh my God

Washing and ducks at Greta Hall.

Greta Hall

another room' and 'oh my God another staircase.' It was very institutionalised – there were beds left all over the place from the days when it was a boarding house for Keswick School – and there was pink paint and bathrooms and toilets everywhere, and that musty, unlived in smell because it hadn't been lived in for three years apart from a caretaker. But right from the word go I felt that I had come home.

"I remember when I brought the family back one February morning and we drove up the front drive and at that time the house was covered in this old grey original render."

"It was a horrible day," recalls Jeronime, "the entrance was overgrown with trees and it was like Bleak House."

Scott: "And the grass was long and there were big rose bushes growing out of the front of the house. I was so excited and Jeronime was thinking 'oh my God.' It didn't help when we opened the door and there was a strong smell of wet and dry rot and dampness.

"But it was such an amazing project to take on. For years everywhere we looked there was a job to do. That was quite intimidating and we had to learn how to do it all as best we could. The house was very forgiving in that respect and in teaching us how it wanted to be looked after. It's been a really nice way to work with it."

Greta Hall as it is today.

Jeronime: "We let the house grow on us before we made any decisions about colours. We have had a lot of time to get the feel of the house before doing anything."

As you will doubtless have gathered Jeronime's initial reaction – and that of the children who were happy in Hong Kong – to the move to Greta Hall was not as warm as Scott's. In fact I suspect Jeronime may have been quite unnerved at times in those early months and years.

"For me it's different because it's more about the women who lived here," Jeronime explains. "I had this really weird feeling – and I'm not a great believer in ghosts and things like that – but I did feel that we weren't welcome in the house. I felt I was being watched and I remember quite distinctly being outside and feeling there was somebody looking out of the windows at me. And then going up the stairs to the very top balcony and feeling that there was somebody up there looking down. Over the years I had really bizarre feelings that when I was vacuuming there was someone there who was thinking 'Oh my gosh, look at that machine.'

"It was almost like we were being tested to see what we were doing with the house. I think we have passed the test and I feel that the house has accepted us. It's a bizarre thing but the house is full of children – just as it was in the 1800s – the house is decorated in a way that's sympathetic, the people who come and go love it and we haven't done anything that's incongruous or out of keeping.

"It's really settled. I feel very comfortable here now. I love it when Scott and the children are out of the house because I have this extraordinary feeling that as a woman I am continuing the roles that the women did in Southey's time – cooking and cleaning, washing clothes and baking. I'm doing all of those primary roles that the women of Greta Hall did many years ago in this house. And it is quite interesting just to be filling someone else's shoes, on the same flagged floor of the very same kitchen. All the women would have been cooking and cleaning and washing and providing beds and there'd be no running hot water, no central heating, no proper oven and all these demanding men in the house. The appliances that I use are clearly very different, but that feeling of just being part of the history is quite astonishing. When you look out of that window, give or take a few trees, you are looking out at exactly the same landscape that they looked out on and that is extraordinary.

Greta Hall

"These days the house has found the perfect balance between the past and the present. It's still full of children, it's still visited by people and people stay here, there are strong links to universities, literary and arts organisations so it's still got lots of people who are artistic and literary crossing the threshold."

Scott: "We are stewards of it. This house can't be owned. We are just looking after it until the next generation."

Of course, the house was not always a happy place to be. It has witnessed lots of sadness over the years, especially in the Southey years, a period when child mortality was high. Robert Southey's favourite son, Herbert Castle Southey, was born at Greta Hall on October 11, 1806, and died, of consumption, at the house on April 17, 1816, aged nine.

"His death," wrote Southey, "has drawn a broad black line between the years which are gone and those which may be before me."

Jeronime observes: "They apparently carried out the autopsy in the kitchen, in this very room where we're talking now, to confirm the cause of death. We are all so cosseted these days in so many ways. And yet they were making those sort of decisions . . . to have your child autopsied on the kitchen table certainly shows the very different lives they lived. It doesn't bear thinking about. They were hard times."

An adventure playground for the children at Greta Hall with dens and swings over the river.

Today advances in medical science mean that longevity for the young and old is greatly enhanced and for the 21st Century children at Greta Hall life is a provider of infinite entertainment with plenty to stimulate the mind and exercise the body.

The children of today's Greta Hall and the many other local children who visit the house run wild and use the garden and river bank and trees below the orchard as a glorious adventure playground with tree houses and ropes attached to high branches from which they can swing to and fro over the steep bank and the river. I wonder if Southey and Coleridge's children also had swings over the river and revelled in childhood games close to the Greta?

The Greta . . . a river runs through it

The interior of the house is an Aladdin's cave of fascination and interest, paintings and drawings and old photographs adorn the walls, and musical instruments are everywhere, as are shoes and wellies. One of the favourite games played by the children is Hide and Seek. But when the winter nights draw in and all the lights in the house are turned off and not even the street lights of Keswick can fracture the gloom of the house on the hill, the children play another game called 'Murder in the Dark,' a scarier version of Hide and Seek where – especially in Greta Hall – you never know who you might meet in a darkened corridor at dead of night.

If, in the course of the game, you happened upon the spirit of Robert Southey I think you might find that he would be perfectly affable and stand aside or allow you to walk clean through him. He was undoubtedly a good man, as transparent in death as he was in life. I like to picture him now, sitting contentedly on a seat down by the eternal River Greta in the early summer when the mass of wild garlic is dark green etched with white flowers, and its strong aroma fills the air. The washing on the lines at the back of Greta Hall, at the top of the slope leading down to the river, is pure white and brilliant as it rolls and flaps in the breeze and the flashes of sun.

And a blonde-haired girl shouts with joy as she careers wildly back and forth on a swing over the river and urges her older brother to push her higher and higher . . .

This is fun. A swing from the trees at Greta Hall with the river below.

Greta Hall

The Brazilian Connection

Robert Southey's *History of Brazil* was published in 1810 and his name and the book he wrote are revered to this day in the South American country. The Brazilian Government renovated Robert Southey's grave in the churchyard of St Kentigern's Church, Crosthwaite, in 1961.

The connection between Southey, Greta Hall, Keswick and Brazil was recognised on Thursday, July 5th, 1877 when the Emperor and Empress of Brazil, Dom Pedro d'Alcantara and Donna Theresa Christine and their entourage paid a special visit to the town.

The newspaper of the day *The Lakes Visitor and Keswick Guardian* reported: "The memorials of Southey seemed to possess the most interest for the Emperor, who remarked that Southey had written a very good history of Brazil. His majesty on entering the church (St Kentigern's, Crosthwaite) was attracted to the monument of the Poet Laureate of a past generation, and read the inscription on it from Wordsworth's pen. On leaving the church he went to the poet's grave, reading what was recorded on the stone.

"The imperial party then repaired to Greta Hall where they were received by Miss Brindle who showed them all that was associated with Southey – the room in which the poet died having especial attraction for his Majesty. On their departure Miss Brindle's pupils (Greta Hall was a Dame's School at that time in the days long before it became a boarding house for Keswick School) made them an offering of fresh gathered flowers, which was well received."

Returning to the Keswick Hotel, they sat down at 10 o'clock to a recherché dinner of Soups: Mock Turtle; Julienne. Fish: Turbot, lobster sauce; Salmon steak, piquant sauce. Entrees: Curried chicken; Rissoles of veal and ham; mutton cutlets and tomato; Boiled leg of lamb with gooseberry sauce; Roast beef. Poultry: Boiled chickens and mushrooms; ducks. Sweets: Sweet omelette and gooseberry pudding; tarts; stewed fruit; jelly; creams; custard. Desserts: Melon; grapes; dates; Normandy pippins; oranges, pineapples etc.

St Kentigern's Church, Crosthwaite.

Facing page: A watercolour by Lucy Gipps of Barf, High Hill and the River Greta, only a stone's throw from Greta Hall. Watercolour courtesy of Keswick Museum and Art Gallery.

Floods
HELL AND HIGH WATER

The River Greta running pell-mell and in spate is exhilarating in sight and sound. With its waters muddied brown and carrying along tree trunks and assorted debris, including the occasional flying pig*, unwilling passengers all on an unstoppable journey to the sea, it is a formidable spectacle. But even when the river is at its fastest, loudest and most intimidating I never find it frightening or alarming. On the contrary it heightens the senses as I stride the riverbank on a stormy day, the rain and wind in my face, ominous black clouds sweeping in over the fells and the treetops swaying crazily in the gale. It all adds to the life-affirming drama of a river in full cry.

My favourite time to walk the river is when it is at its wildest. It is at times like these that I like to get as close as I can to this lion of nature as it races manically and almost triumphantly through the valley and the Skiddaw rock which it has grooved, eroded and occupied for thousands of years; usually quite contentedly but, from time to time, in an angry, unruly and untamed manner.

When in spate, this is a beck that has Attitude with a capital A.

My attitude towards the river might be somewhat different if I personally lived in danger of perpetual flooding, but as someone whose house is on relatively high ground I can sleep easy in my bed (although low flying jets can be a worry); unlike the people who live in fear of their homes being repeatedly violated by the river. However, I suspect that even they, the victims who watch each and every year the rising waters with varying degrees of trepidation, depending on the height of the river and the weather forecast and flood alerts, cannot fail to be struck by the force of nature and the awesome sight of the Greta at full tilt.

Facing page: The River Greta in spate races under Calvert Bridge.

*Once, while fishing for salmon on the River Greta above Low Briery, at an area known locally as the Pigfields – so called because it at one time had a tin sheeting hut in which pigs were kept – I was fishing in the pool known as High Yak, when a very real, very pink and very drowned pig, floated down the far side of the river in spate. It was one of those daft moments and coincidences in life – dead pig floats through Pigfields – that only happens once in a lifetime.

This image, date unknown but possibly 1950s, shows the extent of flooding at High Hill. The AA sign says the road is impassable but it would appear that plenty are prepared to give it a try.

Perhaps it is something that they may now be able to enjoy in a more relaxed frame of mind thanks to the millions of pounds, £6.1m to be precise, that was spent by The Environment Agency in 2012 on flood defences in Keswick along the banks of the River Greta as a direct result of repeated and devastating flooding in the early years of the 21st Century, especially in 2005 and 2009; the latter, well-documented in words and images, produced the worst flooding in living memory.

But, as you might expect, flooding – as long as rain falls from the sky – is nothing new to this region. Perhaps its effects were not so badly felt in years gone by when there were not as many houses, the lower part of the town where the flooding is most severe and prevalent these days, was largely non existent and, in any event, a lot of houses would be so basic and rudimentary that they might even have benefited from flood water sweeping in through the front door and out the back.

So this chapter reflects on the floods in the 19th and 18th centuries, beginning with what was described as 'the great flood', of August 1749, one which had a dramatic effect on the higher ground of St John's in the Vale, south east of Keswick.

Devastation and the 'great flood' of 1749

The year 1749 was an unusual one in that it snowed during the summer and snow was to be seen on the fell tops as late as June 16. On Tuesday, the 22nd of August, there was severe flooding in the Vale of St John and the following account was published in the *Gentleman's Magazine* of 1754: "There happened, about four years ago, a most dreadful storm of thunder and lightning in these parts, which, bursting over the mountains, was attended with such a torrent of rain, as considerably changed the face of the country, and did incredible damage in the vale below. The vale is called St John's and, as I lately passed through it, I send you a more particular account of the effects of the storm, than has yet been published.

"The precipices on the left of this vale, as you pass along the road from Keswick to Ambleside, very much resemble volcanoes, and look as if they were half burnt. The ascent is for several miles covered with rude fragments, of different sizes and figure, which storms and torrents have torn from the native rock, and is ploughed into many hollows, down which the cataracts have poured, when a water cloud has been broken at the top, which very frequently happens, and produces such rain, as the inhabitants of level countries have never seen . . .

"In the afternoon which preceded the storm, it was perceived to thunder and lighten incessantly beyond Skiddaw; the cloud from which the tempest proceeded, came at length up to the mountain, but, not being high enough to pass over it, divided; one half of it went north east, and, meeting with no opposition, it discharged a great quantity of water on the plains of Wigton and Carlisle, over which it hovered, till about nine o'clock at night, and then moved farther in the same direction, but so slowly, that its explosions were not out of hearing till two in the morning.

"The other half went through a vale called Threlcot (Threlkeld), and over the rocks on one side of Keswick, called Lady Rocks, meeting no opposition till it came to the mountains which bound St John's Vale, and by these it was stopped. It became every moment more dense, by the accession of vapours, which, being still in motion, pressed upon it, and soon after it poured down a torrent of rain, which lasted eight hours. The thunder still continued, and the darkness, which might almost be felt, became more dreadful by the flashes, which broke it at short intervals with a sulphurous light. To the noise of the thunder was added that of the cataracts, and of the fragments of the rock which they drove before them; the fences were overturned in a moment, the fields covered with the ruins of the mountains, under which the cottages were first crushed, and then swept away by the torrent.

"The inhabitants (of the cottages) who were scarce less astonished and terrified, than they would have been at the sound of the last trumpet, and the dissolution of nature, ran together from under the roofs that sheltered them, lest they should be beaten in upon their heads, and, finding the waters rush down all round them in an impetuous deluge, which had already covered the ground, such of them as were able climbed the neighbouring trees, and others got on the top of hay stacks, where they sat exposed at once to the lightning and the rain, discovering by the light of every flash some new ruin, and every moment expecting that the trees to which they had fled for safety should be torn up by the roots, and the hay overturned by the inundation.

"It is perhaps impossible for the strongest imagination to accumulate circumstances of greater horror, and these were produced by a concurrence of various causes, which perhaps may happen no more. To this account it is necessary to add that several cottages were swept away from the declivities where they stood; the vale was deluged and many of the cattle were lost."

Rain in the hills over Troutbeck. Deluges there would soon be felt in the Greta system

Other accounts of the deluge were recorded and the following (taken from *Hutchinson's Cumberland*) suggests that some reports of the event were sensationalised. It reads: "Near the Eleven mile stone flows Mosedale beck, which has its source between the two eminences called Wolf Crag and the Dodd. Travellers have been amused with various fictitious accounts of an inundation on the 22nd day of August, 1749, and exaggerated circumstances have crept into the productions of hasty writers . . .

"We believe the following account to come very near the truth. On the evening of the 22nd of August, noises were heard in the air, gusts of wind at intervals burst forth with

The Greta . . . a river runs through it

great violence, and were almost instantaneously succeeded by a dead calm. In this country the inhabitants are accustomed to the bottom winds and whirlwinds, the howling of the tempest among the rocks and mountains gives them no serious alarm: on this evening the inhabitants went to repose at their usual hour. About one in the morning a heavy rain began, and before four o'clock, the whole face of the lower country was covered with water many feet in depth. Several houses were beat down by the torrents, and others filled with sand to the first story; Legburthwaite mill was totally destroyed, and not one stone left upon another; even the millstones were washed away, one of them has not yet been discovered, the other was found at some considerable distance.

"The affrighted inhabitants climbed the roofs of the houses for preservation, and there waited for the subsiding of the waters. One Mounsey, of Wallthwaite, when he came down stairs in the morning, found his doors burst open by the violence of the floods, and utensils and timber floating in his lower rooms. At Lobthwaite, the most remarkable vestiges of this inundation are to be seen; stones piled upon each other, to the height of ten or twelve yards, many of which are upwards of 20 ton weight. The distance between Lobthwaite and Wolf Crag is not more than a mile and a half, and very little water

Another early image of Keswick suffering from flooding.

could be collected above Wolf Crag; the fall of rain or waterspout did not extend above eight miles, so that it is astonishing such a quantity of water could fall in so small a space of country.

"At Fornside all was devastation. Trees were torn up by the roots, and immense beds of wreck and gravel covered the lands, whilst at Mell Fell, three miles distant, the countrymen were leading home their corn all night, in fair weather; a practice not unusual when there are signs of a change.

"In this vale is a place called Guardhouse, where are the remains of some strong walls, probably a watchtower belonging to the

Threlkelds, where they secured their domestics and cattle on the incursions of the borderers."

Another account which "seems best to be relied upon" reported as follows: "This remarkable fall of water happened at nine o'clock on the 22nd of August last, in the midst of the most terrible thunder and incessant lightning, ever known in that part, in the memory of the oldest man living. The preceding afternoon having been extremely hot and sultry; and, what seems very uncommon, and difficult to account for, the inhabitants of the vale, of good credit, affirm to having heard a strange buzzing noise*, like that of a malt mill, or the sound of wind in the tops of trees, for two hours together, before the clouds broke. I am not so much a philosopher, as to find out what would occasion such a vast collection of clouds or vapours, particularly at that time or place, but am satisfied, from the havoc it has made in so short a time (for it was all over in less than two hours) that it must have far exceeded any thunder shower that we have ever seen; most probably a spout, or large body of water, which, by the rarefaction of the air occasioned by that incessant lightning, broke all at once upon the tops of these mountains, and so came down in a sheet of water upon the valley below.

"At the bottom of Catchety Gill stood a mill and a kiln, which were entirely swept away in five minutes time, and the place where they formerly stood now covered with huge rocks and rubbish three or four yards deep. In the violence of the storm, the

The Greta in spate from Forge Bridge.

mountain has tumbled so fast down as to choke up the old course of this brook and, what is very surprising, it has forced its way through rock and now runs in a great chasm, four yards wide and eight or nine feet deep. Such monstrous stones, or rather rocks, and such vast quantities of gravel and sand, are thrown upon their little meadow fields, as render the same absolutely useless, and never to be recovered.

*Humming, crackling, hissing, or buzzing noises indicate that a lightning strike is imminent. Sometimes even rocks make buzzing sounds in the presence of the large amount of static electricity accompanying an electrical storm. The rapid movement of electrons causes the noise.

The Greta . . . a river runs through it

"It would surpass all credit to give the dimensions and weight of some rocks, which are not only tumbled down the steep parts of the mountain but carried a considerable way into the fields, several thrown upon banks larger than a team of ten horses could move. Near a place called Lobwath we had the curiosity to measure one carried a great way, which was six hundred and seventy six inches, or near nineteen yards, about.

"The damage done to the grounds, houses, walls, fences, highways, and the loss of corn and hay then upon the ground was immense. One of the brooks, called Mose or Mosedale Beck, which runs north from the other side of the Legburthet (Legburthwaite) fells, continues still to be foul and muddy, having worn (as is supposed) its channel so deep in some parts of its course, as to work upon some mineral substance, which gives it the colour of water flushed from lead mines, which is so strong as to tinge the river Derwent (into which it eventually empties), even at the sea, near twenty miles."

Another writer noted that he had met with someone who "seemed to be of the opinion that this vast discharge of water was not from clouds, but an eruption of the mountain; and that uncommon noise, such as is heard from the mount Etna, or Vesuvius, some days before a violent eruption of fire and combustible matter, labouring to be discharged from the bowels of those mountains – but this to me seems too chimerical."

What impact all this had on the River Greta and Keswick is not known and I can only surmise that because the storm was centred on a specific area in the fells around Threlkeld and St John's Vale it probably resulted in a flash flood in the lower reaches of the river, perhaps similar to one in the recent history of Keswick when a wave of dirty brown water unexpectedly swept down the river in the middle of a summer's day.

However, it is unlikely that the flash flood of 1749 caused any significant damage in the town

The flooding in 2005 and the road at High Hill has been transformed into a raging torrent.
Picture by Stuart Holmes.

and immediate area as the water would perhaps not reach the sort of high levels usually linked to the widespread prolonged rain and snow melt that caused such devastation as recently as November 2009 (and before that in January 2005) when Keswick, Cockermouth and Workington and surrounding areas were badly hit by flooding. In 2009 the River Greta was already bank high when the heaviest rainfall since records began (in 1766) fell on Seathwaite, the wettest inhabited place in England. It was recorded at 377mm in 36 hours. The resulting floods in 2009 were described as being of "Biblical proportions" and a "one in every 1,000 years event." It was certainly the worst flooding that the town of Keswick has experienced in its recorded history. I ventured out to witness the worst of the flooding at first hand on the night of Thursday, November 19.

I reached the conclusion that the rain we experienced on that occasion, almost monsoon like, the high winds that invariably accompanied the rain – rising to a crescendo during the night – and the increased risk of flooding, all smack of climate change. There are many people who still doubt the authenticity of claims of this nature but all the evidence points to Man and our pollution being to blame for what is happening, not just here in the Lake District, but all over Planet Earth and in many different extreme forms – icecaps melting, excessive heat, rain, storms, flooding, mudslides, and the sun scorching through holes in the ozone layer.

Post flooding and storm damage in Lower Fitz Park in 2005.
Picture by Stuart Holmes.

The warning signs are clearly there and for me, after the floods in Keswick of November 2009, it was the sight of a twisted spiral of tarmac, ripped away from a nearby footpath like a strip of carpet, and deposited in the centre of a playing field, a bizarre sculpture next to its creator, the River Greta, as it flows alongside Fitz Park and, occasionally, straight through it.

The Greta . . . a river runs through it

The flood of 1888 and drowning of 'Priest' Brown

Other significant flooding was reported in the Keswick area in the 19th Century – in February 1822, November 1863, three times in 1874, in March 1881 and October 1888. *The English Lakes Visitor and Keswick Guardian* in its edition of Saturday, November 3rd, 1888 reported: "The heavy rain which fell at the close of last week caused a serious flood in this district, and, owing to the rapidity with which the watercourses were filled to overflow, serious damage has resulted, yet not so serious as has been reported in some newspapers.

"Isaac Bristo, farmer, Borrowdale, lost twenty one sheep on Saturday morning. These sheep, along with others, had been brought down from the mountains for the winter. The violence of the storm waked Mr Bristo and he went as quickly as possible to look after his flock, but he was unable to rescue them all . . .

"Rain continued to fall all day on Saturday and during the night. On Sunday morning the water from the river had backed up through the sewers into Main Street and from the extra quantity flowing from the lake the Derwent spread its waters over the lower lying meadowland between Derwentwater and Bassenthwaite. Some fear was felt that the Greta would burst through the wall at High Hill, and possibly it might have done had there been no precautions taken.

"The road through the Howrahs, the Portinscale Road and the road to Crosthwaite Church were flooded and impassable to pedestrians. For the first time for many years service was not held at Crosthwaite Church. The scene at the lakeside on Sunday morning was one of wreck. A goodly number of boats had been drawn high up on to the road, but not before some of them had been very much clashed. The landings were greatly damaged. Many boats were more or less injured on the Isthmus, where they had been put for the winter, and a quantity of boat furniture is still missing. Mr Harker's and Mr R Mitchell's boats on the Portinscale side of the lake were washed away and went down the river. The lake was higher than it has been for six years.

The valley, as seen from Castlehead, looked like a vast watery waste in which the higher grounds stood out as islands. It was curious to note the different articles washed down by the waters. Among these was an apparently new cricket bat down the Greta.

From Borrowdale there came part of a roof, a gate, and a rail with hat pegs. The suddenness with which the flood and storm came was surprising, for the barometer was high and firm and there had not been even a hint from cousin Jonathan (a reference to Jonathan Otley, geologist and meteorologist in Keswick).

An account by Canon Hardwicke Rawnsley, published in 1902 as part of his book *A Rambler's Notebook – at the English Lakes,* provided a particularly colourful report of the flooding in Keswick vale on the Sunday morning of October 28th, 1888. Rawnsley (September 2nd, 1851 – May 28th, 1920) a famous resident of Keswick, clergyman, poet, writer, conservationist and campaigner who went on to be a founder member of The National Trust, wrote: "In our Lake country, if after a hard, dry time in October as dry as the driest summers – when the salmon are waiting down in the lake, and cannot make for their spawning beds; when children run across the river weirs, and the wells are beginning to give out at farms; if then, with hardly a fall in the barometer, a south-west wind rises, and drives the wild Atlantic mists in moving mountains of cloud ashore, and if rain falls for two consecutive days to the depth of four inches and then the wind increasing almost to a cyclone, drives sheets of water upon the fell-side breasts, so that in twenty four hours another four inches of rain is chronicled in the rain gauge, then we may expect just such a flood as it was my fortune to witness on Sunday morning.

"All day, as it seemed," Rawnsley continued, "on Friday and Saturday the sun was hid, the air was full of the noise of rain and rush of lying leaves. The salmon, waiting in Bassenthwaite till they might have despaired of revisiting again their old haunts up the

When two lakes become one. Derwentwater (left) and Bassenthwaite in the flooding of 2005.
Picture by Stuart Holmes.

River Bure (St John's Beck) in the Vale of St John, were seen to be leaping the weir just above Robert Southey's old house (Greta Hall) at the Greta side. The mill wheels at various mills were stopped, for the head of water was too great; the pencil maker, who had been obliged to work short time for want of water, was obliged to work shorter for the fullness of supply. And still the winds roared and the rain fell."

Skiddaw was veiled in cloud and when it lifted silver streams of water poured down its purple-brown flanks. Shepherds started to worry about their flocks and herds. On Saturday afternoon many sheep and cattle were gathered from pastures beside the rapidly rising waters of the Derwent.

"Explaining why precisely sheep are particularly vulnerable to drowning, one shepherd said: 'You see a sheep has a girt cwoat on and cannot set it aside when they've a mind to, and yance in't watter they sink the seame as a stean (stone).'

"Farmers left the market early, fearing that they might not get home. 'Dar bon,' said one old peasant, reverting to early Norman / French days, 'but it's garn to be t'end of t'world. Fwolks was buyin' and sellin', as Book tells us, when the fust flood cem, and it'll be the seame now. . .' Darkness set in early and the noise of rising water and the storm made for a terrible night. Few slept soundly in their beds."

The arrival of dawn gave the writer the distinct impression that the Greta was determined to wipe the little town, situated beneath storm-dark Walla Crag, from the face of the earth.

"Boiling round its corner and hurrying towards the town, the torrent had risen to what, from our vantage ground, looked like within a foot of the rampart that is built

between it and the houses at High Hill," Rawnsley wrote. "If that bank gives way there will be death and disaster."

The nearby Howrahs was under water and Derwentwater and Bassenthwaite were joined by the flood, a sight not uncommon in the early years of the 21st Century and in other flood years during the preceding century.

"Lost was the Greta, lost the Derwent river, lost the northern confines of the lake, and had it not been for the upstanding of the grey parapet of the Long Bridge, near Portinscale, with the white flashing close beneath it of the tremendous torrent, one might have felt that Derwent and Greta had ceased to be. As far as the eye could see, a calm white lake possessed the plain and the hedgerows and trees might have been so much flotsam upon the water, a huge net cast upon the flood . . ."

Rawnsley, who had been appointed vicar of Crosthwaite Church (dedicated to St Kentigern - also known as St Mungo) in 1883, and was made honorary canon of Carlisle Cathedral in 1891, succeeded in reaching the ancient church, which is situated on raised ground, and there he met the sexton who had, in his own words 'kindled chuch fire and rung t'bell but me an chuch cats is aw th' congregation for today. They tell me Newlands Beck is burst. Fwoaks cannot git what ivver from Portinscale or town. And I should not ha' bin here missel but for t'railway where I rose be-times and climmed 'bankment so I'se here.'

The river at Brigham.

Rawnsley and the sexton went up into the church tower to survey the scene: "Derwent Hill, the How Farm, and salmon-guards stood out like green islands from the wild deluge," Rawnsley relates. "With these exceptions the Keswick valley, from the gates of Borrowdale to beyond Bassenthwaite, looked just one large lake. Bassenthwaite's older name of Broadwater seemed to have been deserved, today it might well have returned to it.

"There was a pause in the storm and Skiddaw, for a moment, ceased to hide. Dark purple, stained with the iron rust of the drenched fern, the shales upon the High Maen leapt up angrily against the cold wet sky. The milky cataracts in fine thread lacework twisted themselves together and plunged from the heights to Millbeck and Applethwaite and the full becks hustled through the lower grounds. Far away Lodore showed like an avalanche of snow . . . a horseman-shepherd went by to see to charges bleating on a knoll; flood imprisoned cattle lowed pitifully from upper pastures, and with much splashing, their udders touched the water on the roadway, they were driven towards the milk pail and safety by men in carts.

"Then the huge skirts of another storm wiped out all view of Barf and Wythop, and trailing after it a majestic train of rain-wove cloth of silver, another burst of rain fell heavily upon the flanks of Skiddaw and the tower of the ancient church. . ."

It was all very dramatic but at least there was, it seems, no loss of human life.

That, regrettably, was not the case in February 1822, a market day Saturday when every yeoman felt obliged to come to Keswick, stable his horse at the inn, put down 3s for his dinner and drink success to his host. Tragically, a man known as 'Priest' Brown, of Bassenthwaite, lost his way home, the Greta was high and his horse (or its drink-fuddled rider) somehow mistook the main stream for the main road and Brown was swept to his death down the river below Greta Bridge.

"It was Candlemass Saturday," someone recalled, "that was t' day Priest Brown was found drowned. Deal of ice cem' down t' beck, washed away machines at The Forge, mashed up Shulecrow brig and fult houses wi' watter. Mi father kenned it weel. We've a clock at yam shows mark o' t' water on t' case, and father used to crack on aboot how t' auld clock was flayte o'watter and was nivver quite seamme in its head efter that."

But let's move forward in time to October 1888 and revisit Crosthwaite Church where Hardwicke Drummond Rawnsley has left the sexton in the belfry.

Glass topped flood defence wall at High Hill. Unfortunately there were reports that kingfishers had been found dead after presumably flying into the glass.

"I left my old friend in full grin at the gathering waters," he wrote, "one chuck cat on his shoulder, the other mewing at his feet and, getting on to the railway embankment that passes the end of the churchyard, set face for home. A sense of indescribable loneliness possessed me as I turned to take a last look at St Mungo's Church, lonely and flood-girdled, its Sunday use gone; its glorious peal of bells for that day to be silent in the tower ... 'Crostet's (Crosthwaite is) not the only place where a priest will ha' nowt to dea this day,' said an old friend as I crossed the only part of Fitz Park still above flood water, passed the bowling green, now in possession of ruder hands than the hands of men. 'They tell me St John's beck's out anaw and neabody can git to chapel today on Naddle Fell.'

Flood defences at Keswick. The big slate wall as seen from Upper Fitz Park.

"One remembered, as he spoke, how the waterspout, which wrought such mischief from Legburthwaite right down the dale, fell as long ago as 1749. But the fact is, that in this Lake country, where all the vales are just so many conduits for the storm, where when it 'siles down reet gaily, every road becomes a sike, and every sike a beck, and every beck a river' one cannot tell what is to be the result if, when the becks are full, a storm cloud breaks far up upon the hills.

"As I spoke, just such a freshet came down the Greta, now surcharged and boiling along into the back lanes of Keswick. The sound, as this freshet crashed down, was as though the torrent had taken a fit. The hoarse crackle and cry of the gurgling wave, as it swept on beneath the bridge had a really human note of pain and distress within it, and a kind of tidal surge swept into the Park. And still the heavens opened and the rain fell.

"About noon the downpour ceased for a while, but the wind seemed to gain strength and, with less heavily-weighted wings, rushed against the woods. Rooks were sent whirling up into the sky. The sea gulls come up from the coast alone seemed able to manage their white sails and steer their wonderful ways above the flood . . ."

Later in the day, after Rawnsley had visited Derwentwater and struggled on to Lodore to see the fall in full flow, the weather changed dramatically: "Bassenthwaite, as pale as a dead man's face, visibly glowed and gleamed with new life. The cloud wrack suddenly parted, the curtains of the storm seemed to be looped back by invisible hands, and such an aery pageant of sunset glory was enacted between Barf and Skiddaw Dodd as it has seldom been my fortune to behold . . ."

And later still: "Twenty-four more hours without rain, and I stood on the Vicarage terrace, from which at sunset on a calm October day in 1769, Gray, the poet, saw 'the sweetest scene he had discovered in point of pastoral beauty.' I believe he would still have gazed with satisfaction. The grasses on the long back of Helvellyn and Glaramara were washed into strange whiteness, the fern on Grisedale and Skiddaw was still dusky red from the recent rainfalls, but the fields had reappeared, children sang along the roads, and men and cattle came as of old across the valley.

"The Greta, murmuring loud, had sunk from sight, the Derwent shone clear and brimming as it swept through emerald meadows toward the sea."

The Greta . . . a river runs through it

Otley's Well and the man who loved water

Part of the major flood prevention work completed in Keswick in 2012 involved the creation of a substantial slate wall that towers over the bank of the river opposite to the beautiful trees, gardens, lawns, footpaths, tennis courts and bowling greens that make up the town's Upper Fitz Park. To anyone driving or walking along Penrith Road it would seem to be an impressive piece of slate walling – which it undoubtedly is on the outside – but appearances can be deceptive. Anyone who watched the wall being built will know that the centre is made up of solid concrete slabs, sufficiently strong for a nuclear fall out shelter and pinned together by metal rods.

The wall, designed and built to thwart the worst advances of the River Greta in flood, has a sister construction (built under the same Environment Agency scheme) at High Hill, just upstream from Greta Bridge, where the wall has the added benefit of what can only be described as a glass fence stretching out along the top of its entire length and in which, somewhat surrealistically, the images of nearby homes, cars and passing traffic are reflected onto the scenery beyond of Skiddaw, Latrigg and the river.

The plaque to Jonathan Otley's well set into the big slate defence wall opposite Upper Fitz Park.

Whether all these formidable constructions can actually prevent the river from flooding roads and homes remains to be seen. Nature and especially water in its extreme form (floods of Biblical proportions and all that) take some stopping and only time and the elements will tell whether 'slate' walls, reinforced glass fencing atop them and enlarged embankments in key locations have done their job and justified the time and expense. If they do not then there could be some very red faces, not to mention very wet feet.

Anyway be that as it may, the reason for mentioning all this is that sometimes in the construction of the new a flavour of the past can be irretrievably lost. But in the area of the new slate wall overlooking Upper Fitz Park a little piece of Keswick's history has, thank goodness, been retained. Viewed from the other side of the river the slate wall is very tall and substantial, stretching from the site of what used to be Wren's Mill to the footbridge over the river into the park. Look closely at the wall from the park side of the Greta and you should be able to make out an entirely different coloured stone in one small area of the expanse of grey-green slate. And if you walk along the parapet directly below the wall you will see at close quarters (virtually opposite the entrance to Greta Street) an old, dark stone plaque set into the slate half way up the wall.

The original plaque, formerly a lintel, bears the legend 'Otley's Well.'

Now you might think it unusual nowadays to find the source of a well, or at least a plaque to mark its whereabouts, half way up a 21st Century flood defence wall. And you would be right. But this plaque marks the place above which Otley's Well was situated and once emerged, pure water, out of the ground and into the river. Of Otley's Well in 1903 it was written: "A few yards from Shu-le-Crow is seen a break in the quite sufficient fence and, from that, steps lead down to a spring of the clearest water. It is, however, so hidden away under the bank that hundreds of passers-by have not noticed it; and even from the Fitz Park side one sees more of the steps that lead down to it than of the spring itself. The words Otley's Well are on a lintel."

The next question is why Otley's Well and where does the name spring from?

Well (if you'll pardon the pun), Jonathan Otley (January 19, 1766 – December 7, 1856) was a remarkable figure from Keswick's past and his name, again in plaque form, also crops up on the side of the house in the middle of the town where he lived and worked from 1797. The property is made easy to spot by the row of steep steps (it became known as 'Jonathan's up the steps') leading to its door and situated in King's Head Court, just off Market Place. Otley was a geologist, minerologist, meteorologist, botanist, topographer, cartographer, and watchmaker / repairer.

He certainly spent a lot of his time out and about tracing streams to their sources, discovering fountain-heads on distant fell sides, quiet woody places or, closer to home, carefully cleansing them of fallen leaves and planting flowers here and there. He also observed winds and storms and flood, made a study of the Floating Island on Derwentwater, and marked high and low lake levels on the rocks at Friar's Crag. He was often found in the higher fells with a barometer making observations on altitude and frequently returned home laden with botanical examples and with his pockets full of various specimens of lava and volcanic ash.

One friend noted that Otley, aged 87 (he died in his 91st year) had walked two or three times a week to Barrow Side, and spent hours amusing himself forming little wells of the springs that arise in the mountain side. In his Journal for March 16, 1852, Otley recorded: "At spring on Barrow Common, planted now and before, water-cress, scurvy-grass, veronica, and forget-me-not."

Jonathan Otley has not been forgotten and there is a plaque at his former home in King's Head Court (near the Moot Hall in the heart of Keswick) and another by the old well near the River Greta to demonstrate the fact. Given his meteorological background, Otley would doubtless have appreciated that his name is not only linked to a spring of pure water in the town but that it is also washed over by the spate water of the River Greta, drawn from a thousand and one little becks and streams and, of course, wells of pure water.

Flooding at High Hill in 2005.
Picture by Stuart Holmes.

Wildlife
THE GOOD, THE BAD AND THE UGLY

Wild Atlantic salmon and river otters, two of the most precious species to live on Planet Earth, have reached a crossroads as they continue their struggle for survival on the greatest little river in the world – the Greta. The otter, after years of persecution and being hunted down, to the point where very few, if any, lived on the river, its tributaries and surrounding lakes, has been undergoing something of a renaissance. A UK policy of reintroduction appears to have worked and otter sightings are now a regular occurrence in and around Derwentwater and Bassenthwaite and the rivers Derwent and Greta and related streams.

It is good to see otters on our rivers and long may they thrive. Unfortunately it appears that while the otter is on the way back another great species, the salmon, could be on the way out or, at the very least, in serious decline.

The future of the Atlantic salmon on the Greta is not looking so positive. In fact the species on these waters is currently under considerable threat. As a child and later as a youth I can recall that in the late summer and autumn of the 1950s and 1960s vast numbers of salmon used to run the River Greta. On Sundays, while out for an afternoon stroll, families would gather by the weir (long since destroyed) in Lower Fitz Park to watch hundreds of salmon leaping the man-made barrier or plough forcefully up the shallow water slipways at the sides, their backs and fins slipstreaming out of the water as they made their way upriver on the spate-high coloured water to the spawning grounds.

It was a similar scenario further down stream at Greta Bridge where anglers would peer over the parapet to see if the salmon were coming over the small weir that once existed there. Up river, once the water had dropped, and the fish had stopped travelling and settled into pools, it was often said that dubs (pools) were so thick with fish that you could run from one side of the river to the other on the backs of the salmon. This, clearly, was impossible, but it was an apt way of indicating the large numbers of salmon that once ran the river.

Facing page: The dipper.
Picture by Mike Lane, NHPA.

Not only that, when the salmon eggs in the redds (raised sections of finer gravel and stone where the hen fish lays and buries her eggs and the cock fish fertilises them with its milt) hatched and developed into young salmon fry and parr, the number of young fish was prodigious. As young lads fishing for trout with worm we were constantly plagued by salmon fry and parr tugging at the worm on the hook and repeatedly stripping it bare. Nowadays you are fortunate to see a salmon fry or parr. They are there but their numbers are greatly reduced and are constantly being eroded by predation and other factors.

Since the days when salmon ran the river in vast numbers several factors have combined to make the survival of the species a cause for concern. These include: deep sea trawler fishing with sophisticated location devices and techniques; climatic changes which are affecting the salmon's ability to grow and survive at sea; loss of and damage to habitat in the rivers of their birth and on the spawning grounds; the disease Ulcerative Dermal Necrosis (UDN) which wiped out thousands in the late 1960s early 1970s, so much so that it is questionable whether stocks have ever really recovered; pollution in various forms; contamination of the breed from escapee farmed salmon; predation from cormorants, mergansers and goosanders. And then there are mink and the otter. Finally, there is the river angler and while many fishermen these days, conscious of the scarcity of salmon, return any catches to the water, there is always the temptation for some to keep 'one for the pot.' The combined impact of all of these is undoubtedly giving the salmon a hard time and the odds are heavily against its continued survival on the Greta and its tributaries in any meaningful numbers. Fish stocks in the early years of the 21st

The Atlantic salmon.
This cock fish is sporting
its red livery.
Picture Laurie Campbell, NHPA.

Century are arguably at an all time low and I fear that the species – just like the otter previously – is now in danger of eradication from some of the smaller rivers where it has survived and evolved for thousands of years. This, in fact, has probably already happened on some of the higher fell streams in Lakeland which flow into the Greta and where the Atlantic salmon previously spawned but no longer does so.

It is arguably an environmental nightmare, yet another indictment of Man's negative impact on the planet. If we allow a species as marvellous as the Atlantic salmon to 'die-off' on the Greta it shows yet again that we are only prepared to pay lip service to wildlife and the environment on those occasions when it suits. As soon as the cold wind of a financial front blows in over our morally devoid cityscapes and financial institutions, the moneymen take precedence and the environment loses out as politicians take what they simply love to call 'tough decisions' or 'hard choices.'

The protection of the environment and the world in which we live should always be our first priority; it is not a matter of choice. Alternatively, the seriousness of a situation is badly misjudged and warning signs ignored until it is too late.

The life cycle of the salmon is nothing short of amazing. For thousands of years the salmon has bred in the selfsame river, or its tributaries, where it was spawned, on virtually the same area of gravel. That a grown salmon can find its way back from the oceans of the world to the same river and the exact location where it began life as an egg in the redds is miraculous. The way in which salmon, as night follows day, have for centuries found their way from the place where they were created, high in the Lakeland fells, to the seas where they feed and grow and then return to repeat the cycle all over again, time after time, generation after generation, world without end, remains a mystery. It is thought the salmon's navigational skills are made possible by a number of factors. These include being guided by the stars and 'the use of receptors sensitive to local differences in the earth's magnetic field.' And we thought we were sophisticated?

Ocean currents may also play their part and, when nearer to the coast and seeking out the river of its birth, the salmon is apparently guided by a 'chemical memory' that allows it to recognise and home in on substances, including pheromones present in the water in very minute traces. In short they can sniff out where they belong and where they should be headed.

The otter.
Picture by Mark Hamblin,
NHPA.

But if the salmon is increasingly experiencing a tough time in the survival stakes then we should reflect on the fact that it is not all that long ago that the otter was hunted almost to oblivion on the Greta. The otter was not always a protected species under UK and European law and most people now look back with a sense of abhorrence and incredulity to the days when otters were hunted with hounds in local rivers.

The death of an otter

Even in the days when the otter could be hunted legally it caused a degree of controversy as can be seen from an exchange between the Editor of the *Lakes Visitor and Keswick Guardian* and a 'sportsman' writing in the columns of the newspaper about otter hunting in the tributaries of the Greta. The June 10, 1882 edition of the publication contained the following report and comment on an otter hunt: "During the last few weeks several otters have been seen both in St John's and Threlkeld becks (Glenderamackin). Mr Jonathan Stanley's terriers had a severe encounter with one just a little above Wanthwaite Mill. Fishermen were naturally desirous to have the waters freed from the otters which are very destructive animals among fish, and it is said that some intended to shoot them as opportunity offered unless the otter hounds were brought shortly.

"From what follows it would have been better had they carried out their threat. On Saturday the Cockermouth otterhounds were booked to Threlkeld (railway) station and after being uncoupled near the Glenderamackin, they soon began with a lusty cry to 'rend the thin air.' Taking a splendid drag from Mr Sawer's field they scampered up the beck as far as Lamb Bridge but as here they could not get the otter to make his appearance, pick and shovel were called into requisition and soon effected an exposure. Then began what cannot be considered sport. The otter was taken by the nose with a pair of blacksmith's tongs and a whip thong was noosed round its body. Thus it was dragged from its lair and let off again in shallow water, with a greater certainty of its falling prey to the dogs. The 'deep mouthed band' began their 'forest music' and they were not long in killing the vermin, which was a male and weighed about 20lbs. A large number of people were present at the kill and as their 'joys are in the chase' no doubt they felt highly gratified at the sport.

"It is necessary for the protection of fish these animals should be exterminated, but because it is so there is no need to torture the brutes in the manner described – by the prelude of blacksmith's tongs to the fangs of the dogs. It would have been more merciful to have killed the otter outright in its lair than that it should have been put to unnecessary pain, just to give 'sportsmen' the gratification of seeing its body torn and bleeding in the beck in such a position that it had no chance of defending itself."

The following week the newspaper carried a Letter to the Editor, from someone writing under the pen name 'Nimrod', defending the actions of the huntsmen:

"As the concluding remarks in your account of the otter hunt at Threlkeld condemns the way in which it was killed, may I, as a sportsman, defend the means used? In the first place, was it not the better way to let the otter have a chance for its life, however small, than by killing it outright in its lair as was suggested; and again, why not let the dogs delight themselves if it is only for the development of the special faculty they have for hunting down the otter?

"As regards the prelude of pincers and noose, they were used with as little pain to the otter as circumstances would allow. It would be very difficult indeed, without the aid of the 'deep-mouthed band' to prevent otters from becoming too numerous, yet we don't wish to exterminate them; but when the occasion requires, 'A hunting we will go, my boys'."

In responding to this the editor wrote: "We do not see that our correspondent's pleas at all affect the position we took in respect to the 'hunt.' The 'small' chance which he claims was given the otter was so very small that possibility of escape was beyond question; and we maintain that it would have been more humane to end its misery at once – that is, admitting the necessity of killing it – than that it should have been subjected to the increased torture of being dragged by the snout with a pair of pincers from its lair. Besides, we have since been informed that in order to effect this means of ejectment it was necessary first to thrust a stick into the animal's mouth – perhaps throat – before it was ventured to apply the pincers. So much for the little pain which 'circumstances allow.' The delight of the dogs would have been just as great had the newly killed carcase been thrown among them; but the spectators would have missed the 'sport' of a worry, in which a poor brute is torn and mangled to death.

"We have no objection to our friend 'going a hunting.' All that we desire is that he and his merry 'boys' would show a little more of that sensibility which would not "heedlessly set foot upon the worm'."

Otter hunting in the UK was made illegal in 1978.

Birds of the river bank

The dipper is a flier, hurtling up and down the Greta at great speed, low to the surface and the central current, its wing beats a blur. It is a busy little round bundle of brown and grey with a strikingly white bib and stubby tail. It is a bird that is invariably to be seen – when not whirring its way up and down the river – standing on a stone in the middle of white water, doing what it does automatically, dipping up and down to camouflage itself against the constantly moving water, bobbing and weaving like a nimble ring boxer and occasionally taking a dive in and out of the bubbling foam and emerging with food, insect larvae and the like.

Stop to study this master of the stream and you will see that it is an effective hunter and forager, an accomplished underwater swimmer and one of the river's great characters. It may build its oval-ball, wren-like nest under the arch or in the sidewall of one of the eight old metal railway bridges spanning the river between Threlkeld and Keswick. But, then again, it may not; there are plenty of alternative places along the river.

The kingfisher.
Picture by Mike Lane, NHPA.

Other birds I love to see on the Greta are the grey wagtails, much more colourfully yellow than their name suggests, with a bouncy tail that appears as if it is permanently attached to a puppet master's string; the rare and exquisitely blue flash of a kingfisher as it sweeps upstream and, among the upper branches of oaks in Brundholme Woods, the red, white and black of the Greater Spotted woodpecker, flitting like a giant moth up the tree trunks. And not forgetting the smaller, beautiful birds like the nuthatch, the tree creeper, the goldfinch, the tiny wren and the even titchier goldcrest with its snazzy golden-streak hairstyle.

The red squirrel puts on a show

The red squirrel is the entertainer of Brundholme Woods and other locations along the Greta. Watching a pair of squirrels engaged in a game of chase – either a pre-mating ritual or just for the hell of it – through the branches of the trees is a wonderful sight that will keep you amused for ages. The best way to spot the red squirrel is to walk along with your eyes raised to the tree canopy watching out for sudden movement or a twitching of branches and foliage. Alternatively, keep your eyes down and the shell of a hazel might crack you on the head.

The red squirrel pictured in a pine tree after feeding on hazel nuts provided by Eric Bainbridge and his wife Kath from a feeder at the back of their house, Riverside, at The Forge, Keswick.

While out trout fishing I once saw a red squirrel heading towards me through the low-slung branches of an avenue of hazels. I quickly lay down stock still and flat on my back and watched as the squirrel went through the trees directly overhead. When it saw me it paused, raised itself on its hind legs, and appeared to become quite agitated. It issued an aggressive chattering sound while switching its impressively bushy tail to and fro. For a moment I thought it was going to go straight for the jugular!

The red squirrel is more often to be seen in the early morning and early evening. This is very much a Cumbrian squirrel, not to be confused with the invasive and bigger East European grey, carrier of a virus that is deadly to the red. Hopefully the red squirrel can survive the invasion. It is a marvellous little creature and the star turn of the riverside woodland it shares with other animals such as deer, badgers and the fox, all of which will visit the river to drink. And, who knows, take the occasional dip in the heat of summer.

The heron in his great cloak

The walkers streaming over the old railway bridge near the tunnel on the railway path next to the Greta have failed to spot the heron as it stands on sentry duty in the shallow water at the foot of Scar Dub. It looks rather miserable and forlorn in the light drizzle, its grey plumage wrapped around it like a great coat and its orange beak the one flash of colour in an otherwise drab scene. The heron's long spindly legs, spreading marginally outward from the knee, emerge from beneath the cloak and provide an almost comic effect. But the heron is no fool. It is a cunning hunter, stealthy, precise and calculating with the patience of a saint. The deadly strike, when it comes, is cobra-like in its speed as the pointed beak spears its prey.

The heron on the Greta.

While the heron is a perfectionist and extremely graceful when hunting in the shallows of the river, it is anything but that in the sky where it is slow moving and ungainly. Long, laborious and troubled wing movements are more of a flap than a beat and the protruding underbelly gives it all the appearance of a low flying bomber yet to discharge its cargo.

Herons appear to have favourite places on the river at particular times of the day. On winter mornings there is usually one on the far side of the island at the bottom of Windebrowe Avenue where I live. Like experienced anglers who know the river well, I suspect that the heron knows where and when the river affords the best opportunities for food.

Mick Tinnion brings a trout to the net in the middle pool in Town's Field.

The Greta . . . a river runs through it

Fishing
CASTING OUT A LINE

The entire culture of fishing on the River Greta has changed significantly in recent years. There was a time, not all that long ago, when salmon caught by local anglers were sold to the chefs of local hotels and money and fresh run fish changed hands at the back door to the hotel kitchen. Anglers would also keep trout and salmon to be eaten at home; so as well as enjoying the experience of angling on a very scenic river, the fisherman could also provide for his family and friends and, from time to time – when the salmon were running – supplement his income.

And then, of course, there were fishermen and downright poachers, who were not too fussy as to how the salmon were removed from the river or the streams that feed the Greta. Down the years a team of water bailiffs, or beck watchers as they are still known, was employed to counter the worst excesses of those who took salmon by illegal and unfair means.

In late November, 1880, for example, a report appeared in the local press which gives a strong flavour of the times: "On Saturday night and Sunday morning last there was the highest flood in the Vale of St John that has been seen for some years. It came,

A salmon fly tied by
Terry ("The Heron") Appleby.

however, too late for the salmon fishing, which in that branch of the river has this year been a total blank, no fish having reached it before the commencement of the close season. No doubt there will be a great run of fish just now, and when the water goes down the watchers of the new Board of Conservators will need to have their eyes open, and to exert their utmost vigilance to prevent the poaching fraternity from destroying the fish on the spawning beds.

"The flood came just at the time of year when that wonderful instinct possessed by the salmon tribe prompts them to make their way into the very smallest tributaries, where, when the water goes down quickly, they are sometimes left almost stranded. In some former years they have been found far up into Mungrisdale, as high as the Matterdale road, in Mosedale Beck, up to Shoulthwaite in Naddle, as far as Seathwaite in Borrowdale, and through Thirlmere, at the foot of Dunmail Raise.

"In olden time, some 80 or 90 years ago, there was a common saying when a high flood occurred at this time of year that 'it would make a rich St John's,' and the people were wont to rejoice, much the same as the Egyptians do at the rising of the Nile. If we may believe the traditions handed down from the latter part of last century, the numbers of fish which come into the river now, at best of the seasons, are as nothing compared with what came at that time and the dales people then (statesmen, farmers and labourers alike) vied with each other which could get the most and boasted who got the largest. All that is altered now.

"Everything is changed since then, and nothing more than the popular feeling regarding the salmon. Since more liberal enactments have been made in the Salmon Laws, the fish have been suffered to pass into the upper waters earlier in the year, and rod fishing has become a very general and favourite amusement, in consequence of which, there are now very few dalesmen who would kill a salmon during the close season under any circumstances."

Brown trout.
Picture by Terry Whittaker,
FLPA.

Nowadays it is questionable whether there are sufficient fish to even justify a poaching trip at dead of night. Rod and line anglers are legally not permitted to catch and kill a salmon until after a date in late June and many fishermen – understanding the scarcity of the fish and the very real threat to its existence – are loathe to kill any fish at all and practice 'catch and release.' They also use barbless fishing hooks (a far cry from the days when salmon were cruelly hauled from the river on the sharp point of a gaff) to minimise potential damage to the fish and to ensure its fast and safe return to the water. The same principle is applied by many trout fly anglers who now go to the river, not for food or financial incentive, but simply to enjoy the act of fly-fishing in beautiful surroundings. One such in Keswick is Mick Tinnion who has fished the Greta man and boy for almost 50 years. Mick, who lives on Latrigg Close, is Manager for the England Rivers Fly Fishing team, having had his first taste of competitive angling with a team of local lads back in the Seventies.

"I think the whole mindset of fishing has altered," he says. "As kids and men in the Seventies, when there were a lot more salmon running the river, we all used to knock them on the head. Everybody did it. But now there is a complete change in the approach to fishing. The Atlantic salmon is in very real danger of becoming extinct in the Greta or is very close to it. Various agencies keep going on about the importance of habitat improvement and that it will fix everything. Well, you can have perfect habitat for tigers but unless you have some tigers in the first place it's fairly pointless and it strikes me that that's the way we're heading with the salmon."

He contends that a lot of the blame is due to the growing impact of invasive fish-eating birds on the Greta and reckons, as do a lot of local anglers, that the birds, mergansers and goosanders in the main, are stripping the river bare of salmon fry and parr; although there are other factors affecting the survival of the species (see wildlife on chapter 8).

As someone who has enjoyed fishing all his life, Mick, 54, now prefers the art of fly-fishing for wild brown trout on the River Greta and returns all the fish he catches to the water. He fishes by walking up the river in waders and expertly casts his line over broken water, or breks, as well as the deeper pools. In the course of an afternoon's angling he will catch and return several good-sized trout to the river. But the catching of fish is not the be all and end all; it is part of being by – and in his case quite literally in – the river and enjoying all that the Greta and its surroundings provide in sight and sound. I suppose it may also satisfy, deep down, some well-hidden hunter-gatherer instinct that goes back to the cavemen.

"Once you are in the river trout fishing and walking upriver other wildlife seems to accept you and doesn't take a lot of notice of you," he says. "You become part of the environment. I love trout fishing on the Greta. You don't get many stretches of water that are similar to this river. It's fast and boulder strewn, occupies a tiny, short valley but

CAUGHT A WEASEL

D Melvin has broken his long frost, having caught a beauty last Thursday weighing 15 and a half pounds. Two days before a jovial friend met him coming home despondent and tired, and he noticed a carefully made up parcel, carefully carried under his arm, and thought it was a fish.

"What luck?" says Will.

"I'll show you," says Dave as he proceeded to unfold from his numerous wrappings a small creature.

Will stretched it out and said: "It's a wizzle (weasel). What did tag it wid?"

"Neither with fly, spoon, nor worm, but by speed of foot, activity and cunning, and at the risk of my precious neck," says Dave. "I caught it. Now I cannot understand how it is that all the duffers are catching fish and I am left in the cold. Is there a man along the river who can catch a weasel awake, let alone a sleeping one?"

"Thoo'll fummle on tul thoo gits a good un efter a bit," says Will cheerfully.

And now he has.

A 19th Century report.

Fishing

once you get in the valley bottom and in the river it's like a little hidden world. There's the old Bobbin Mill, all the railway bridges, the surrounding woodland and fells and you just get on the old railway line footpath and the river comes round and it's a lovely place to be. I never go up the river now without seeing a kingfisher."

Fishing for trout and salmon on the River Greta is no longer as popular as it used to be in the days when The Twa Dogs pub on Penrith Road was very much an unofficial HQ for local anglers who would fish for salmon on a Sunday morning and then go to the Dogs (sometimes quite literally) as soon as landlord Gerald Hayes opened the doors at 12 noon; this was in the days when Sunday opening was from 12 noon to 2pm and 7pm to 10pm. Rods and catches were left outside at midday as the anglers got wet inside. Some would return to the river for the afternoon but most would drink their fill of beer and go home for the Sunday roast and a snooze and the rumblings of post-prandial thunder in front of the fire; the combination of Gerald's mild and Brussels sprouts with the Sunday meal could have powered a small bobbin mill.

These days the Twa Dogs still has strong fishing connections and regularly holds fly tying sessions in the evenings for local youngsters but there are no longer the numbers of adult anglers on the riverbank, and they were all characters. In my day, to name a

TIGHT LINES
October 6th. 1900

Thanks to the brimming rivers, salmon steaks grace the boards of not a few houses in Keswick. Many fishermen have during the week experienced the thrill of a tight line which has amply repaid them for aching limbs, soaked hides, and the hungry yearnings of a wolf. For instance, two gentlemen after a day's fishing cleaned up a potato pot containing half a stone of potatoes and half as much mutton.

Anglers three.
From left to right: Terry Appleby, Bruce Frampton and Mick Tinnion.

The Greta . . . a river runs through it

few there was Jackie Bertram and his son Rodney, "Lanty" Barnes, "Buzz" Cowp (Harold Cowperthwaite on a Sunday) "Pinky" Rose, "Shinner" Martin, the Lowden brothers, Walter and Jim, Jimmy Miller, Alf Tonkin, Alfie Price, Roy Graves, Mike Readman, "Pop" Mawson, Willox Graves, Alf Gaskell and the younger mob (in the early Sixties this is) of "Mowdy" Maughan, Howard "Nezzie" Nesbitt, Terry "The Heron" Appleby, Bruce "Stack`" Frampton, Kevin Wilde, Jimmy Moffat, Ralph Swainson, John "Shapes" Dennison, and others.

The pools on the river also have their names and down bank from Threlkeld Bridge they are as follows: Crozier Pool, Cat Craggs, Tunnel Dub, Scar Dub, Rock Dub, Ashtree, Brundholme Breks, High Flats, Willie Dub, Half Circle, High Yak (where there is a memorial bench to Alfie Price) Pig Fields, Fore Dub, Turn Hole, Tommy Wilson, Hewletts, Bobbin Mill Weir, Forge Weir and Garden Pool. From there down bank until you reached the River Derwent, the names of the pools on the town water were not well known to us, although I did come across a document that provided some very useful information on that front, not only on the names of the pools but also the town's industrial past.

Entitled *A Walk Down the River* it read: "Starting at Calvert Bridge, we will go downstream with an old fisherman as guide. On the high side of the bridge is the site of the old smelting works used in the days of Queen Elizabeth when copper ore was mined in the neighbourhood. Between the two bridges is Stank Dub which leads to the weir (now directly beneath the old railway bridge over the road) where a sluice conveys water to drive a water wheel at High Mill, originally a pencil mill and, later, a flour mill (the mills were situated opposite what is now the Millfield retirement home).

"At Station Bridge (over the road leading to the Keswick Hotel) we come to Deep Whol (or Hole). Here fleeces were washed in the river when a tannery was in existence. The big weir (since demolished) is just below and Fitz Dub extends to t'laal weir (situated directly below Greta Hall) where another sluice takes water via a tunnel to the Southey Hill Pencil Works. Below the small weir (still visible) is Ladies Dub. Here, generations of children paddled in safety until a wall was built by the park

Top: "Buzz" Cowp and salmon at Willie Dub on the River Greta.

Above: Wilk cartoon of Willox Graves.

Caricature courtesy of the Wilkinson family.

Terry Appleby's salmon fly box.

trustees. Roddery Stream (opposite the current Keswick AFC field) leads to Bullfield Corner (opposite the lower park gates), where the river turns towards High Hill, skirting Donkey Field before it makes a sudden turn at the Turn Whol which, at the time of writing, is full of salmon (the Turn Whol is now the widest part of the river after extensive flood prevention work on that corner as the river turns towards Greta Bridge).

'Passing Carding Mill Field the river passes under Greta Bridge, past the old woollen mill to Tenterfield dub. Woollens were hung out to dry or bleach in the field alongside (they were hung on hooks attached to frames and it is from this that we get the term 'on tenterhooks'). Close to the old school playing fields is Lands Dub, and just below is Cement Point, or Kiddam's Corner, where the Derwent (emerging out of Derwentwater) joins the Greta and remains as the Derwent until reaching the sea at Workington."

The pools through the town were the places where we went fishing as kids, starting in Town's Field and working our way down through the park where we discovered that fishing with floating bread was a highly effective bait for trout. But the real fishing, the proper, grown-up fishing was up river when the salmon were running. It was something we aspired to and Jackie Bertram showed me how and where to fish for salmon. In return I dug the worms he used for bait. I have vivid memories of my father trout fly fishing in the pool above the Bobbin Mill weir and being fascinated by the beautiful patterns and spots on the flanks of the gleaming wet fish. Dad fished with trout flies that, for me, had attractive names such as Woodcock and Yellow, Partridge and Orange, Greenwell's Glory and Snipe and Purple. I caught my first salmon, an 11 pounder in

Fore Dub on the Greta when I was 11 years old. I did not even realise the fish was on until I drew back my line to make another cast and felt the heavy pull of the fish as it began to fight. When we were young we always killed the fish we caught, provided they were big enough to keep. Now I would never kill a fish; they are too few and too precious, especially the increasingly diminished salmon, to take from the river. In truth I am reluctant to hook fish at all but the pleasure of being by a river and sending a fly line snaking across the current has never lost its appeal.

Whenever you are among fishermen there is always an abundance of stories to tell, and not necessarily about the size of the one that got away. Terry "The Heron" Appleby spends more time on the River Greta and Derwentwater – the latter when the May fly is on the lake – than any other fisherman I know. And if he is not fishing he is always looking at the river. It is his life and whenever you talk with him about fishing he becomes energised and enthusiastic and loves to reminisce over a pint or three.

He recalls that at one time anglers, rather than carry their salmon catch up and down the river with them, would hang them in a tree and return to collect them later. Unfortunately there was another kind of predator who might take advantage of their laziness.

Terry explains: "One local character, Ronnie Capes, who was not averse to taking the odd bit of game, nivver went fishing. 'I didn't need to fish or to poach either,' he telt us ya day. 'When I went for a walk up the river they were aw fishin' away and there was salmon hanging in the trees all ower the bloody spot. And when they were fishin' away they always had their backs to you and I just used to sneak in and tek yan off t'tree and back down to Keswick and sneck it in'."

Terry Appleby casts a long line over Sandy pool at Town's Field on the River Greta.

Fishing

'Sneck', a phrase very popular with this particular character, means 'cash'.

Terry, it transpires, is full of stories and I am initially incredulous at one he tells me about the morning he was fishing in High Yak, standing in the shallows just beyond the row of stones that edge the pool.

"This laal red squirrel cem running along the line of rocks at the beck edge," says Terry. "It got roughly opposite and it stopped and sort of looked at us. Next thing it lowped right onto us, ran round mi shoulder, round the top of mi jeans – its claws went through mi jeans – and it started ratching in mi fishing bag. Nobody believes us but it's true, it really happened . . . and then I notice there's a dog coming round the corner and I recognised it as one of Tant Bland's, and he has two, and the other one comes up as well. The squirrel saw them and shot off into the undergrowth and a laal bit later Tant comes up and I says 'now then' and he says 'now then' and I said 'you won't believe this' and he says 'what?' and I says I've just had a bloody squirrel running all round us and ratching

Angler on the River Greta at Fore Dub in the Pigfields. Pastel drawing by Keith Bowen.

in mi fishing bag and he says: 'You're nut fishin' wid bloody hazel nuts are yer?' That's exactly what he said. I wouldn't mek that up, honest."

I believe Terry. While I have never known a red squirrel to be so brazen The Heron's explanation is that it must have been hand-fed at the caravan site at Low Briery and had become used to contact with people.

As young lads you were always a little hesitant to approach other anglers who you regarded with some esteem. One such formidable character was "Buzz" Cowp and my first encounter with "Buzz" up the beck was one day on the railway line by the Greta when he was returning from fishing in the morning and we were just setting out.

As he passed us on the path I asked, as you do, "Owt doin'?"

"Buzz" replied: "What the hell, it's like fishing in a bloody dolly tub."

He was clearly a wordsmith and an expert in the local vernacular, or dialect. Terry recalls that "Buzz" always fished fly and one day Terry and Nezzie (Howard Nesbitt) were on the river bank watching him work his way down a pool.

The Greta . . . a river runs through it

"Buzz cast out and you could see this salmon following his fly," says Terry. "It was a decent fish and I made the mistake of standing up and pointing. We didn't dare caw him Buzz, we knew him as Mr Cowperthwaite and I said summat like 'Mr Cowperthwaite, there's yan coming for your fly.' And you know what he said: 'Hi' doon you buggers, hi' doon. Fine fish, 10 or 12 pund, warnt come again, thoos scared it, hi doon thee buggers, hi doon!' And that's exactly what he said."

I take it that in the vernacular 'hi' is a bastardisation of 'si' and is a unique Cumbrian combination of hiding and sitting!

Terry's supply of stories also encompasses the legendary figure of "Lanty" Barnes.

"Shapes (John Dennison) was fishing at Willie Dub when he was a young lad and Lanty was there," Terry explained. "Lanty was Mowdy Maughan's uncle and if they weren't tekken well he was prone to snigging (intentionally foul hooking a salmon – he was not alone in that practice). Any way, Lanty got into this fish, played it in and he said to Shapes 'right I've got it into the side, I'll just tek the gaff out and I'll have the bugger out.' Shapes said he let fly with the gaff, missed the fish completely and the gaff went straight through the bottom of his wellie and out through the top of the toe. It went straight through his foot. There was blood aw ower the spot and that was the day the river ran red wid Lanty's blood."

I was also tickled pink by Mick Tinnion's story of how Alfie Price was once fishing Tommy Wilson dub and was standing at the head of the pool with his back against the big rock on the bank. Alfie advised Mick that he had better watch his step as he made his way upriver as all kinds of branches and other debris had suddenly started floating down the beck; a sure warning sign that the river was about to suddenly rise in a flash flood as a result of a torrential downpour somewhere higher in the tributaries.

"Heeding Alf's advice I walked up the river to the Turn Hole – out of sight of Alf – and there was Roy Graves in among the debris that tends to collect at that point. He was throwing branches and all sorts into the river just to kid Alf. And there's poor old Alf, fishing away quietly further downstream, convinced there's gonna be a flood coming at any moment."

Anglers six from Keswick. They are (left to right) Mick Tinnion, Kevin Wilde, Tony Stephenson, Roy Graves, Ralph Swainson and Alf Price.

Below: A wild brown trout from the River Greta. Note the distinctive markings.

Fishing

Alf occasionally took his ferret up the beck and its head would pop out of his fishing bag or jacket pocket as you stood talking to him while he fished. He said that he had brought the ferret out for "a bit of an airing." Alf would also, if the fish in a pool were sluggish, send his golden Labrador Rusty in for a swim to stir them up.

Many anglers would take their dogs with them when they went fishing up the river. The route to and from the beck was via the railway line which, at that time, was still a working railway with regular passenger trains, diesels, travelling the line. It was, of course, illegal to walk the line but everyone did. Even so, the unexpected arrival of a train could give you quite a start.

Ralph Swainson tells the story: "Mike Readman, Robin Telford and me were coming down the line to the Twa Dogs for a pint after fishing up the beck in the morning. Any way we were just below the tunnel and the next thing we heard a diesel train coming fast round the bend behind us. We looked round and old Prince, Mike's dog, is walking down the middle of the railway line. Robin went to grab it but Mike pulled Robin back and shouted at Prince. The dog lay down on the sleepers in the centre of the line and the train went right ower him. We thought he had had it but when the train had gone by there he was. He stood up and all he had was a mark down the middle of his head where the train had parted his fur. He shook himself down and was perfectly all right."

But there was a sequel to the incident. Word had got back to the railway authorities about the close call on the railway line and the next day, when Mick Tinnion's father Eric went up the river fishing, he was caught trespassing on the line and prosecuted.

You also had to be careful for another reason when taking a dog up the river. As lads of 14, Mike Readman and Roy Graves had caught a number of trout worming on a full beck.

"Roy had half a dozen trout and I had mebbe three," recalls Mike. "They were all good trout. Roy had put his down on the bank and he was baiting up. I had a dog – a mongrel – and as Roy looked round the last tail was disappearing down its throat. It ate the bloody lot, all six of Roy's trout."

Alf Price, Roy Graves and Mike Readman all worked at the Bobbin Mill at Low Briery where there was quite a community of local anglers among the workforce. "We worked with Noilly Bertram and Jack Bertram who were also fishermen," Mike added.

"They used to fish above the Bobbin Mill weir when it was the right height. They used great big greenheart rods and fished the spoon. I've seen them catch salmon during their midday break at work. There were a lot more fishermen then. Twag (Norman Tonkin) used to keep his fish in the bath to keep them fresh. He used to fish the Turn Hole down at High Hill. I've seen Twag and Lanty Barnes there with the prawn on as if they were fishing it properly. They were still good fisherman as well mind . . ."

Occasionally an angler would be taken to court for foul hooking a salmon and in one instance while Tommy Harrison was at court and the beck watcher, Sandy Coutts was there to give evidence against him, Tommy's workmates at the Bobbin Mill took the opportunity to poach salmon out of the mill race and sold them to the Millfield, then a hotel, in order to pay any fine.

Fishing tended to run in families and in Keswick two devotees were Fred Bowness and his son Les, of High Hill. Old Fred, who died when he was 97, was so keen that he took to practising his casting in the back garden or the nearby field. Fred, who looked after the horses that hauled the gun carriages during the 1st World War, caught his last salmon when he was 90. Les's wife Mary recalls: "Grandad going out into the field to try out his rod casting was a regular occurrence – it was well known (she laughs). He had a little gate put in the railings at the back and he used to go through there and a neighbour Tom Wilson had a weather recorder which he had to keep clear of. Grandad and Les used to go up the Greta in all sorts of weather when the river was in full flow. I don't think there are any salmon now. In the Turn Hole (just up from Mary's house) fish used to gather in the pool there and people used to come from all over to see them. And, of course, when the weir in Fitz Park was still there they used to take their kids up to see the salmon jumping over the weir. It was lovely. There were lots of salmon then.

"Grandad would go out anytime on his old bike. He would leave his bike at the old stone bridge down the river and fish his way back up to Greta Bridge. Sometimes, when he was getting older, Les would go and keep an eye on him but he had to hide so that he didn't know he was being watched. He was well into

Les Bowness with the first salmon he ever caught. In the garage behind him is the old green Bedford van which would take Les, his father Fred and pals on fishing expeditions.

A fresh run salmon leaps the old weir in Lower Fitz Park, Keswick. The weir was situated just down stream from the YHA building and it is a great pity that it is no longer there, like all the other weirs on the Greta.

Fred Bowness, fishing below Greta Bridge.

Facing page: Willie Dub.

his eighties by then. And Les would come and say "he's caught summat" and then shortly after granddad would arrive on his bike and he always tied his fish on the cross bar, pedalling away, and we always pretended we didn't know (she laughs). He was a grand old fella, a marvellous man. They were big Methodists so he couldn't drink, or at least he couldn't be seen to be drinking. But he did like his little bottle of whisky in the garage when he was tying his trout flies.

"He was always tying his own trout flies. May flies, oh gosh, there were May flies for ivver more. But you were banned in England from buying the feathers of a particular bird, the Bird of Paradise. Les bought him a wing in Sweden. He brought a lot of fishing tackle back from Sweden for grandad, including this wing from a Bird of Paradise. Well, you would have thought we had given him a pot of gold."

A next door neighbour of Fred's at High Hill, the poet Chris Pilling, wrote a poem about the old fisherman who cast his fly line in the garden. The poem appears in Chris's book *Coming Ready or Not* (Bookcase 2009):

A GOOD DAY'S FISHING

The old man, he must be nearly
ninety, is standing in his garden
with, of all things, a fishing rod
and he's casting it, the early
bird, to catch whatever is lurking
in the lobelia bed, an odd
centipede or a worm? Are there
really fish swimming round the flowers
that only he knows about? Gherkin
trout no hotelier would recognise?
He reels in his line, turns to where
our fence divides us. In the hours
that pass his muscles will not tauten
for he casts again among the fireflies
hovering above our compost heap
with an easy turn of the wrist, a wily
savoir faire, flexing like fish that leap.

Fred Bowness (left) and George Stuart who used to run the grocer's store at the junction of Helvellyn Street and Leonard Street, Keswick, with an 11 and a quarter pound trout he caught on Crummock. Fred helped George to land the fish, caught while trawling minnow. The trout is to the back of the picture. The fish at the front is, of course, a pike.

The Greta . . . a river runs through it

MAGNIFICENT BLENCATHRA . . . BUT POLLUTION FROM THE LEAD MINES ON ITS
LOWER SLOPES REGULARLY WIPED OUT FISH LIFE IN THE GRETA

The Greta . . . a river runs through it

Pollution
A STREAM OF PURE POISON

The water quality of the River Greta today, while not entirely pure, is a considerable improvement on the latter years of the 19th Century when the beck was to all intents and purposes a running sewer with another deadly element in the mix. Lead waste, a product of mining on Blencathra, occasionally added more than a dash of toxic flavour to the pollution already being carried along on the current of the river and deposited in the deeper pools, especially in the summer months when the river was running low. Sanitation was, to say the least, basic if non-existent and the solution to many waste problems, industrial and domestic, was quite simply to dump it in the river for it to be washed away.

The effect on wildlife, principally fish, was blatantly obvious when thousands of them turned belly-up overnight, wiped out by the occasional flushing-out of lead-contaminated water from the mines. The effect on humans of this fatal combination of raw sewage and toxic and other waste, especially on those people who used the river system for drinking water, does not bear thinking about. It seems certain that many people must have died as a result, but that their deaths were masked and attributed to causes other than the water they drank. The poisonous river, probably the real culprit, was able to hide behind a multitude of other sins.

The wildlife suffered just as badly. The toxic lead pollution of the river certainly wiped

The bed of the River Greta.
But it was not always as clear.

out all the fish, and goodness only knows what else, on a fairly regular basis. It also went largely unpunished and the perpetrators, the Threlkeld Mining Company, quite simply did not seem to care about the consequences of their actions and went to great lengths to avoid any admission of guilt or sense of responsibility.

The environment, as we know it today, had not yet been born.

On July 5, 1884, the *Lake District Visitor and Keswick Guardian* newspaper reported as follows under the headline A STREAM OF POISON OF THE WORST ORDER – "A large number of dead fish, both young salmon and trout, have been taken from the river below the Threlkeld mine. A few have been sent away for purposes of analysis on the supposition that the cause of death is due to lead poisoning. It is to be hoped that no one will be so unscrupulous as to collect fish for sale."

The same edition carried a Letter to the Editor which read under the heading: THE FISH MASSACRE – "In four days of last week 694 dead fish were taken out of the Greta, suffocated by the fine quartz in suspension, or poisoned by the lead washings from certain mines up Threlkeld way. This amount of dead fish taken from the river represents only a share of the wholesale fish murder that, by divine permission of people who have the law to prevent it in their own hands, has been and is being allowed to go on in a stream that is largely used for drinking purposes both by men and cattle.

"Fish have a way of dying under stones and their bodies putrefy at the bottom. I write this letter to caution all who fill their kettles, or who use the Greta water supply for any household purposes whatever to be most careful to avoid it. What the Greta really now is can best be described as a stream of poison of the worst order, flowing within easy tempting reach of a lot of thirsty cattle who can't be warned and of the hands and homes of a lot of thirsty people who, unless warned, are ignorant of the poisonous properties of the stream which in the old days was the clearest, sweetest river God ever gave for the service of men and for the home of fish. How long are we going to sit idle by our fish-emptied, plague-smitten, mine-fouled, sewer-festering river, and refuse to call in the law to prevent its pollution?"

The letter was signed 'A LOVER OF PURE WATER.'

In August of the same year The Derwent Fishery Board reached the conclusion that pollution from the Threlkeld mines was responsible for killing over 600 fish (taken out of the river) and did not accept the mine manager (Mr Bawden's) explanation that sheep washing poisons were to blame.

It was agreed that the board's clerk should write to the company and say that "the board is not satisfied with the means that they have taken to render harmless the liquid poison from their mines, and if they do not at once adopt more efficient means the Board will be compelled to take proceedings against them to compel them to do so."

At the same time that this was happening the miners were involved in something of a public relations campaign (why allow the small matter of wiping out the entire fish population of a river to get in the way of a good PR opportunity?) when it was announced on August 9 under the heading SUCCESSFUL MINING IN THE KESWICK DISTRICT – "The Threlkeld Mining Company have won and delivered upwards of 150 tons of silver lead and spelter ores during the month of July. This enterprising company have under consideration the opening of the Blease Ghyll mine, also the eastern part of Brundholme mine, both of which are within their royalties. A shaft is to be driven from the Glenderaterra Beck . . ."

One year later and the mines were again polluting the river. And this time it was particularly bad, judging by the tone of the newspaper report of July 11, 1885. DESTRUCTION OF THE GRETA AS A TROUT RIVER – "A cruel blow has been inflicted upon Keswick in the complete destruction of the Greta as a trout river. Last Saturday will long be remembered as a black day, because then was witnessed the climax of the destruction which has been slowly going on for some years. It was pitiful to watch the poor fish in their death throes, and the more so because nothing could be done to help them. It was theirs but to die, for their bright crystal home had been converted into a *lethe; the black shadow of death had been cast across the river, and the work of the destroyer was soon complete.

"In the face of magisterial proceedings pending upon the pollution of the river it would be both unfair and injudicious for us to go beyond a mere statement of facts which have resulted from it. Every effect follows a cause, and we trust that no effort will be spared to discover the cause of what is a scandal and a disgrace. The Greta was one of the finest fishing streams in the country.

"There is no exaggeration in saying that hundredweights of its fish were poisoned last Saturday and among them were young salmon, trout from a few ounces in weight up to 5lb and even eels, whose hold on life is most tenacious. On Sunday not a live thing could be found in the river between the head of Bassenthwaite Lake and Threlkeld.

"All the circumstances demand the most searching inquiry and the blame being fixed on the right parties, the most stringent measures must be adopted in the interests of the public to prevent the recurrence of such flagrant outrage."

*Lethe, in Greek mythology, being one of the five rivers of Hades.

In the same edition of the newspaper, a correspondent wrote as follows in a letter to the Editor: "It has been my pleasure to meet with many people intending to visit the Lake District and one of the first enquiries is 'Have you good fishing?'

"Without hesitation I have many times answered 'Yes.'

"What am I to say now that the Greta and the Derwent have been visited by the wholesale destruction of Saturday? I hope Keswick people will not sleep on the matter in their usual apathetic way: it concerns them very gravely and they ought to be up and doing."

Someone at last decided to act (almost a year to the day after the initial incident of July 1884) although the end result could hardly be considered salutary. On July 18, 1885 it was reported under the heading PROSECUTION OF THE THRELKELD LEAD MINING COMPANY – "Threlkeld Lead Mining Company was summoned before Keswick Magistrates for two offences of alleged pollution of the River Greta contrary to section 5 of the Salmon Fisheries Act 1861. The magistrates heard that the dead fish contained lead and unanimously agreed that the fish had been killed by poisonous matter proceeding from the mine, and that the best means practicable at a cost not exceeding £100 had not been used to prevent the pollution. In these circumstances they were bound to convict, and they would inflict the nominal penalty of £1 and costs." A powerful deterrent that must have been.

The magistrates said there was an urgent need to come to some agreement through which an effective method of cleansing the mine water could be achieved. But at a later hearing, before the Divisional Court of the Queen's Bench in London, one of the two convictions was set aside when the mining company claimed that a magistrate who took part in the court's original decision was an interested party.

It seems clear that the mining company was intent solely on clearing its name at all costs, showed little or no remorse for its actions and was not remotely interested in working towards a solution to the problem of pollution from the lead mines.

The strength of feeling, between Keswick and Threlkeld, was clear in correspondence from the Rector of Threlkeld who wrote in defence of the company and claimed that the pollution rife in Keswick was due to gas works, tan pits and slaughterhouses.

In an editorial on July 18th, 1885, the newspaper responded to the rector's remarks with a hard-hitting and vastly entertaining editorial: "Nobody wishes for a moment, I am sure, to stop the working of the mine; but the people who live below the mine have rights as well as the mine owners, and all they want is that their fish and their cattle and their land shall not receive injury from the mine. The enlarged gasworks, tan pits and slaughterhouses are ghosts of the parson's own raising. Tan pits may perhaps be done away with when parsons set the example of going barefoot, and slaughterhouses will be an exception when beef and mutton are no longer articles of diet. The rector regards fishermen as idle men and fools. The fisherman may give the 'retourt courteous' and add that a wet salmon is better than a dry sermon."

Take that!

The same edition also published a letter written by one C. Christopherson, of Acorn House, Keswick, and which read: "I enclose photographs of a dozen poisoned trout taken from the River Greta at Greta Bridge Pool, Keswick. The one marked with a cord I saw die. During Saturday and Sunday some hundredweight of poisoned trout were taken out of the river and used for food; some were sent to Ambleside, Whitehaven and other towns for sale. Among the fish were specimens up to 5lb weight. The poisoning, which has culminated in this wholesale destruction, has been going on for at least three years, yet our Derwent Fishery Board are patiently waiting the lead miners' endeavours to remedy it. Seven or eight miles of river are now without fish of any kind."

And he added: "What is to become of the people of Maryport who drink this water?"

Mr Christopher's letter was originally published in *Land and Water*, a British Weekly Journal. In an editorial accompanying the letter the journal observed: "This is only another instance of the shameful and unchecked pollution of valuable fish producing streams going on at present all over the country. We can, indeed, hardly find sufficiently sorry phrases in which to express our sense of indignation. Still, while the law tacitly permits this cruel destruction of fish life to proceed unheeded, and while Fishery Boards are so confidingly lax as to hope or wait patiently for the lead miners doing anything to remedy the evil, we can but express our sorrow and regret that Carlyle's definition of mankind is so abundantly proved to be true."

A further two years down the line and there is still no respite from the worst excesses of the lead waste from the mines.

On April 23rd, 1887, it was reported: "During the recent period of dry weather nearly all, if not all, of the fish in the Greta, between Threlkeld and Keswick, have died, presumably from poisoning. Samples of water and fish have been taken from the river and it is expected the Board of Conservators will move in this very serious matter."

An editorial added: "The fish have again been swept wholly out of the river, just as the fishermen have taken out their licences for the season. This is a serious state of affairs and one that calls for prompt and decisive action on the part of the Fishery Board. Two years ago the river was similarly denuded of fish, and it was hoped then that efforts would be made to prevent such a catastrophe in the future. But it seems that so soon as the water becomes very low we may anticipate a recurrence of the evil. However much one may feel that it is due to mine water, it would not be wise to say so positively, because certain alterations were made at the Threlkeld mine with a view to meet the requirements of the conservators. But to whatever cause it may be due, something should be done and 'twere well it were done quickly' for what with losing the fish out of the river and the right to go along favoured walks (a reference to a battle with landowners over the right to walk up Latrigg and at Fawe Park on the far shore of Derwentwater) the sum of Keswick attractions will shortly be confined to the main roads."

On May 7th, 1887, a meeting of the Derwent Fishery Board determined that lead washings from the Threlkeld mines were responsible for wiping out the fish in the Greta. The analysed fish contained oxides of lead. It was agreed to take steps to prosecute the company.

June 18th, 1887: The Threlkeld Mining Company was charged with polluting the River Greta on April 17th. The prosecution's case, brought by the Derwent Fishery Board under the Salmon Fishery Act of 1861, was dismissed because the board failed to prove that the mining company had not used the best practicable means at a reasonable cost to prevent the pollution of the river.

The mining company could quite clearly get away with murder; with the sole exception, of course, of that swingeing £1 fine imposed by Keswick magistrates in 1885.

A fresh approach to the problem was made four years later. On May 30th, 1891, it was announced in the newspaper: "Your readers will have seen a notice inviting all to attend at the Court House on Wednesday next at 11am and give evidence as touching the pollution of the River Greta . . . if those interested in preserving their Greta from pollution will attend at the Court House and tender evidence they have seen or known of they will be strengthening the hands of our local authorities very much to deal with a matter that is urgent.

"It seems quite clear that we have it largely in our own hands to determine whether the Greta shall be henceforth pure or poisonous for man and beast; and it is also clear that there need be no interference with legitimate labour upon the banks of the Greta in seeing that necessary precautionary measures are taken to render innocuous either sewage or mine refuse before it is poured into the river." The writer was Canon Hardwicke Drummond Rawnsley.

On June 6, 1891, it was reported: "The County Council inquiry into the pollution of the River Greta was told that the alleged pollution seemed to arise from two distinct causes – one was the introduction of sewage matter from the town and the other by means of water from lead mines."

The inquiry received a letter of complaint from the trustees of Maryport Town and Harbour relating to the discharge of sewage into the River Greta by the Keswick Local Board (the town council of its day). The Greta flowed into the Derwent from which the Maryport trustees obtained their water supply for the district. The trustees also supplied water to Dovenby, Papcastle, Dearham, Ellenborough and Flimby. The trustees were interested in the question how their district was affected? From time to time, since 1884, the trustees had contacted Keswick Local Board to see if something could be done, but "the question had been put off by the Keswick authority and nothing had been done."

Analysis of water from the Greta and from the race (the latter taking water from the Derwent at Cockermouth to supply Maryport) showed that it was seriously contaminated by sewage. Dr Franklin said the water from the Greta was turbid and contained "a considerable proportion of organic matter principally derived from sewage and other refuse animal substance. The water was dangerous and unfit for drinking or other dietetic purposes."

The River Greta was inspected and found to be in a "disagreeably disgusting condition."

One medical witness said: "I tremble to think what the consequences would be in the event of cholera or typhoid fever occurring at Keswick. If it were not for Bassenthwaite Lake there would not be many living to tell the tale."

The inquiry was also told "the death rate of Maryport is considerably higher than it ought to be considering the excellent situation of the town."

Mr L. Collier, of Ormathwaite, told the inquiry: "There is pollution of all the lovely becks which should be a source of joy and health to the inhabitants and visitors. Wherever there is a farmhouse or cottage nearby the beck is a receptacle for all kinds of foul rubbish." He attributed the circumstances to thoughtlessness, ignorance or laziness, and he hoped the inquiry would lead to improvements.

Canon Rawnsley said that three weeks ago he had seen salmon fry dead all the way along the river. Not withstanding all that had been done at the mines, there was a very serious destruction of fish. If the council was firm he thought the mining company would prevent poisoned water from passing into the river.

Mr T. Musgrave, who said he had fished the river for 60 years, considered the mining company had acknowledged the pollution by attempting remedies. His opinion was that the water was polluted day after day, for he had seen dead fish all the year round. When salmon fishing he had noticed at Ash Tree dub that the salmon always edged away to the opposite side of the pool from that on which the mine water came down.

So what happened next in this sorry tale? More of the same I am afraid. In short, not a great deal.

January 30th, 1892: The General Purposes Committee of the County Council reported in their minutes (to be submitted to the next council meeting) that they had asked the Local Government Board to hold an inquiry. This followed the action of the Threlkeld Mining Company in declining to allow an expert to inspect the mines and the settling tanks used by the company to prevent pollution of the River Greta by water discharged from their works. However, on the sewage issue the Keswick Local Board was negotiating for ground to be used for the reception of sewage which would not afterwards be emptied into the river.

September 10th, 1892: A newspaper report stated: "The great majority of the people of Threlkeld are employed in the mine and it would be a serious matter to them if the works should be stopped." The company employed 145 men and boys and the village was dependant on the mine.

April 29th, 1893: "On Monday the river watcher, Mr C. Oliver with Messrs T & J Musgrave, and Mr Alcock, of Threlkeld, made a careful examination of the river between Brundholme and Threlkeld and they picked out no less than 1,327 dead fish, of which about a dozen were trout and the remainder young salmon. Some of the fish, we believe, have been sent away for analysis."

December 9th, 1893: "At the meeting of the County Council it was stated that a letter had been received from The Local Government Board with reference to carrying out analyses from time to time of water entering the Greta from the Threlkeld mines."

May 22nd, 1897: "A quantity of dead fish have been seen in the river and we learn that some have been taken out with a view to get at the cause of their death if possible. The river is very low and there is a great need for a freshet."

How could someone pollute this?

Longtown Field, full of wild flowers and a place, right next to the River Greta, of outstanding natural beauty. Unfortunately it did not escape the attentions of modern day polluters (see over page).

To cut a long story short, where the mines at Threlkeld were concerned it appears that there was plenty of huff and puff but nothing was ever done to effectively deal with the source of the problem; possibly because of the employment factor as there has always been a tendency, unfortunately, for the provision of jobs to override any environmental concerns. Clearly the pollution problem on the Greta was not only confined to the twin terrors of mining and the disposal of sewage, the latter being an issue on which the local council was also loathe to act quickly, if at all. But the great British public, as ever, was just as bad when it came to the way in which they used and abused the river. A letter in the edition of the local newspaper for May 16th, 1891, criticised the dumping of rubbish in the 'clear stream' of the River Derwent at Grange Bridge.

"The river," a correspondent wrote, "seems to have been thought a fit and suitable place to deposit the rubbish of the hamlet and debris of miscellaneous character, broken pots and pans, and especially obtrusive on the sight that particularly objectionable refuse of the present generation – empty tins, meat tins, sardine tins, lobster tins, et hoc genus omne. I did not stay long."

The writer then turned his attentions to the Greta and added: "It is to be regretted that Keswick does not set a better example by worthy treatment of its own river. The traveller approaching the town along the Penrith Road and coming near to the widely and deservedly famed Greta will not be favourably impressed with the sort of love the Keswick people seem to bear to their beautiful stream, or, at least, will greatly marvel at their way of showing it. Surely it is high time that the local authorities should take the needful steps to prevent the degradation and defilement of the banks of the river where they are especially visible and therefore where the great nuisance is especially offensive."

And so we look back in horror at the way in which the river was treated during the later years of the 19th Century. Clearly matters have improved significantly since then.

The lead mines closed in 1928 and there have been considerable and ongoing improvements to the sewage scenario. But this does not prevent the public from damaging the environment of the river and its surrounds. In 2011 people left the rubbish portrayed in the photograph on this page after they abandoned a site where they had pitched a tent in a beauty spot by the River Greta, up river from Low Briery.

I struggle to come to terms with the mentality and attitude of people who go to the

Discarded rubbish left by campers in Longtown Field.

trouble of finding a secluded place where they can, presumably, enjoy the peace and beauty if affords them, only to then despoil that site by leaving masses of unsightly and potentially very damaging (to the environment and to wildlife) rubbish in their wake when they desert the area where they have stayed.

I had previously noticed a largish grey tent – pitched in a fairly secluded corner of what is known as Longtown Field – some weeks previously while walking up the other side of the river on the high footpath through Brundholme Woods. The tent never appeared to be occupied. Perhaps its occupants were out walking or perhaps people were using it only occasionally and had left the tent in place?

Who or what is not the most important factor here and, irrespective of whether they should or should not have been there at all (I strongly suspect the latter) by far the worst aspect of the whole incident was that the people were prepared to, quite literally, rubbish a place of outstanding natural beauty. It is an all too familiar occurrence in these days of our low on responsibility, throwaway society where litter and rubbish, in lesser or larger amounts, are randomly deposited all over the place without any thought whatsoever as to the consequences.

It is almost as though some people – too many for this country's good – seem to think it is almost their right to drop or leave litter and rubbish wherever they please; hanging from trees in plastic bags, in roadside lay bys, over hedges, casually discarded in the street and, of course, by the river. Nowhere is safe from what has become the curse of 21st Century Britain.

Discarded in Longtown field next to the river, a broken down chair and the remains of a fire.

The photographer Val Corbett was, like me, sickened at what we found on close inspection of the site of the deserted camp. The tent had gone but bedding, cushions, clothing, tins, half empty bottles of wine, seating, cooking equipment and more, were all simply left in heaps on the bare brown earth where the tent had stood. The content and extent of the pollution was unbelievable.

The salient point is that litter and rubbish and the people who deposit them are the bane of modern living and, unfortunately, it seems that it is almost getting to the stage where it is becoming acceptable. When was the last time you heard of someone actually being prosecuted for dropping litter, let alone leaving masses of the stuff in a local beauty spot?

I appreciate that there are many people, young and old, who deplore the way in which society today treats its environment with almost casual disdain and an attitude of 'it's all right – someone else will clear up after me.' But it strikes me that those who do care and who are prepared to do something about it are in decline while those who cause the problem in the first instance and who do not give a damn, are on the rise. Meanwhile, the organisations and the authorities we might expect to actually do something appear to be sitting on the sidelines.

Following my discovery of the horrendous rubbish deposited by the River Greta and my subsequent attempts to resolve the situation by drawing attention to it, I was delighted when Pete Barron, Lake Management Ranger for the Lake District National Park, got in touch to say: "We are clearing up the rubbish near to the Keswick railway line. We have done this a few times this summer and are going to report the problem to the police. It is not our land or responsibility but we are in a position to clear it and others may not have the ability to complete the clear up required."

A walk up the River Greta only a couple of days later showed that the work had indeed been done and the place was restored to its natural beauty. So my eternal thanks to Pete Barron and his team for carrying out this important work so promptly and efficiently on behalf of everyone who genuinely appreciates the outstanding beauty of places like the River Greta and its environs and the need to look after them, now and in the future.

My only regret is that the culprits of this modern day crime against the environment were never caught or prosecuted. They had enjoyed and exploited the countryside, left their mess and got clean away with it. In its own way it stands comparison with what happened all those years ago in the 1880s and 90s concerning the lead mines on Blencathra, sanitation in Keswick and the dumping of all manner of rubbish in the river.

And that is extremely worrying.

Facing page:
Sunlight on the Greta.

The Greta . . . a river runs through it

The History Files
A RIVER RUNS THROUGH IT

No 1 is always very special and it was incredibly satisfying to carefully turn the pages of a bound copy of the very first edition of a newspaper that was printed and read for the first time by townspeople, my townspeople, more than a hundred years ago. It was almost voyeuristic. My research work was carried out in an old office – the room where the former trustees of Fitz Park had met since the 1880s – of the Keswick Museum and Art Gallery on Keswick's Station Road in the summer of 2011, just a little over 134 years after that very first edition of *The English Lakes Visitor and Keswick Guardian* was printed and published on Saturday, May 26, 1877. The broadsheet newspaper, No 1 no less, sold for the imperial price of one penny. And that's an old penny as in 1d as opposed to the virtually worthless 1p of our modern times.

Opening the pages of that first edition opened a portal to another world, a world with which I was familiar in that some of its landmarks remain the same – the River Greta, the Moot Hall, the bridges over the river, The Keswick Hotel, and many of the old houses, street names and family names – but a world that was entirely different, one with which in some ways I felt I had a strong link, but at the same time no connection at all. Here was Keswick, my hometown and the place where I have lived all my life yet the Keswick of the period 1877 – 1908 (which I chose to research to illustrate how a river flows through the life of a town) was far removed from the Keswick of 2011 / 2012 when I researched and wrote this book. The past is a foreign country and (in the best traditions of LP Hartley's novel from which those words are borrowed) I felt like something of a go-between.

For the summer of 2011 the bound newspaper files became my constant companions as I spent countless hours going carefully through the pages and writing meticulous notes in the old Dickensian office with its antiquated table and painfully uncomfortable chairs, hemmed in by the bound copies, bookcases and a writing desk that could have come straight out of the offices of Ebenezer Scrooge. The historic resonance of the room was enhanced by the almost surreal presence of a stained glass window, complete with dilapidated and original worm-eaten wooden frame, placed a couple of feet on the inside

Facing page:
The work of the farrier was of vital importance in Keswick in the days before the motorcar took over the world. In this highly evocative image the farrier hammers home the nails on a new horseshoe while a pipe-smoking helper holds the animal steady and a young boy looks on, rather curiously. The name of the photographer, the exact location of the image and date is not known.
Picture courtesy of
The George Fisher Collection.

of the actual window to the room. The curved window, a beautiful piece of work – soon to occupy a prominent place in the new look Keswick Museum and Art Gallery – had come to the museum from The Royal Oak Hotel where it commemorated the soldiers of the town who lost their lives in World War 1.

The reports in the newspaper provided a unique and accurate record of the town and its people at a specific point in its history. I doubt if there is a better record anywhere. And on coming across the original bound copies of the newspapers in the museum I immediately knew that I wanted to use selected extracts from the pages of the newspaper to illustrate the life of the town and how the River Greta flowed through it during a particular period in the town's history. While the Keswick has changed over the years the river has run remorselessly through the town on its journey from the mountains to the sea, its music continually serenading the population, whether they liked it or not; the river an ever present, ever moving, onwards rushing volume of water, sometimes high, sometimes low, occasionally polluted and invariably, during the 19th Century and before, little more than an open sewer, flushed out now and then by heavy rain and spate water. The River Greta was there long before the town took shape and, who knows, may well be there after the town has gone and our world has slipped into the abyss, fallen off the face of the planet, or been blown to smithereens, one way or another.

The newspaper's front page was entirely made up of advertisements but to turn the page was to open up an editorial wealth of local news and opinions followed by national news and international news. I have to say that this particular newspaper – in this former newspaper and magazine journalist's objective opinion – is far better than many of the publications, national and local, that appear in the name of print journalism today.

It is a remarkable newspaper and contains an amazing record of the town at a particular time in its history. This, hopefully, will all become self evident in the following pages through my selection of extracts from *The English Lakes Visitor and Keswick Guardian* from 1877 – 1908. After 1908 I felt that the newspaper, which went tabloid about that time, lost some of its early vitality. The earlier editions, especially those in the 1870s and 1880s, are beautifully written in a slightly archaic but nevertheless very appealing style. The newspaper also did not pull any punches and its reporting of courts, council meetings, accidents, fires, pollution, accidents, drownings, battles between walkers and land owners, health and housing and all manner of issues over the years, were all published in tremendous detail and without, as far as I could see, fear or favour.

On a personal level research work among bound copies of a newspaper comes at a price. My comeuppance occurred one afternoon when, hard at work in the old office, head bent over a newspaper file, pen poised over notebook at the side and with a reading lamp illuminating the entire scene, I sensed, at the door beyond my right shoulder, the presence of two visitors to the adjacent museum. I was quiet, stock still, my back to the door and intent on my work, when I heard one of the visitors (a woman) say to her elderly companion in a hushed voice: "Oooooh, for a minute there I thought he was real."

This, of course, is the first and hopefully the last time, that I will be mistaken for a Tussauds-style exhibit. Not for one moment did I think there was any danger that by sitting in a museum long enough I could inadvertently transform myself, Kafkaesque, into an exhibit. Could I even begin to compete with the museum's prize showpieces, the musical stones, a mantrap or, heaven forbid, the 667-year-old cat?

On Saturday, May 26, 1877 *The English Lakes Visitor and Keswick Guardian* announced itself on an unsuspecting world and in its first editorial set out its intentions for the years ahead.

"It is customary," the editor wrote, "on presenting a new journal to the notice of the public, to state some reason why it has been called into existence, and to define, as nearly as possible the line of conduct which shall mark its after career. In this instance we have no disposition to cavil at precedent and will say, firstly, that we believe the interests of Keswick will be promoted by a newspaper peculiarly its own, and printed and published in the town; and, secondly, we also believe there is sufficient business enterprise in the town and district to support a newspaper, so long as it properly fulfils its mission. Its success, therefore, depends mainly upon the measure of good it can accomplish, in making more widely known the grand beauties of the district and inducing a greater influx of visitors, upon whom the inhabitants chiefly rely for their means of subsistence. So far, then, there is an identity of interests between ourselves and those whom we essay to represent.

"In the literary management of the paper, we shall carefully avoid politics, sectarianism and party leanings, but will give impartial publicity to all shades of opinion. Public topics will be treated with candour and honesty. Special attention will be devoted to the collection of local news, and the reports of meetings, police and county courts will be copious and accurate. Under the usual editorial restrictions, our columns are freely placed at the service of correspondents and we respectfully invite therein the temperate discussion of matters of public importance.

"During the season, as our title implies, we shall publish a list of the visitors at the Lakes. Our aim is to compile a reliable list and to this end we urgently request the hearty co-operation of hotel and lodging house proprietors.

"Further we shall not neglect an opportunity of advocating the welfare of the entire district, and directing our efforts to the recognition of its claims for an earlier season. The beauty of the district never dies, but its wild and majestic grandeur is seen to the best advantage when softened by the freshness of spring."

On the following pages are my selected extracts from the pages of the newspaper:

Winters were hard in the old days. This ice on the River Greta by the silver bridge near Fitz Park is more reminiscent of the Arctic than Keswick.
Picture courtesy of
The George Fisher Collection.

The English Lakes Visitor
AND
KESWICK GUARDIAN.

. XXX.——NO. 1543. | REGISTERED AS A NEWSPAPER | SATURDAY, DECEMBER 29, 1906. | FOR TRANSMISSION IN THE UNITED KINGDOM. | ONE PENNY.

1877

May 26th
HORSE TAKES FRIGHT AT FLAPPING CLOTHES

On Tuesday night John Sanderson, a drayman employed at the Old Brewery, Keswick, met with a serious accident while out exercising a horse, near to the railway station. Some clothes were hung upon a fence, and were flapping about by the action of the wind. The horse took fright, leapt the fence, threw its rider and fell upon him. He was taken home and Mr Dennison, bone setter, of Penrith was summoned to attend him. That gentleman arrived on Wednesday morning and found a dislocation at the shoulder and also some hurt to the right hip. The injuries were attended to and Sanderson, who has also been visited by a medical gentleman, is progressing favourably.

June 2nd
DRUNK IN CHARGE OF A HORSE AND CARRIAGE

The usual fortnightly petty sessions was held at the Court Room on Saturday. The business, which consisted of several cases of drunkenness, was not of public importance, except in the instance of John Story, who was summoned for drunkenness while in charge of a horse and carriage. The Chairman said the magistrates had decided to deal severely with cases of this description, for every summer great danger was caused on the narrow roads by drunken drivers, and they must make an example. As this was the first case they would not inflict the full penalty of 40s, but they should fine the defendant 20s and costs which amounted to 31s. Inspector Richardson proved the case.

NARROW ESCAPE OF BOATMAN ON DERWENTWATER

On Monday last a boatman named Joseph Spark had a narrow escape from drowning. Spark was precipitated into the water (while attempting to bale out a boat) and sank twice before he was rescued by his son. There is no doubt that but for the activity of the son the father would have been drowned.

June 9th
SHEEP KILLED ON THE RAILWAY

At the latter part of last week a ewe and lamb belonging to Mr Edward Hawell, were killed on the railway near Keswick. The ewe and her two lambs had got through the fence and were straying on the line when an engine came upon them and ran over the ewe and one lamb.

SHEEP WORRYING

During the past fortnight the flocks in the neighbourhood of Under Skiddaw have been attacked by one or more dogs and upwards of a score of lambs were worried and disfigured.

June 23rd
TEMPERANCE DEMONSTRATION AT KESWICK

The annual demonstration of the various temperance societies in the county was held in a field adjoining Friar's Crag, Keswick, on Wednesday. The day was fine but almost uncomfortably warm. About one o'clock the procession commenced to parade the town and having gone over the prescribed route, returned to the field where a public meeting was held. There would be several thousand persons on the grounds when the public meeting commenced at three o'clock.

Above: An artist working on a painting of Greta Bridge.

Left: Shops in Market Square, 1850. The alley way leads to the King's Head yard and the shop is that of R Jackson, grocer. This is central Keswick near the Moot Hall. Drawing by Tom Wilson.

July 7th

EMPEROR AND EMPRESS OF BRAZIL IN KESWICK

On Thursday evening the Emperor and Empress of Brazil arrived at The Keswick Hotel where they were received by the proprietors Miss Frank and Miss Cole. During their stay the royal party visited the Town Hall, Flintoff's Model, Ann Banks' Pencil works at Greta Bridge, Mayson's Ordnance model, Lake Road and Crosthwaite Church and Southey's grave … The Imperial party then repaired to Greta Hall, where they were received by Miss Brindle, who showed them all that was associated with Southey – the room in which the poet died having especial attraction for his majesty.

August 4th

THE DEATH OF THE IRREPLACEABLE ABEL BANKS

Many persons connected with Keswick will learn with regret that old Abel Banks, the prince of country fiddlers, has passed away. No ball nor gypsy party was thought complete without Abel and his sprightly performance on the violin. He attained the good age of 74 years, and was much respected for his upright character and genial and unobtrusive demeanour. Latterly he has been heard to say regretfully that when his career was run the young people would have to do without dancing, for he did not see who was to fill his vacant place.

August 25th

OTTER HUNTING

On the 10th inst a brace of otter cubs were killed at Naddle Bridge foot. The dam succeeded in eluding the hunters.

A VETERAN WHIP

On Thursday the services of "old Harry Bowe," who is upwards of 84 years of age, were called into requisition in consequence of the scarcity of drivers to accommodate the visitors. The old veteran had laid aside the whip some years ago, but he handled the ribbons with his former ability and drove out two different parties – one journey being round Bassenthwaite Lake.

ECLIPSE OF THE MOON

A total eclipse of the moon took place on Thursday night, in more favourable circumstances for observation than will again occur until October 4th, 1884. The sky was beautifully clear and the colour, varying from dark grey to copper, exhibited by the moon while passing through the different stages, were well defined.

September 1st

A LUNAR RAINBOW

A fine display of this somewhat rare phenomenon was witnessed in our neighbourhood on Thursday evening last. Our informant was returning along the Borrowdale road towards Keswick about 10 o'clock in the evening in question when his attention was suddenly attracted by the appearance of a magnificent arch of bright light, forming a perfect semi circle and over spanning the western shore of the lake. At the end of about three minutes from its first appearance the rainbow was suddenly extinguished by a dense mass of black clouds rising over the mountains and sending down one of those drenching showers which have characterised the weather in the Lake District for some years back.

ANYTHING YOU CAN DO

In as much as last week's Jehu's rejoiced at the resumption of the "ribbons" by Harry Bowe, the hearts of the boatmen waxed glad at the proof positive that in their calling they still possessed vigorous and venerable comrades. Benjamin Wilson, who is 82 years of age, and as "nimble as a cat" rowed two different parties up to Lodore and back on Saturday last, which is a feat to tax the strength and staying power of a young man. Although Mr Wilson was originally a 'knight of the lapstone' (a cobbler), he has followed boating for upwards of 40 years.

September 8th

A CHEERY LITTLE NUMBER

The poetry of local writer William Gaspey was occasionally published in the newspaper. This stanza from a poem entitled 'The Day of Judgement' is fairly typical of his work and, as you can see, is a cheery little number guaranteed to raise the spirits of the downtrodden working man of the 1870s:

"… *The seas dry up – to dust the mountains fall*
The pyramids, once Art's immortal pride,
Expire with time, which, god-like, they defied.
Oh! Dire the horror, maddening is the woe
Of unrepentant wretches left below, –
Who, from the barriers of redemption hurled,
Sink in the ruins of a burning world!"

Right: Keswick street scene.
A watercolour by John Ruskin (1819 – 1900).
Picture courtesy of Keswick Museum and Art Gallery.

The Greta … a river runs through it

November 3rd
NOT MUCH OF A SABBATARIAN

In a village not many miles from Keswick, there dwells a sturdy farmer for whom the week is too short, just by a day, as evidenced by the fact that on Sunday last, instead of "resting" after the toil of the preceding six days, he was busily employed in packing his wool for the market on Monday. Having completed that job he improved the time still further by shoeing his horse. We should neither like to be either his "man-servant nor stranger within his gates." How the worthy individual would have fared had he lived in the good old days when a 'Cat was hung on the Monday, for catching a mouse on a Sunday,' we are not in a position to say.

November 10th
TUP SATURDAY

Keswick wore quite a busy aspect on Saturday last. The stand below the Town Hall was filled with farmers' carts ranged in an orderly manner and the streets were thronged with country cousins, some on "pleasure bent" and others on what is prosaically termed business, viz, the disposal at from 6d per pound, of an article of diet apologetically termed cheese, which suffers in character from the immense quantity of good butter which the local dairies send to market. In the Pack Horse Yard there was a very good show of Fell Tups, but business was exceedingly dull. In the evening, according to the usual custom, there was a dance at several of the inns in the town. We are glad to be able to say that there was no case of drunkenness such as to call for the interference of the police.

December 29th
A PAIR OF ANTIQUE BUTCHERS

On Monday last, Mr John Mumberson and his "apprentice" Mr Thomas Bragg, both upwards of eighty years of age, were engaged in pig killing at Miss Brindle's, Greta Hall. They acquitted themselves so well that in recognition of their ability Miss Brindle invited them to lunch.

1878

May 18
RARE TREE CULTIVATION

Mr Thomas Ferguson, of Shu-le-Crow, has succeeded in growing out of doors three specimens of the blue gum tree (Eucalyptus globules). These are the first trees of the kind which have grown in the open so far north, the latitude being 54 degrees 36N and the situation 278 feet above the level of the sea. For the information of those who do not know the tree it may be stated that whole plantations grow on the Australian morasses and to it has been attributed properties of an anti-malarial character.

May 25th
GYPSIES AT KESWICK

A tribe of Nomads have taken a field near Greta Bridge for sixteen weeks, so that fortune-telling will no doubt be one of the attractions this summer. Even in these enlightened days there are plenty of simpletons and they and their money will have another opportunity to part.

NARROW ESCAPE FROM DROWNING

On Wednesday afternoon two little boys, sons of Mr Elwin, joiner, were playing by the riverside, near the Station Road bridge, when the younger one fell into the water. His brother made an effort to save him and both were in danger of drowning. Mr T. Postlethwaite, while passing, saw the position of the children and went into the water and rescued both. They were afterwards ill from the effects of the immersion, but have since recovered.

June 15th
WILLIAM SHAKESPEARE, BUT NOT THE BARD OF AVON

A tramp, who rejoices under the revered name of William Shakespeare, was apprehended by PC Booth on Wednesday night for vagrancy. The officer saw him begging and cautioned him, but he afterwards met two gentlemen whom he abused because they gave him nothing. They complained of the conduct of the tramp, and this led the police to take more stringent action. He was brought before J.J. Spedding Esq and committed to gaol for seven days.

June 29th
A CARELESS NURSE

On Sunday evening last a woman, whose age ought to have taught her better, allowed a perambulator, in which a child was sitting, to run by itself down a hill on the Borrowdale Road. Before she could catch it the carriage ran into the roadside and overturned, and threw out the child which fortunately was not badly hurt though it possibly might have been.

July 13th
SHEEP WORRYING

During the past fortnight twenty five lambs, belonging to the farmers in the neighbourhood of Threlkeld, have been destroyed by a dog, the property of Mr Thomas Cockbain, High Row. On Tuesday the animal was caught in the act by Mr John Hall, of Derwent Falls, and hanged.

July 20th
THE EXCESSIVE HEAT

On Wednesday last Mrs Routledge, wife of Mr Routledge, fish monger, was taken suddenly ill from the effects of heat and exhaustion. Dr O'Reilly was called in to attend her and under his care she is now progressing towards recovery.

Right: Horse and carriage in Keswick.
Picture courtesy of The George Fisher Collection.

July 27th
HEAVY THUNDER-STORM IN KESWICK. EXTENSIVE DAMAGE TO PROPERTY

A thunderstorm of unusual violence, accompanied by a heavy hailstorm, passed over Keswick on Sunday afternoon. The morning was almost tropically hot and oppressive, although the sun for the greater part of the time was obscured by cloud. Towards two o'clock the sky in the north east assumed that dark premonitory appearance, and at a little past half past two the storm burst upon the town in full power.

Vivid flashes of lightning were closely followed with crashing peals of thunder, and presently hail stones of what may be termed prodigious size fell in an alarming quantity and with such force that all the sky-light windows facing to the east suffered more or less in breakages. Some of the hail stones measured no less than one and a quarter inches in diameter and would weigh not less than an ounce.

The trees were stripped of a large quantity of their foliage and much fruit has been knocked off while plants and even the rigid bracken on the mountain sides were literally cut to pieces. It is singular that the storm came over in a narrow belt, extending from the Keswick side of Little Crosthwaite to about 200 yards from Thirlspot. The fringe of the storm was only very light on both sides. The whole force appeared to be centred in the immediate district of Keswick. For many years there has not been a hailstorm of equal violence or stones of so large a size, and what makes the circumstance more singular is that ice should fall in such great quantity at the height of an unusually hot summer.

July 27th
A NARROW ESCAPE

On Wednesday morning a boy, the son of Mr W. Pridmore, was riding on a timber wagon on his way to school, when by some reason he was canted off. He fell and was caught between the wagon and one of the hind wheels. His screams prompted the driver to stop at once, but some difficulty was experienced in releasing the lad who was wedged quite tightly in his position. Fortunately his injuries are slight, though there can be no doubt but for the prompt action of the driver the consequences might have been very serious, if not fatal. The lad's dinner basket was crushed to pieces.

August 3rd
'CHEAP' AND 'NASTY' TRIP

A heavy train came into Keswick yesterday from Blaydon, near Newcastle. The trippers were such, as a body, that we hope to see them no more. Their delight was in drunkenness, and their disgusting language and exhibitions a terror to all decent people.

September 28th.
CATAPULT NUISANCE

A good many juveniles have lately been going about the town with catapults, and the other day a lad discharged a stone which broke a large pane of glass in a front window of Mrs Simpson's house in Station Road. Though there can be no objection to boys using these instruments in the country they are a cause of damage and annoyance in the streets.

October 5th
A RUNAWAY

At Underskiddaw on Tuesday evening a horse the property of Mr Rathbone started off with the carriage to which it was attached, and was not recaptured until nearly at High Hill. No damage was done.

DEATH OF ANOTHER OLD INHABITANT

In our obituary of today is recorded the death of Mr Thomas Howe, of High Hill, at the age of 82. Formerly he was a farmer at Applethwaite and was looked upon as a remarkable character. He was, in his prime, a big, strong man, and could do a wonderful day's work in the harvest field, and with the scythe, having, it is stated, moved no less than three acres in one day. He leaves a widow but a few months younger than himself.

November 2nd
INSUFFICIENTLY ARDENT SPIRITS

John Bailiff, the "Black Lion," Dinah Pearson, "Shoulder of Mutton" and Jane Lowden, "Packhorse," were severally summoned under the Food and Drugs Act for selling adulterated spirits. These were the first cases brought before the Keswick Bench for selling spirits adulterated with water. Each was fined 10s.

In the same edition of the newspaper there was a letter to the Editor, which read – Sir, I understand that this day certain publicans of Keswick have been fined for selling weak spirits, to me a commendable act, and why the law should do so (inflict fines) I cannot tell. Certainly the weaker the grog the less fear of their customers becoming drunkards, for the more you reduce one the more you reduce the other. We live in strange times certainly . . . poor fellow! When the Liberals were in power he (the publican) lost many friends; and now the Tories are there he seems to have no friends at all. Fined, vexed and perplexed on every side what can he do? The letter was signed THE POOR MAN'S FRIEND.

The Vale of Keswick from Ambleside Road, 1836. Artwork by William Westall (1781 – 1850). Picture courtesy of The Wordsworth Trust, The Jerwood Centre, Dove Cottage, Grasmere.

November 9th

AN AMOROUS FARMER

A worthy gentleman, of bucolic habits, while returning to the Vale of Newlands on Saturday last (the occasion of the Martinmas Tup and Cheese Fair) fell into an awkward predicament through the flow of amorous and other spirits. It appears that he was so beside himself with joy that nothing would prevent him attempting to kiss the good lady of his choice. Whether she was unwilling to receive the tender tribute from her Lord, or battled with that charming coyness of her sex and gave him a playful tap over the head with a butter basket, or the horse started at the unusual circumstance or something had previously displaced the centre of the farmer's gravity, is not known; but the result of the little by-play was a man falling astride one of the cart shafts, and some difficulty to put him straight again.

December 14th

THE FROST

Winter seems to have fairly set in, the thermometer has shown freezing to have been the order since the latter part of last week. Skating and curling have been vigorously enjoyed on Derwentwater. The moon has been favourable for evening skating, and every night during the week the lake has been thronged with a merry crowd. A ladder and rope were provided to render assistance in case of emergency.

December 21st

SOUP KITCHEN

At the commencement of the present week a soup kitchen was opened at the old Almshouse for the benefit of the poor people of the Old Church district. On Tuesday 112 quarts were given out at a penny per quart but through the kindness of Mr S. Ladyman the pennies were returned. Yesterday about 120 availed themselves of the soup kitchen, and each was presented with a cake, the gift of a tradesman in the town.

1879

January 18th

ONE MONTH WITH HARD LABOUR

A woman was sentenced to imprisonment for one month with hard labour for unlawfully concealing the birth of her child by secretly burying the dead body at Dyke Nook, Bassenthwaite.

February 15th

SKATING AT KESWICK

The long continuance of the frost, which has permitted skating on the lake for over ten weeks, has been extremely prolific in the genus "skater." Numbers of youths have acquired a remarkable proficiency in the art.

Below: Gates to Upper Fitz Park, Keswick. Right: Toll Bar at High Hill, 1846. Drawing by Tom Wilson.

April 29th

THE DEATH OF AN OTTER

The Cockermouth otter hounds were at Keswick on Tuesday and got on game in the River Derwent. They hunted well up the river and came up with their prey near the junction of the Greta and Derwent where the otter was seen to be completely spent after the severe chase. A good number of spectators witnessed the finish, and several of them in their excitement went into the stream. Mr Robinson Mitchell, who was the huntsman, picked the otter up by the tail and threw it among the dogs to be worried. As a finale the otter's head was held under water until its death was assured. It was a fine mammal of its class and weighed upwards of 20lbs. For part of the day the carcase was hung, as a trophy, at the door of The George Hotel for inspection, and many went to see it.

June 14th

BAND OF HOPE TRIP

The annual trip of the St John's Band of Hope when 600 / 700 people, including children, sought a day's pleasure at Morecambe. The sun was shining and everyone was in high glee as the long train moved out of Keswick at 7.10am to the lively mirth of the juveniles. Unfortunately it rained all day and faces changed to those of disappointment. In Morecambe the children (230) were entertained indoors at the Victoria Music Hall. Others took excursions across the Bay in a steamer while others repaired to the aquarium and botanical gardens, the pier and the observatory. Before the hour of departure (from Morecambe) nearly all had taken their seats in the train, which left punctually at 7pm and arrived at Keswick at 9.45pm. There was no casualty save the loss of a few youngsters' caps from pushing their heads out of the windows.

In June 1880, 900 went on the Band of Hope trip to Blackpool and the weather was sunny with many swimming in the sea.

June 7th

A REMNANT OF WINTER

Mr John Jeffery, who has been twice at Scawfell during the week, states that there are still some deep drifts of snow, one of which, on Great End, was no less than eight feet deep.

A DRUNKEN VIRAGO

A drunken blackguard woman, a stranger, who gave the name of Margaret Usher, was apprehended by Inspector Richardson for begging in the streets on Monday night while in a state of drunkenness. She was brought before a magistrate on Tuesday and sentenced to fourteen days imprisonment.

August 9th

A MAN ON FIRE

On Tuesday evening a volume of smoke was observed issuing from the clothes of a man standing upon the platform at the station. He was seized by one of the porters and the fire, which was probably due to a lighted pipe having been placed in his pocket, was subdued.

September 8th

TUP AND CHEESE FAIR

This annual fair was held on Saturday last. With the exception of a cheap jack and a strength indicator there was nothing of an exciting nature and the town wore its usual quiet aspect.

CUT HIS OWN THROAT

A Keswick man was charged with attempting to commit suicide on the 6th of August last by cutting his throat. He was reprimanded by the chairman and discharged.

September 27th

A VULGAR, FOOLISH HABIT

Letter to the Editor written by J Clifton-Ward, Keswick: Sir, A Fellow the Society of Antiquaries has drawn my attention to the injury done to our fine stone circle near Keswick by the practice of that very vulgar and foolish habit, the carving of names and initials. A new notice is about to be placed beside the circle, warning future offenders that they will render themselves liable to prosecution, and it is earnestly hoped that the inhabitants of Keswick will use their utmost endeavours to check this idle and wanton habit, and will take pride in preserving this and all other ancient monuments entrusted to their keeping.

October 18th

THE SCAVENGER

The newspaper published a letter congratulating the Local Board (Town Council) on the flagging of footpaths throughout the town. "You may now get from one end of the town to the other dry shod, even on a wet day. It is a boon that natives as well as strangers will alike enjoy." In a previous edition it was noted that the unsurfaced roads became dusty in the summer months. So much so that a worker was employed to keep the streets in good order (he rejoiced under the job title of Scavenger) and his duties included dispensing water from a cart to keep the streets clean and the dust down.

December 27th

WAS IT A UFO?

A most curious light was seen over Walla Crag between five and seven o'clock yesterday morning, by several persons. It seemed to contract and expand and, when at its largest size, oscillated like a kite in a steady wind.

Right: The Queen's Head. Licensed in the name of Wm Banks to sell ale, porter, wines and spirits. Next door is Mayson's draper. Drawing by Tom Wilson.

1880

February 7th

FIRST INSTALMENT OF EARLY RHUBARB

Mr Edward Greenhow showed in his window the other day several very fine sticks of rhubarb of his own growth.

KILLED ON THE RAILWAY

On Tuesday morning on the line opposite "Willie Dub," Mr William Dixon found a fine, full-grown otter which had evidently been killed by a train.

May 1st

A FACT FOR THE CURIOUS

There is a street in Keswick in which there are not more than five and twenty houses, and of these fifteen are occupied by widows, and every one, in the event of the woman's suffrage would be eligible for electoral franchise.

In its edition of September 25th the newspaper reported as follows:

WOMEN'S SUFFRAGE MEETING AT KESWICK

On Wednesday evening a meeting was held at the Oddfellows Hall, Keswick, when an address on the "claims of women householders and ratepayers to the Parliamentary franchise" was delivered by Mrs Oliver Scratcherd, of Leeds. The chair was taken by Miss Becker, of Manchester, the pioneer of the movement. There was a moderate attendance.

June 26th

NOT A WEE DROP

Within the licensing division of the Keswick magistrates there is a Boniface who has been a publican for the last 46 of his 76 years of age. Taking an average of his daily "wet" at ten pints – some days he has managed twenty and others less – he has consumed no less than 20,976 gallons. Divided into barrels, three of which are considered a cartload, this would make a procession of nearly 200 carts. Taking the value at 2s per gallon, the cost of wetting the whistle of mine host is represented by £2,097 12s. The duty paid upon the drink, at 6s per barrel, would amount to £174 18s. After all this the man lives and thinks he has not yet had his share.

September 25th

HORTICULTURAL SHOW MORALITY

The committee of the Keswick Horticultural and Cottage Gardeners' Association have devoted four meetings within the past few weeks to inquire into alleged illegal practices at the recent show. Firstly, Messrs M Postlethwaite and W Telford charged Mr Joshua Dobson with having received prizes for vegetables (cabbage, cauliflower and peas), which were not of his own growth. At the third meeting, Mr Dobson and his accusers were present and the latter failed to establish their case. However, Mr Dobson, when called upon to sign the "declaration" said that he did show potatoes which were not his own. In making this confession he said that he had exchanged some celery for the potatoes with Robert Smith, one of the committee, and who he further alleged showed the celery and took second prize with it.

The case of Dobson was considered; the prize for the potatoes was withheld and he was debarred from exhibiting for one year. (The case against Mr Smith was not proved at a later meeting).

Right: Dover's Court, off Main Street, 1890. Drawing by Tom Wilson.

October 16th

BECK RACING

On Thursday morning two men (whose names are Jimmy and Bob) agreed to race across the beck and back for half a crown. The consequence was that the spectators had the pleasure of seeing a good rough and tumble in the middle of the stream. Neither completed the "course."

November 13th

THE FOX AND THE GEESE

Master Reynard paid a visit to Goosewell Farm on Saturday night last and killed two geese.

1881

January 22nd

THE FROST

The intensity of the frost on Saturday and Sunday nights has not been equalled for many years. The temperature was quite Arctic, and everything it was possible to freeze, both inside and out of doors, succumbed to its influence. Many gas meters have ceased to work in consequence of the freezing of the requisite water, and many others have only been kept going by occasional additions of boiling water, while not a few have been debauched with spirits in order that they might thereby resist the cold. If this method succeeds our temperance friends will be able to recommend a new way of getting rid of "heavy wet."

The Greta . . . a river runs through it

August 27th
INDECENT BATHING

It has lately become the practice of some young gentlemen visitors to bathe from the boat landings at about eight o'clock in the morning and occasionally during the prohibited time after that hour. Not always have the bathers complied with the rule as to wearing of bathing drawers; but even supposing they had done so the sight of so many naked forms could hardly fail to shock the feelings of any unsuspecting ladies who unknowingly took an early walk to the lake.

Persons whose training should at least make them gentlemen ought to set a better example and, especially for the modest outlay of six pence, a number can take a boat to a part of the lake where they may enjoy their "dip" without giving cause of offence to anybody. We throw out the suggestion that bathing from the landings should be entirely prohibited; indeed we believe the police have power to interfere but we trust this note of warning may prove sufficient to put an end to the objectionable practice.

A Keswick man would never think of bathing at such a place, when there is a sequestered spot behind the Isthmus.

September 17th
DRUNK IN CHARGE OF A HORSE AND CART

Isaac Miller, hawker, Braithwaite, was summoned for being drunk while in charge of a horse and cart. P.C. Garnett deposed that at 6.30pm on the 30th of August he received information that the defendant had driven his horse's head through a shop window. He found the defendant in the George Hotel yard very drunk. He was fined 5s.

October 29th
POST BOYS' SUPPER

On Monday evening the post boys of Keswick had their annual supper at The Pack Horse Inn and upwards of forty sat down to an excellent meal prepared by the hostess, Mrs Spedding. After the withdrawal of the cloth the evening was devoted to harmony.

1882

June 17th
SNOW IN JUNE

The great fall in temperature experienced from the close of last week was strikingly demonstrated on Monday morning, when the higher mountains were covered a good way down with snow.

September 16th
A SUSPICIOUS CHARACTER

Between three o'clock and four o'clock on Thursday morning near Greta Bridge the policeman on duty was startled at a peculiar sound accompanied by the jangling of chains. Turning his light on he discovered one of the elephants belonging to the circus, which had broken away and had come to the river for a drink. The brute had been chained to a stake which it had pulled up.

1883

March 31
DEATH OF DERWENT COLERIDGE

The Rev Derwent Coleridge died early in the morning of Wednesday, the 28th (of March) at Torquay. He was the last surviving son of the poet Samuel Taylor Coleridge and was born at Greta Hall in September 1800. He was much attached to this county, the home of his childhood, and until age and infirmities prevented him taking a long journey, he was a frequent visitor to Keswick. He was himself a poet and a learned and gifted man. The bell of Crosthwaite Church will toll on this day.

October 13th
BLACK SPOT IN SOCIAL HISTORY

'Immorality, vice and disease.' My attention has been directed to one of the black spots of social history in this otherwise model town of ours. The case pointed out to me is as painful as it is disgraceful, and in calling attention to the general facts I do so in the hope that steps will be taken to remove all such predisposing causes to immorality.

I am credibly informed that in a two-bedroomed cottage there live representatives of three generations of one family and a lodger – in all three females and three males. Of these, five persons occupy the same small bedroom, and, with the only approach to decency, the female lodger sleeps upon chairs in the kitchen. While folks have such surroundings, is it to be wondered that immorality, squalor and misery follow?

What moral agency can compete with conditions so wretched? The details, which were given to me in respect to the particular instance, are too deplorable to make a public show of. For humanity's sake something needs to be done, which shall remove a cause so fruitful of immorality, vice, and disease.

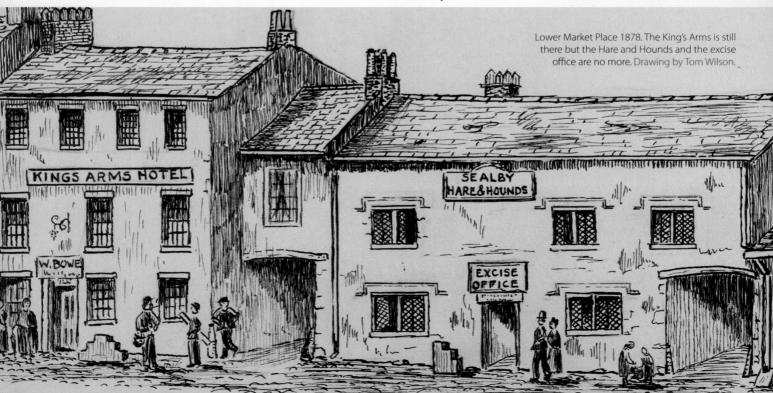

Lower Market Place 1878. The King's Arms is still there but the Hare and Hounds and the excise office are no more. Drawing by Tom Wilson.

November 3rd

LAST PAYMENT
TO PIKE KEEPERS

Poor Mr Weller, senior, if he be alive and kicking now, will not be able to "devote the remainder o' his days and energies to a pike" in this district at any rate, for the tollgates were disestablished effectually on Thursday. The barriers have been taken down and the maintenance of the roads will henceforth be thrown upon the different districts. I understand the portion which falls to the lot of Keswick is about a mile in length and the maintenances of this additional road will have to be borne from the rates, so that those who do not run even a perambulator or a one-wheeled omnibus will have the honour of doing his little towards paying for the road mending.

I understand some affecting scenes took place on Saturday last, between the farmers and the "pike keepers." The last payment, no doubt, came more cheerfully from the rustic pocket than any previous contribution to the P.K & C (Penrith, Keswick and Cockermouth) Turnpike Trust Fund.

The adieus and waving of hands and fervent "goodbyes" were sufficiently indicative of the sorrow which the jovial farmer is capable of when put to his mettle.

Below: Shops in Lower Main Street, 1870. The sign reads 'Isabella Eliot, grocer.' Drawing by Tom Wilson. Right: Couple by the millrace at The Forge.

November 17th

MARTINMAS HIRINGS

On Saturday the town was somewhat thronger than it is ordinarily in consequence of the Martinmas Hirings, but business of that kind was not very brisk. The Market Square in the afternoon and evening was occupied by some of the commoner fair rabble, and dancing was permitted at two of the inns; the only other distinguishing feature was that there were rather more cases of drunkenness than on ordinary Saturdays.

1884

January 5th

LETTING IN
THE NEW YEAR

The ringers at Crosthwaite Church observed, as regards this district, a new method in their celebration. For the last ten minutes of the dying year the tenor was tolled as a "passing bell" but as soon as midnight had passed the whole of the eight iron tongues in the tower made a joyous clamour in honour of the birth of 1884. The fife and drums played up and down the street for a time shortly before and after midnight, but the good people of Keswick were spared any further infliction of festal music.

The spirit of mischief was abroad and kept the policemen actively at work for a long time, both at the close of the old and beginning of the New Year. It is a pity that malicious damage cannot be dissociated from the fun of the rollicking youths of Keswick.

May 18th

OTTER KILLED AT
YEWLETT WHOAL ON
THE GRETA

The West Cumberland Otter Hounds came by train from Cockermouth to Braithwaite on Wednesday morning and were cast off near Stocks Bridge. They hunted up the Derwent to Portinscale and afterwards were transferred to the Greta. In the neighbourhood of White Moss an otter was found and it gave the dogs more than an hour's work. It fought bravely for its life and left its mark on some of its pursuers, but eventually it was overcome in deep water, at the part of the river known locally as "Yewlett Whoal." The dogs were drawn off after the kill although other game had been seen. The otter was a fine dog and weighed 19lb.

May 24th

THE TELEPHONE
IN KESWICK

Mr W. Wilson of the Keswick Hotel has got his telephone in perfect working order, the work for which has been most efficiently done by Mr Frank Kenyon of the Railway Telegraph Maintenance Department. The instruments are Bell's patent and the necessary electricity is generated in bichromate batteries. Conversation can be carried on with ease and with quite as much rapidity as were the speakers face to face.

August 30th

KESWICK PONG

(Letter to the Editor) – I had occasion to go to the station today and will only say that the stench (which arises I believe from a tan yard adjoining the bridge) was so intense and horrible that I could not shake off the recollection of it for some time, and my lunch was quite spoiled in consequence. The letter was signed 'A VISITOR.'

In the same edition it is reported that there were pigsties and middensteads in the heart of the town. These were attached to local hotels and inns and, in some instances, were closed down because they were, not surprisingly, "a nuisance." Pigsties and middens were also close to housing and "blood and garbage were thrown on the midden and allowed to accumulate for several weeks."

Incidentally, the bridge referred to above is the silver bridge situated on Station Road. The tannery was on the left of the bridge on the Keswick side of the River Greta as you made your way towards Fitz Park, the Keswick Hotel and the then railway station. The site is now occupied by Riverside Lodge flats and the verandah that leads along the side of the river to the YHA building. It all suggests that Keswick at that time had its own distinctive aromas and these doubtless included that from the effluent in the river.

The Greta . . . a river runs through it

August 31st

WORKHOUSE CHILDREN'S TREAT

The children from the Cockermouth Union, accompanied by the matron, schoolmaster, and several friends, spent a very pleasant day at Keswick on Thursday. At the expense of Mr Stockdale, of Leeds, they were entertained to an excellent dinner of roast beef, pudding etc at Mr Greenhow's dining rooms, and later on to tea. The youngsters enjoyed themselves heartily in Fitz Park, Castlehead, and at the lake side, and, happy in the remembrance of a bright day in their lives, left for home by the 6.30 train.

Above: Turnpike gate on Ambleside Road, 1860, with the steeple of St John's Church in the background.
Drawing by Tom Wilson.

October 4th

THE QUACK DOCTOR

Last Saturday night I stood in the Market Place to watch the antics of a quack doctor and listen to the "patter' with which he approached the gullible portion of Keswick. After some introductory remarks which were but doubtfully complimentary to his audience, he produced an array of bottles containing a bright red fluid, which he offered as a specific for corns, warts, bunions, toothache, earache etc. In fact I question whether the medicine was not qualified to cure all the ills that graduate between soft corns and consumption.

He asked but a shilling a bottle for this concentration of the British Pharmacopoeia!

What a wonderful amount of faith the purchasers must have had! And there were enough buyers to exhaust the stock. The contents of the bottles I judged to be coloured spirits of wine in as much as the "doctor" wet the tip of his finger from one of the bottles and then, passing it through the flame of his naptha lamp, showed the pale blue light of the burning spirit.

He next sought to raise the wonder of his audience by the display of a variety of bottled worms which he scientifically described as 'Animal culey.' He explained that they were only samples of what succumbed to his skill. Having fully dilated upon the horrible character of the infesting creatures and his absolute power over them, he commenced to offer some remarkable pills. They contained the concentrated powers of certain herbs which were good for this, that, and the other complaint, and therefore could be taken for any manner of disease with assured success. He only asked six pence a box, or three boxes for a shilling.

When will the people learn sense to button their pockets in the presence of charlatanry?

October 25th

THE FIRE ENGINE

The Keswick fire engine was actually got to work at the fire at Millbeck yesterday morning before the whole of the smouldering was extinguished. This was a feat worthy of record because it shows the earnestness of a body of men who dragged the poor feeble thing all the way there and then set to pumping. There was no horse to be got, and if there had been there were no means for yoking it. Besides it is unfit to travel because of the small wheels, and any but Cumberland men would have been too exhausted to do anything more after sharing the labour of transporting it between two and three miles. The men worked well and hard, as did all who could be of use and it speaks very highly of the sympathy one has with another in this time of trouble that so many turn out of their warm beds and carry their own buckets to assist in putting out a fire.

October 25th

NUTMEG GRATERS

(The following letter to the editor was intended to promote the benefits of vaccination in the treatment of smallpox): When I was a boy, fifty years ago, you could not walk up Keswick street on a market day without encountering two or three people with faces like nutmeg graters. Now you may travel through the Lake District and scarcely see one. Why is this? How comes it that, in spite of the filth and want of medical treatment among a portion of the poor, people do not take small pox as they once did? There is only one common sense answer: vaccination. The letter was signed ANTI-HUMBUG.

1885

February 25th

THE MOUTHS OF LIBERTINES

The Divorce Court during the past week has given two painful examples of the weak-kneed morality of two clergymen – one a Cumberland rector, and the other connected with the county by marriage. The details of the cases are the more disgraceful by reason of the position of the two respondents. They have been educated as gentlemen or they could not have attained to the offices they hold; but they have proved themselves to be wolves in sheep's clothing. Sunday after Sunday their duty would be to read the commandments for the warning of their flocks, and yet it appears they have had no faith in the punishments which they should and doubtless have taught as following a breach of the Decalogue. But I think they should preach no more. Purity is too sacred a subject to become the mouths of libertines.

In the same edition of the newspaper a second editorial read: A man can procure the decree nullifying his marriage on the proof of his wife's adultery, but a woman must prove cruelty as well as adultery before the law will give her more than a judicial separation. The sin is surely as great morally on the man's side as the woman's, yet the law does not recognise it as such. Some day, perhaps, we shall have advanced far enough to agree with the old adage that "what's sauce for the goose is sauce for the gander."

March 14th

THE NEW FIRE ENGINE

I am glad that we in Keswick have something to think about in the way of saving life rather than the taking of it. By a remarkable effort to get out of the old slough of "stand over for a time," the Local Board have determined to send off at once for the new fire engine. We may expect to be better prepared against an emergency than we have been in the past, but a brigade will be required to work the new engine and an opportunity presents itself for praiseworthy voluntary effort.

Old property backing onto the Greta near Penrith Road and its junction with Wordsworth Street. It is the location for the former Wren's Mill.

'FIERY FRENCHMAN DREW A REVOLVER'

Mr J.L. Knubley, of Keswick, who was apprehended on the charge of threatening to shoot the Editor of *La France* in Paris a fortnight ago, was released without dishonour on Wednesday.

It will be remembered that Mr Knubley (a journalist) supplied the French press with some particulars of a meeting of dynamitards to which he had gained admission, and the Editor of *La France* described the report as a work of the imagination and repudiated its veracity. Mr Knubley called upon him and asked that the statement should be withdrawn. They got to high words and Mr Knubley's exasperation was expressed in a blow, whereupon the fiery Frenchman drew a revolver. Mr Knubley followed suit, but before a shot was fired the porter at the office seized him, and he was afterwards hauled into the custody of the police. The reports of the occurrence which have appeared from Paris correspondents to the London dailies have been remarkable in their contradictory character. First the onus of blame was thrown entirely upon our townsman, till the *Daily Telegraph* correspondent gave the above version of the affair, and he said that although this fact was much in the Englishman's favour the case would go hard with him unless official interference was made in his behalf. We are glad, however, at being able to announce, on the authority of himself, that he was released as stated.

In a later edition it was reported that a court case ensued in which it was revealed that J.L. Knubley had in fact struck a journalist on the staff of the French newspaper, one Terrail de Vermont. He was convicted of assault and sentenced to 48 hours detention and fined 200 francs with costs. The report added: "As Terrail de Vermont left the court an indignant Englishman shook his fist at him and called him a lache (coward)."

BOYS BIRCHED

Three boys were each given six strokes of a birch rod after admitting theft of 12s from a master's desk at Keswick High School.

PEPPER'S GHOST

Mr E. Pryce's spectral opera company will open at the Oddfellow's Hall, Keswick, on Monday evening for six nights. The entertainment visited Keswick a few years ago and then gave unbounded satisfaction, not only in reference to the wonderful illusions but also to the very refined acting and singing of the artistes engaged. The company has been making a tour of Cumberland and has been very well received all round.

One week later it was reported: Mr E. Pryce's adaptation of the scientific illusion known as "Pepper's Ghost" to the purposes of drama and opera has been exhibited at the Oddfellow's Hall during the week. The chief pieces presented have been Dickens's "Christmas Carol," Gounod's "Faust" and Schiller's "Storm of Thoughts," and it is impossible to praise too highly the admirable management which obtains. The characters are cleverly sustained by the company of artistes, and the manipulation of the ghost illusion is simply perfect. The opportunity of seeing such a high class entertainment does not often occur in small towns and therefore the people who care for entertainments should not lose the chance now presented.

April 18

TRAGIC CASE OF OLD WOMAN WHO "TIRED OF EARTH"

An elderly woman was charged with attempting to commit suicide by cutting her throat with an old razor. The magistrates ordered her removal to Garlands Asylum, Carlisle. Though for some years the woman had been eccentric in her ways she became unquestionably unfit to live alone after the stroke with which she was afflicted a few months ago. Her memory had entirely gone and owing to her strange manner most of the persons for whom she worked as a charwoman had been obliged to discontinue her services. This preyed upon the old lady's mind and she became, as she expressed, "tired of earth."

Latterly she had no food except that which her neighbours gave her, although it is said she had a little hoard of money. She was taken to the asylum on Monday by the noon train.

The Main Street, Keswick. Showing bollards outside what was the Poor House and is now the Post Office. Drawing by Tom Wilson.

The Greta . . . a river runs through it

April 25th
"DERWENT" THE NEW FIRE ENGINE

This very important acquisition of the Local Board of Health arrived on Wednesday and is now stationed at the premises in Penrith road. A trial of its powers will be made shortly and the public will have an opportunity of judging upon its merits. For convenience of moving it is arranged either for horses in case of long distance, or hand drawing for short. Ten men and the driver can be accommodated with seats on the engine which carries also a ladder, hose, and a few other necessary implements. Its name "Derwent" is conspicuously painted on the hose box.

September 5th.
THIS HIDEOUS INFLOW OF FILTH

I have frequently had occasion to pass along a narrow roadway leading to the Forge cottages, and each time my nose has been assailed by a most fearful stench, proceeding apparently from a drain running across the road from the vicinity of the brewery on Penrith road.

I surmise that pigs were kept on these premises and their foul drainage, of an inky blackness, is conducted in an open sewer into the River Greta, to the fatal destruction of fish and, worse, seriously imperilling the health of the vicinity. Many school children constantly pass this way three or four times each day and I fully expect an outbreak of fever will, in this hot and dry weather, call the attention of the sanitary board – only when too late. As a fisherman myself I do bitterly regret to see such a fine river poisoned, not only by mine water, but, needlessly, by this hideous inflow of filth.
A SUFFERING VISITOR.

October 3rd
THE END OF ALL THINGS IS AT HAND

A young man named Joseph Akitt, who had advertised himself as a gentleman who would address a public meeting in the Oddfellows Hall on "The end of all things is at hand," was present at the appointed time on Saturday night. It was soon evident that the young fellow's mind was affected and that he would have been better in the charge of his friends than on a platform, as a butt for the jokes. The greater part of his audience soon left the hall, but a few remained behind, and after a time somebody turned off the gas and summarily closed the meeting.

Lower Main Street with Greta Bridge in the background.

1886

October 2nd
PLAYING AT SUICIDE

On Saturday night between eight and nine o'clock, a young man ran down Main Street bidding "good night" to everybody, invoking a blessing among them, and adding the information that he was going to drown himself. Two female relatives followed him and requested several people to stop him. But they did not do so, as probably they either thought that the young fellow was not in earnest or that he knew his own value best.

The delinquent pursued the uneven "tenor of his way" to Greta Bridge, crossed over and turned into the water at the place where sand is taken from the bed of the river. He went no more than knee deep and then stood, as if waiting for the water to rise and save him the trouble of lying down, or perhaps he feared to get too wet at once. The womens' cries brought two men to the bank. They called to the foolish fellow to come out but he heeded them not and braved the cold. Meanwhile they consulted what to do, as they saw no immediate danger of the extraordinary threat being carried into execution. One of the men remarked to the effect that though he felt as light as a cork he could not swim a foot. The other laughed because he saw no need of the exhibition of any feat of natation whatever.

At length they walked into the water and got hold of the amateur suicide whose passion had subsided with the reduction of the temperature and restored him safe and sound to his disconsolate female relatives. He was not satisfied to be merely called back; he desired to be fetched. A course of hydropathic treatment – a forced dip in the lake – would most likely complete the cure of his malady.

November 13th
AN OLD MAN'S FIRST TRIP TO LONDON

Mr Thos Atkinson, barber, who in a few days will complete his 77th year, took advantage of the recent cheap trip to pay his first visit to the Metropolis. He left here on Monday evening, 1st November at 7.30pm and arrived in London at 7 o'clock the next morning. A friend was in waiting and took him to lodgings secured at The Waverley Temperance Hotel.

He visited St Paul's Cathedral, Westminster Abbey and the exhibition. A "night cap" of real London stout was the climax of the first day's visit. The next day he went to the Tower, Docks and Bonded warehouses, Covent Garden Market, Trafalgar Square, Nelson's Monument, St James Park, Buckingham Palace, Thames Embankment, The Houses of Parliament and Cleopatra's Needle. He spent the night at The Adelphi Theatre where "Harbour Lights" had been playing for more than 300 times in succession. Friday morning saw him at Madame Tussaud's Waxworks. Of all the places he visited he liked this best.

From here the old gentleman made his way to Euston Station and, after a brief nap in the waiting room, took train at midnight for the journey home to Keswick, where he arrived at 11 o'clock on Saturday morning, quite fresh and struck into work at once.

(The newspaper subsequently reported that Thos Atkinson lived only a few more months. He died in April 1887 at the age of 77 years).

FOOTNOTE: Thos Atkinson is one of the characters on the Keswick street scene, next to his barbers pole. See page 255.

December 4th.

'I AM NOT DEAD AS SOME IMAGINE'

The writer and poet William Gaspey penned the following verse after hearing that a report of his 'death' had been circulated in the town and area:

Though, after long and weary years,
Little remains that life endears,
"Good natured friends" I am not dead
As some imagine they have read;
But both my health and strength retain,
Of time have nothing to complain,
Can perpetrate a pun or verse
And get along without a hearse.
In Shakespeare's lore I have been taught
"The wish is father to the thought"
And maybe those kind folks who spread
The pleasant news that I was dead,
Would not have much been put about
Had the sad tidings true turned out.
Be as it may I've no ill will
Since rumour's important to kill;
And when at length I bid adieu
To earth, and friends both old and new,
Not sorry for that sweet release
Which, ending trouble, brings us peace,
Those who despatched me prematurely
Ample amends will make most surely
If for my grace a flower they seek,
And of my memory kindly speak.

This amazing image of people outside their houses was taken on Lower Main Street directly opposite the Crosthwaite Parish Room. Picture courtesy of The George Fisher Collection.

December 11th

THE WEATHER

The changes of weather have been very trying to all but the most robust. Following that of temperature we have had quite a vicissitude of atmospheric pressure. Mr John Birkett, jeweller, has kindly furnished us with readings of his barometer and informs us that he has never before noticed pressure so low. This sudden and immense decrease of pressure was accompanied by strong wind and increased danger in the working of coal mines.

1887

April 23rd

THE LATRIGG FOOTPATH

We are informed that Mr J.J. Spedding, Greta Bank, has fenced across one of the roads up Latrigg, and that upon another he has caused young trees to be planted thickly.

June 4th

GOODBYE TO ALL MOUNTAIN PATHS

If Latrigg be permitted to be closed against the people – if there be the right to take that extreme course – goodbye to all mountain paths. Skiddaw will be next, then Helvellyn, Scawfell and the rest. Some flimsy excuse will be raised to the effect that the few stones on the top are being shifted about in such a reckless manner as to seriously interfere with the earth's centre of gravity, and that the safety of the world's population depends upon a proper restraint being exercised over their pleasures.

June 25th

KESWICK AND DISTRICT FOOTPATH PRESERVATION SOCIETY

The blocked footpath to Latrigg became a serious issue. The local people formed a protest association and determined to walk the path in question. On Latrigg they were met by a welcoming committee and a barrier.

"Tar was streaming under the gate," the newspaper reported, "and the heterogenous backing of timber, an old iron plough and other rubbish was coated with tar as thickly as it would stick from the bucketfuls which had been thrown at it. Besides this the gate had been chained and locked and a good length of the wall top had been tarred. The force of valiant men, who looked ready to do battle, stood within the field.

"The protestors removed the barriers as best they could and proceeded to the top of Latrigg."

A total of about 2,000 protestors went to the summit of Latrigg in October 1887. They went up by way of the Latrigg Terrace and returned via Spooney Green. Later in October it was reported that the landowner, Mr J.J. Spedding, had decided to take legal action against the Footpath Preservation Society (see 1888 reports for further developments).

November 12th

THE CAUSE OF PURITY

The Rev A.R.Goddard, in his magazine, *The Keswick Gleaner* has called attention to a matter which requires careful handling. He refers to the sad results which may follow a too dangerous liberty being given to young girls. There is need of the advice given. Last Sunday night, in Lake Road, I saw three or four young girls romping about among a lot of lads, and heard language which would not trip lightly from the tongue of innocence. A more careful parental surveillance may save a burden of shame and misery, and I am glad to echo a note of warning in the cause of purity.

November 19th

THE GRETA CLUB

Last week I felt it my duty to refer to the behaviour of some girls in the street. This week I should like to ask the young men who are members of the Greta Club if their dignity would be any the less if they came in and went out with less noise. There is never a meeting in the Battersby Hall that is not disturbed by banging doors or noise of some other kind. It may be important to know when one or another of the young gentlemen enters or leaves the building but those whose attention is occupied with less weightier matters upstairs would be glad to admit the fact, to save the said young men the trouble of stamping their feet or making a noise in any other of the orthodox ways of annoying a quiet assembly.

1888

February 4th
AN ECLIPSE OF THE MOON

The eclipse of the moon on Saturday night was witnessed here in the most favourable conditions for ordinary observers. The night was bright and a few fleecy clouds were passing between us and the moon about half an hour previous to the announced contact, and these reflected a coppery coloured halo. Gradually, as the face of the moon was covered by the shadow of the earth, darkness came upon the town, and the appearance of the moon through its veil, was a dark brownish red. The obscuration lasted a long time, and the phenomenon as a whole was one that does not often fall to the sight of wondering humanity.

March 12th
GIRL CARRIED AWAY IN THE RIVER

On Saturday last a young girl, named Shannon, lost her hat in the river by the Town's Field and she went into the water to get it out. As there was a fresh she was carried off her feet and brought down into the slack above Calvert Bridge. A neighbour saw her perilous position, and called attention of Mr D. Melvin, of The Twa Dogs Inn, to the circumstances. He at once ran to the river, got the girl out, and took her to his house where she was properly attended to.

May 26th
SOCCER PLAYER SINKS TO NEWS DEPTHS

On Wednesday afternoon the Blackburn Rovers football team went up the lake for a row, and as the water looked so inviting, Almond, the centre half back, decided to have a bathe. Without due calculation as to the depth he jumped into water too deep for a non-swimmer and was in danger of drowning. An oar thrown to him hit him on the head but fortunately did not hurt him severely. In the meantime one of his colleagues, who is a good swimmer, jumped into the water and helped Almond out little the worse for his mistake.

Blackburn Rovers played at Lower Fitz on Monday, May 21, 1888 and won 6-0.

June 9th
THE SIEGE OF LATRIGG

We are now within a measurable distance of the battle of the Law Courts in respect of the Siege of Latrigg. The Commission of Inquiry held on Wednesday was the preliminary call to arms and in the short interval before us it is necessary that our ammunition is got ready in plenty. I am informed that £2,000 will be necessary to meet an adverse decision. Shame that justice should be so dear!

If the Society (Keswick and District Footpath Preservation Society) win the Latrigg case – as I believe and hope they will – conclusions ought at once be tried for what are reasonably and honestly believed to be public rights on the Derwentwater estate. If, on the other hand, the case be lost, through want of support, Keswick may as well put the shutters up for our landed gentry will keep the county to themselves; yet a couple of yards will satisfy their needs at last.

June 30th
GREAT BATTLE DRAWS NEAR

Our great battle will be decided one way or the other at Carlisle next week, but I hope the Footpath Society will be successful. Interest which it may be stated Keswick has aroused in footpath questions has been exhibited up and down the country in a remarkably striking way, and one need not be a prophet to say that legislation will be passed in favour of greater freedom than is felt at present.

Saturday, July 14th
COMPROMISE IN BATTLE OVER FELL RIGHTS

The settlement arrived at during the Latrigg case was that "the Association abandoning the claim to the Terrace road while Mr Spedding would recognise the right of way to the top of Latrigg by Spooney Green Lane and the zig-zag. Each party to pay their own costs."

Left: The River Greta where it flows through Lower Fitz Park. The YHA buildings, in white, are in the top right of the image. Below: Keswick Vale by J. Douglas, 1894. Drawing courtesy of Keswick Museum and Art Gallery

September 1st.
"BRUTAL BARBED WIRE FENCES" ON LATRIGG

Mr J. J. Spedding subsequently erected fencing on the top of Latrigg to keep walkers in a particular area, not permitting them to stray from the path. They were described in the newspaper as "brutal barbed fences which outrage the feelings of all decent people and sully the face of the earth."

The writer, in an editorial comment, did not pull any punches: "Mr Spedding has a strong liking for barbed wire fences. Wherever he can possibly put up a length he does so. I am informed that he even had a piece (not yet barbed) fixed partly into the river.

"Barbed wire fences adjoining highways have been held to be illegal in Scotland, and common sense would say they are equally so in England. I heard of a gentleman stranger having his overcoat torn by the fence on Latrigg a few days ago, and later of a lady visitor's dress. They will go away with pleasant feelings to this and towards this Yankee innovation. The best plan would be (for landowners) to clear out of the country and settle down by themselves in the heart of Africa, or some uninhabited island, or make a cocoon of their barbed wire and go into chrysalis state till they emerge into the world again with better feelings."

September 22nd

WOMAN INJURED HAND ON BARBED WIRE

Last week Mrs E. Long, when returning from a journey up Latrigg, forgot for a moment the barbed wire fence and sustained a painful injury to one of her hands in clutching at the wire for support while crossing the boggy portion of the path. We have heard of several cases of injury to dress through being caught on the barbs.

November 17th

RUSTICS ON HOLIDAY

The presence of a goodly number of male and female farm servants in the town on Saturday last was the only evidence of the fair time, up till afternoon, when a couple of the "three-balls-a-penny" gentlemen rigged up their apparatus for extracting superfluous coppers from the rustics on holiday. Street hiring is not very extensively practised at Keswick nowadays; but still there is a little. Known men get £10 to £12 for the coming half year; boys from £5 to £6.10s; females from £6 to £8.

Later on rain fell very heavily for a time and those who had had enough of the day went home, while others bent on further enjoyment went to the dances held at some of the inns. There was not much drunkenness.

November 17th

FISTICUFFS OVER WATER

We hear that the other day a mining dispute occurred between the employees at Brandelhow and Barrow mines, over the water at Stair Mill, and that in an argument of fisticuffs the Barrow men proved to be the better reasoners.

1889

September 20th

A VOICE FROM THE ANTIPODES

Before the late poet laureate, Mr Southey, died, I had frequently been on foot and on horseback to the top of Latrigg by way of Calvert Bridge (which was haunted in those days) passing three road ends (also a haunted place) on past Mr Spedding's and, if I remember right, through a gateway on a road fenced in certainly on the one side where the climb commenced. I must have gone up dozens of times and was never interfered with by anyone nor did any of us in those days have a sense of being trespassers. But then at that time there was more of the spirit of "live and let live" than that which characterises modern days, when everybody tries to grasp what they can.

I have been in every corner of the globe, have gazed on the mighty mountains of the Andes, have seen the lovely islands of the western Antilles. Have been struck by the marvellous scenery of the New Zealand sounds, charmed by the almost magical islands of the Pacific, and have travelled through the most celebrated districts of this great Australian country, but nowhere have I met with the exquisite loveliness spread out with so free a hand as meets the gaze of the spectator standing on a bright, clear day on the summit of Latrigg or Castle Head. It is getting on fast for forty years since I enjoyed those scenes, but my recollection of them is as vivid as if they dated only from last year. AN OLD KESWICKIAN. Sydney, New South Wales.

March 23rd

A PLEA TO MR SPEDDING

I continue to cherish a deferred hope that Mr Spedding will wake to the fact that the best pleasures of life increase the more they are shared, and so soon as he does he will want everybody to partake with him of the bounteous feast which nature has spread for his invitation. Our allotted time above the turf is too short to be marred by constant fretting and fuming, and really, if we are to live in interminable suspicion, the sooner we each get below the latter (turf) then the better it will be.

March 23rd

FLOWER BOX STUNS CLERK

On Wednesday evening Mr Daniel Crosthwaite, chief clerk of the Post Office, met with an accident through the storm. One of the window flower boxes at the Bank Tavern (formerly The Wagon and Horses) was dislodged from its fastenings and in falling it struck Mr Crosthwaite on the head. Fortunately his hat was a hard felt one and protected his head; but he was knocked down and stunned somewhat, and a large skin wound was inflicted upon his left hand.

1890

January 11th

LET THERE BE LIGHT

It had been commonly understood that the electric light would be turned on in Keswick on Monday evening last and although the weather was rainy and uncomfortable the Market Square was thronged by people anxious to see the new illuminent. Though as early as six o'clock had been named it had gone nine before the lamps at the Royal Oak Hotel, Messrs Graham, Mr Cartmell's, Mr Townley's, Mr Gatey's, Mr Birkett's and Mr Wilson's simultaneously shone out in striking brilliance. The light was beautiful and steady as a rock. The untoward day had retarded the work of the linesmen, but when the current was put on the result was most satisfactory. We are informed that already lamps have been applied for to nearly the full extent of the power available.

New developments. The silver bridge (foreground) and in the background (far right) the Railway Hotel (now the Keswick Hotel) and the railway station and goods yard.

January 11th
'LIFE IS A RIVER'

The public tea meeting of the Keswick Co-operative Society held in the Victoria Hall: "In spite of the unfortunate nature of the day about 250 sat down to a substantial meat tea. Three long tables had been erected for the people of Keswick, Borrowdale and Threlkeld, respectively, and were presided over by ladies selected from each locality. The committee's appeal for help to bake the bread, buns, cakes etc, to boil the hams and beef and for waiters and carvers, had been liberally responded to and there was no lack of willing assistance. After tea the tables were removed and the large room was well filled with an appreciative and attentive audience. An attractive musical programme had been arranged. This included the song 'Life is a River' sung by a Mr Richardson. Apparently it was "tastefully rendered and much appreciated."

September 20th
THE PHONOGRAPH AT KESWICK

This most wonderful invention of Mr T.A. Edison was exhibited at the Drill Hall on Tuesday afternoon and evening by Mr C.R.C. Steytler. The machine excited considerable interest and wonder by its marvellous reproduction of all sorts of sound. It is well that Mr Edison lives in the nineteenth century. Such a piece of mechanism in darker times would most probably have been thought positive proof of a league with the author of evil, and efforts to reform the inventor might have commenced at the stake.

September 20th
LEAD KINDLY LIGHT

On September 12th, at 12.45pm, as four persons (two of them resident in Keswick) were on their way from the top of Scawfell Pike, with the intention of returning by the Piers' Gill route, just as they reached that part of the path where the road diverges to the gill they were astonished and delighted to see in the mist below, lit up by the brilliant afternoon sun, a beautiful and perfectly formed luminous ring set full against the white mist which filled the ravine. The colours were clear and prismatic all round the margin and circumference of the ring, while the centre was beautifully white and the shadows of the four tourists seemed literally to walk into the middle of it, having a halo round the whole, as definite and sacred as ever surrounded the heads of saints in illuminated manuscript or aids to devotion in quiet cathedral aisle.

The wonderful spectacle continued, after being first noticed, for about six minutes – sufficiently long to enable the observers to be quite sure that the four figures thrown upon what appeared to be a twelve or fourteen feet disc, were their own. This was ascertained by going through slight extension motions faithfully followed by the moving shadows within the halo; then gently the beautiful circle faded away, but leaving its "memory green" to be carried like a "kindly light" "oe'r moor and torrent – along the narrow, ragged" path of life.

September 27th
'SPECTRE OF THE BROCKEN'

The optical phenomenon lately observed by the party on Scawfell Pike was simply an example of the so-called "Spectre of the Brocken." Although in name associated with the well known mountain in the Harz district, it is not peculiar to any one mountain locally. I saw it myself once in my life, and that was on top of Snowdon, very early one summer's morning. For a considerable time my form was reflected on a screen of mist, and framed in a sort of halo, but which presented but little colour. I believe the sun's rays came on my back through some opening in a bank of clouds. I was, if my theory be correct, a living slide (so to speak) in a solar magic lantern. My impression is that these "spectres" are frequently seen by shepherds and others who pass much of their time in the mountains, but that they are seldom reported. A far more remarkable phenomenon (if one must use that somewhat vague word) is the appearance of horsemen among the crags of Souter Fell, and which has been on several occasions observed by persons of undoubted veracity. My father saw this when out shooting, some 35 or 40 years ago. A man who was with him saw it also - J.R. Campbell.

September 27th
MR ABRAHAM'S LAKELAND ENTERTAINMENT

Mr G. P. Abraham has given a series of his popular entertainments at the Victoria Hall. The entertainment is enhanced in local characteristics by a capital set of music stones, which Mr Abraham has completed only this year. He and his two sons perform a selection of pieces on the instrument at each entertainment and they invariably meet with flattering reception. The instrument contains upwards of sixty stones and the compass is five octaves with semi tones.

November 29th
HOUSES UNFIT FOR HABITATION

(Letter to the Editor): I am pained to learn that Keswick is in such an unsatisfactory condition and that there are so many houses unfit for habitation crowded in close streets, surrounded as it is by so much open country with the clear streams and fresh health-giving breezes from the mountains.

Keswick Museum and Art Gallery on Station Road.

1891

May 2nd

"DEADLY EMANATIONS FROM A SLAUGHTER HOUSE"

A comment piece appeared in the newspaper on the subject of part of Keswick town centre having been declared an "unhealthy area." This referred to the back of Main Street including courts and yards and the space from New Street to Barron's Court together with Back Lane and tenements on either side.

The writer berated the local authority for its lack of action and criticised the reluctance of local proprietors to be more altruistic. The writer went on: "It is a pity that they (landed proprietors) do not remember that while enjoying the scent of flowers and the glorious sunshine from their own happily placed mansions, that their poor brothers and sisters have no sunshine, literal or figurative, in their wretched homes, such as many a rich man would be ashamed to have for his dogs or horses, and that the odours that come to those poor folks' nostrils are perchance the deadly emanations from a slaughter-house. Nature has done much for Keswick; it is possibly the most beautifully-situated town in England; but of the town itself we can only say that it is ugly, built without the least taste or judgement. But need this continue? With a little public spirit, with a little unselfishness, the town might grow from ugliness to beauty, from comparative unhealthiness to become one of the healthiest towns in the kingdom."

May 23rd

AN ENGLISH TRAMP

An elderly tramp, who gave the name of George Brown, was brought up at the Keswick Police Court on Thursday, on the charge of being drunk and disorderly in Main Street the previous night. As he would not take the warnings of the police he was locked up. He said he wanted to see an English magistrate and the interview resulted in a fourteen days visit to an English gaol.

June 13th

MISS EVERARD'S COOKERY CLASSES

It has been found more convenient for attendance to hold on Tuesday evenings, at the Parish room, at 8 o'clock, the cookery classes conducted by Miss Everard.

Miss Everard is an accomplished teacher and has the happy quality of being able to impart her knowledge to her pupils. Health, as well as economy, is so largely dependent upon the right preparation of food that nobody can afford to ignore the correct methods of cookery, and we would earnestly persuade as many as can possibly attend to take advantage of the exceptional chance afforded by Miss Everard's engagements in Keswick.

October 10th

SLAUGHTERHOUSE AT SHOULDER OF MUTTON INN

Keswick Local Board. Nuisances. Recommended that notice be served on Mr Turner, Shoulder of Mutton Inn, to remove pigsty and to abate nuisance caused by slaughterhouse.

1892

August 6th

A NATIVE AND YET A STRANGER

We hear that on Wednesday last a Keswick wife between sixty and seventy years of age was on Friar's Crag for the first time in her life, although bred and born in Keswick. Such a fact can hardly be credited, but the old lady herself told our informant it was the truth.

August 20th

NEWSPAPER'S FIRST PHOTOGRAPHIC IMAGE

The first black and white photograph to appear in the pages of the *Lakes Visitor and Keswick Guardian* newspaper was of the Mary Hewetson Cottage Hospital which had been opened only the day before. The photograph was taken by Mr G.P. Abraham.

September 24th

A RUNAWAY HORSE

Yesterday afternoon a horse belonging to Mr Wallace took fright in the station yard and bolted. It was yoked to a carriage but the shaft pin gave way and the horse galloped as hard as it could along Station Road, colliding with a carriage belonging to Mr J. Wilson, and doing some damage. The cross bar of the shafts was broke, and as the horse turned at the Royal Oak corner the near shaft struck Mr Hilton's plate glass window and broke it. Continuing its wild career down Main Street the horse turned into Atkinson's Court, behind the Bank Tavern, where it was caught.

September 24th

THE GIANT PENCIL, NO LESS

An extraordinary feat was performed at Mr J.W. Grisdale's black lead pencil depot, Lake Road, by Mr Taylor, police constable, Ecclefechan, who cleverly wrote his name and address with Mr Grisdale's giant pencil which measures 4ft 6in long, 1ft 9in in circumference and weighs 2st 10lb. The dexterous performance excited some interest for the pencil is probably the largest in the world.

November 5th

"ONE OF THE WEEDS IN HUMANITY'S GARDEN"

At the Keswick Police Court on Tuesday, Robert Rigg, one of the weeds in humanity's garden at Keswick, was brought up on the charge of sleeping out. PC Thornburrow apprehended the prisoner in an outhouse near Fieldside the same morning. Tobacco and matches were the only property found upon him when searched. Rigg, who has been several times punished for similar offences, was committed to Carlisle for a month with hard labour. Not many weeks ago he was found in an outhouse in the same neighbourhood in a very weak condition, and he was sent to the workhouse at Cockermouth, from which place he came as soon as he could move about fairly well, and speedily relapsed into his old ways, never being able to afford food and lodgings while he had the means to prevent beer becoming sour.

Drawings courtesy of Keswick Museum and Art Gallery.

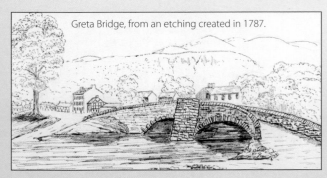

Greta Bridge, from an etching created in 1787.

King's Head Court with the Moot Hall towering over it in the background. The court was the home of Jonathan Otley who occupied rooms at the top of the stairs.

November 12th

MISS CAINE'S PROGRESS

Miss Hall Caine (sister of the famous author who has taken up his residence with us at Keswick) is steadily making her way into the front rank of celebrated actresses. Her portrait, with a brief notice of her achievements on the stage, occupies the first page of the ninth issue of the *Daily Programme*. The writer of the notice says: "Miss Hall Caine's theatrical career has been short. But she has already achieved something, and will do more as she works on; for she is an artist who loves her art, who toils and slaves without remission. And upon such, Thalia is wont to bestow her favours." For the record Miss Hall Caine's Christian name was Lily.

November 12th

THE GUNPOWDER PLOT CELEBRATION

The fifth of November was celebrated by a much larger display of fireworks than ever before were discharged by the youth of Keswick. This was due not so much to commemorate the deliverance of King James I and his Parliament from the machinations of Guy Fawkes, as to the fact that Mr Chaplin had lain in a stock of squibs and crackers, rockets and bombs, and lots of other concoctions known to the pyrotechnist.

November 22nd

CHAPLIN FINED

Arthur Chaplin was fined 10 shillings for selling fireworks to a boy under 13. Nine youths were fined for unlawfully throwing fireworks in the street.

December 17th

"A DEVILISH INVENTION"

An editorial on the subject of war read as follows: "What a travesty of civilisation – to say nothing of the boasted religious character of nations – is that constant effort to outstrip each other in the strife for the means of maiming and killing! Saving life is counted as nothing in comparison with destroying. One learns that 'highly satisfactory experiments' have been conducted at Silloth this week with a new smokeless powder, the devilish invention of a French officer, and which surpasses all other explosives of a similar character. Appalling as were the revolts of the Franco-German war, one shudders at the contemplation of what the slaughter will be when next the world is cursed with war."

1893

February 25th

BOBBIN MILL DESTROYED BY FIRE

The newspaper carried an in depth report of a serious fire at Low Briery which virtually destroyed the Bobbin Mill. "Two or three of the men had narrow escapes, for their clothes were somewhat caught by the fire." The roof fell in and the building and machinery could not be saved. The damage was estimated at £4,400. Neither the mill nor the contents were fully insured. Between 60 and 70 were employed at the mill and it was feared that they would lose their jobs until the mill could be restored. Three weeks later, on March 11, it was reported that the mill was to be rebuilt and that the workers would be employed in the process.

June 10th

IN SEARCH OF HEALTH

I came here to enjoy this beautiful part of the Lake District and in search of health, but the first day I entered a public convenience opposite the boat landings I found one of the most abominable, filthy places ever heard of. Who ever is responsible for this nuisance ought to be prosecuted, considering the threatened visitation of infectious diseases. This is sad neglect and ought to be remedied at once – perhaps the proper authorities will see to it now.

July 8th

"THE PHILOSOPHY OF BETTY CWOATES"

A couple of dialect readings – "Betty Cwoates' advice til her dowter t'neet afooar her weddin," and "A Bit o' Betty Cwoates' mind," have just been published by Mr J. Telford under the title of *The Philosophy of Betty Cwoates*, copies 2d each, may be purchased at the *Guardian* office, or at the railway bookstall.

August 19th

"SWEET TORTURES OF BUSKERS"

The promenade band has fled. The little man with great confidence has led away his trumpets and fiddles. Perhaps it is well that he has done so, for the natives were beginning to feel there was somewhat of a monotony in the strain after sweet sounds, and further they were tiring of the excess civility with which their "small encouragements for the band" were returned.

At the beginning of the season when there were two bands scraping away for public favour, on what must of necessity have been small takings, it seemed likely then, between the odd visits of the German soul distressers, barrel organs, mechanical pianos, and the rival fiddling and tootling of the two claimants to the title of the Keswick Promenade Band, that the good people of Keswick would be played to death. They have, fortunately, survived the sweet torture and are now, it is hoped, enjoying a brief respite from the rasping of cat gut and the blowing through trumpets of brass.

How much longer will a tender British public provide half pence to make misery for themselves?

A popular café in Keswick Market Place was Storms Café with its first floor windows opening up onto the market.

September 2nd
NOT FOR THOSE THICK AS PLANKS

Mr Ross-Scott, the young society entertainer and satirist, is to give two of his immensely humorous and music recitals in the Victoria Hall. People intellectually slow need not go to hear him for they will fail in grasping the depth of his witty and sarcastic hits, but those who can appreciate him will find his performances a delightful intellectual treat.

August 19th
VESUVIUS ON DERWENT STREET

In the neighbourhood of Derwent Street and Lake Road there have been several upheavals of the road through explosions of gas ignited by electricity from the underground wires. The explosions were sufficient to scatter the macadam in a way which frightened the inhabitants in close proximity to the place of the upheaval.

November 11th
TEETH PULLING FOR THE POOR

An advertisement appeared in the newspaper which announced that Mr V.C. Mallan, dental surgeon (of London) had decided to attend daily at The Queen's Hotel, Keswick. Part of the advertisement read: "Mr Valleck Mallan particularly wishes to impress upon the public that the teeth supplied by him are fixed without the least pain – the extraction of stumps not being necessary – and also the teeth are fitted without large and bulky frames or plates, upon the best of the American system."

Not only that, the advertisement added: "Mr Mallan, during his visit, will be pleased to extract teeth free of charge, from 10 to 11 in the morning, for those who are too poor and not able to pay a fee."

1894

April 14th
SWALLOWS IN FLIGHT

While two fishermen from Brigham were plying their art they were agreeably surprised to observe a quartet of swallows in flight. This is a few days earlier than common. In the year 1878 the late Mr W. Greenip recorded their arrival on the 7th of April. In 1880 they were as late as April 26th.

The impressive building in the foreground to the right is still there. It was formerly the Trustees Savings Bank and is currently a café.
The other buildings, behind the bikes and the pram, are long gone and where they once stood is a road leading to Heads Road and the Derwent Close housing development.

June 2nd
ALL THE FUN OF THE FAIR

It would seem that Keswick is a happy hunting ground for the showman and steam hobby horse proprietor, or they would not linger so long in our midst. Last week there were steam hobby horses, swing boats, a waxwork show, shooting galleries, and other attractions in the Sawpit Field. Owing to the combined efforts of two barrel organs, one being constantly turned by steam, the Friday evening service at the Parish Room had to be abandoned.

In the circus field over the bridge things were even brisker. There are still there two sets of hobby horses each with an organ, a conjuror's show, a shooting gallery, and several "establishments" for testing skill in the pitching of rings and throwing of balls, and for the extraction of pence from that class of people who are credited with an early parting from their money.

The din at times has been something appalling. Some faint perception of the noise may be imagined when it is said that the barrel organs, each grinding out a different tune, are occasionally supplemented by a loud toned bell, steam whistle and a big drum. The residents in the immediate neighbourhood must have nerves of iron to be able to endure this nightly horror.

November 10th
ELECTRIC SHOCK TREATMENT

On Thursday night owing to the breakage of one of the electric light wires crossing Main Street near the Royal Oak Hotel, quite a number of people, and dogs also, were affected by electric shocks. The broken wire got in contact and the current was carried by an iron down pipe and spread by the rainwater on the pavement. It is said that a boy named Robinson had to roll off the parapet by Miss Adamson's shop, unable to get away otherwise.

Picture courtesy of The George Fisher Collection.

The Greta . . . a river runs through it

November 17th
"SOMETHING TRULY MARVELLOUS"

The following is an extract from a letter from a literary man of Boston (US) addressed to Mr Baddeley: "I must ask leave to express myself very freely on the amazing attractiveness of the English Lake District. I am familiar with most of the countries of Europe, including Italy and Greece. I have travelled extensively in my own country and am familiar with the most beautiful parts of New England, Virginia, Kentucky, Tennessee and North Carolina, and I know the Rocky Mountains which lie within the borders of Colorado, New Mexico and Utah; but never anywhere, in Europe or America, have I found a district so limited in space and which yet contains so much beauty and so much variety of scenery as does your Lake District. It is something truly marvellous."

December 8th
ABRAHAM BROTHERS CONQUER NEEDLE ROCK

Messrs G.D. and A.P. Abraham were successful in making the ascent of the Needle Rock, Great Gable on Monday last. We understand that the feat has been essayed by several Keswick climbers, and although the rock has been discovered since 1884, this, to the best of our knowledge, is the first time the top has been reached by local men.

1895

February 16th
"NEVER IN THE MEMORY OF MAN"

The frost continues with great intensity and causes much inconvenience as well as distress. It may safely be said that never within the memory of man has there been such a time for keen frost. On Tuesday some of the blown timber on Derwent Island was dragged across the ice by a horse. The Greta is frozen and the skaters have been able to run from the weir in the Fitz up to Brigham by climbing the weir near the railway. All kinds of birds are becoming tame through hunger.

April 13th
SAM HAGUE 'DIES' ON STAGE

This troupe visited Keswick on Monday and gave a performance at the pavilion. There was a bumper house. It is said that Sam Hague has not been at Keswick for 25 years and it would be well for another such interval to elapse before he comes again, in order to afford the public a chance to forget.

April 20th.
HOW MANY MORE WILL DIE?

In the name of our common humanity how many more victims does the Urban District Council require to have sacrificed before it will take any steps to remedy the present shameful condition of things throughout the town? The repeated and earnest warnings of competent authorities, the quite recent outbreaks of scarlet fever in Lake Road and Station Street, seem to have had no effect in rousing their slumbering energies. Will the seizure of an entire family in Stanger Street, and the death of one of them, have no better result than the previous warnings?

What single practical step have they taken or are they contemplating to prevent the frequent recurrence of these outbreaks for which the town is now gaining an unenviable notoriety? Have the drains in Lake Road been examined and set right? Have the houses long ago condemned in Back Lane been demolished? Are Frying Pan Square and other congested areas about the town at present in a sanitary condition?

April 27th
BOYS SAVED FROM DROWNING IN MILL RACE AND RIVER

On Tuesday evening a boy, named John Williamson, while playing on the edge of the mill-race in Penrith Road, accidentally fell into the water. The cries of his companion attracted the attention of Mr Robert Wren, carter, who happened to be near, and he promptly got the boy out. He suffered little worse than a wetting.

The same evening a boy of about five years of age, son of Mr Geo Whittam, gas stoker, accidentally fell over the wall into the river at High Hill, where the current is rather swift. It was fortunate that the accident was observed by Mr George Birkett who went into the river and rescued the lad from his perilous position.

May 18th
GENTLEMAN WITH CANE FELLS RUNAWAY HORSE

Yesterday (Friday) morn some excitement was caused by a runaway horse, the property of Mr Richardson, butcher, Southey Street. The horse's bridle had been removed to give it opportunity to feed and for some reason it started off with the cart up Church Street, down St John's Street, across the Upper Market Square and turned down the street, narrowly escaping a run into Mr Strong's shop window. Goods from the cart were scattered here and there along the route. While the horse was coming at full speed, a gentleman with his cane struck it between the ears and felled it. In its fall the animal hurt its knees somewhat severely and made its mouth bleed.

Summer days. Not sure of the exact location for this photograph but it is either Stoney on Town's Field or at the Hewletts on Longtown Field above Low Briery. I am more inclined to think it is the latter.

HE, SHE, IT

One of Mr Weedon Grossmith's companies played 'The New Boy' at the Pavilion on Monday and Tuesday evenings. The comedy was preceded each night by the farce 'He, She, It.' A moderate house only rewarded the company on Monday and the attendance on Tuesday was disheartening. Mr H. Hallowell (FRCO – Fellowship Diploma in organ playing) played selections on the pianoforte during the interval and was warmly applauded.

1896

February 8th
SLEEPING IN A HAY SHED

On Tuesday Richard Greenip and an elderly man named John Ibbotson, were brought before two magistrates on the charge of being found sleeping in a hay shed at Briar Rigg at 1am on the same day. Greenip was committed to Carlisle gaol for one month with hard labour. The other prisoner, who was suffering from rheumatism and bronchitis, was ordered to be sent to the workhouse.

February 15th
LAND OF THE PAUPERS

In Cumberland there were on the 1st of last July 1,237 indoor (those in workhouses etc) and 5,659 outdoor paupers, a total of 6,896, an increase of 78 on the previous year.

May 30th
A PLEA FOR THE INDOOR PAUPERS

It is most desirable that earnest support should be given to our Keswick guardians in their endeavour to obtain for the inmates of the workhouse at Cockermouth the right to a few hours freedom from the confinement and necessary restraints of the 'house' so as to enable them to enjoy intercourse with their friends and walks in the streets and country, at least once a week.

April 18th
RUNAWAY HORSE AT GRETA BRIDGE

Yesterday afternoon as the last of the circus people were nearing the halting place at High Hill Farm, the weight of the wagon appeared to get the better of the horse as it was going down the incline from Greta Bridge. The man at the horse's head did all he could to hold back and drew the animal towards the fence / bank, against which the wagon wheels came with the result that the off fore wheel was broken, and let the concern down. The shafts pin was shaken out and the horse started off, trailing the shafts.

A gentleman stranger, seeing the horse and wagon coming at a great rate, turned in to the bank for safety, but unfortunately he was caught by the body of the wagon and had one leg jammed against the bank. The driver was also held by the wagon but only sustained a slight cut on the face. The gentleman was taken into the farmhouse by Messrs J.H. Wilson and M. Stamper, members of the Ambulance Brigade, and they afterwards removed him in a carriage to the Royal Oak Hotel where Dr Crawford was called to examine the leg.

The horse, in running away, upset a perambulator in which two children were sitting. The ironwork of the perambulator was bent but the youngsters were not injured. Meanwhile, the horse ran into the orchard and is said to have jumped over the fence onto the Howrahs footpath and careered on towards Portinscale. When it was captured it was found that one of the shafts had been broken, but the horse itself was little the worse for its escapade.

NOTE: At this time horses and carriages, especially of the runaway variety, were an ever-present danger in the town and surrounding countryside. In addition to genuine accidents of the type described above, there were criminal offences called 'furious driving' and also 'drunkenness while in the charge of a horse.'

It also begs the question – which is the more dangerous, an unsafe motorist in the 21st Century or a runaway horse and cart in the 19th? Probably the former in view of the potential these days for multiple fatalities on the road; although, having said that, a runaway horse and wagon coming towards you at full pelt must have been a frightening prospect. Not to mention its collision with a perambulator containing two children. Sadly, children had limbs amputated as a result of accidents involving horses and carts, some while attempting a free ride on a footplate.

June 27th
THE MISERIES OF A MUCH-MARRIED MAN

On Monday, Tuesday and Thursday evenings (the latter being by request) in The Queen of the Lakes pavilion, Mr Terris' Burlesque Company played "The Miseries of a Much-Married Man." The piece throughout was of mirthful character and afforded much amusement to the audiences. The company included some good dancers and singers. Wretchedly poor houses must have depressed the spirits of the performers.

July 4th
PREVENTION OF CRUELTY

Under the "Prevention of Cruelty to Children" Act, a man was jailed for 14 days for allowing a boy under 11 to be in Station Street, Keswick, selling lavender seed. The mother took charge of the children, seven in number.

August 15th
DRUNK AND DISORDERLY TRAMP

At the police court on Monday a tramp named David Collins was brought up in custody, charged with having been drunk and disorderly on Saturday night. The magistrates, Messrs Crosthwaite and Carrick, discharged the prisoner on his promise to leave the town at once.

The pencil works which once stood opposite Lower Fitz Park. Drawing by Tom Wilson.

BANKS & COMPANY
GRETA PENCIL WORKS ESTABLISHED 1832

SHOCKING BUSINESS AT MR GATEY'S SHOP

Some consternation was caused on Tuesday evening through the escape of electricity from one of the main cables above Mr Gatey's shop in Market Square. The paint on a rain spout was burned and appearances were such as to justify the thought that a conflagration was being started. Mr Strong went out with a can of water to pour upon the burning matter and he received an electric shock as the steam from the can established a connection between him and the electric current.

The electricity was spreading over a larger surface than had been expected, for a little girl about three years old got her left hand upon an inch iron pipe which carries the water from the cornice above Mr Gatey's shop. The child commenced to scream and the attention of Mrs T. White was attracted to it. Mrs White assumed that the little one had got its fingers fast and she ran to its help.

Naturally she got hold of the child to pick it up and, in doing so, received a shock which all but knocked her down and compelled her to drop the child which fell with its head on the pavement. The flesh on the child's little finger appeared to be burned to the bone between the knuckle and middle joint and the backs of other fingers were also badly burned. Mrs White was also painfully burned on the left wrist. There was a hole as if she had touched a piece of hot metal and her arm was quite numbed.

PONY ALMOST DROWNED IN MILL RACE

On Tuesday afternoon Mr W. Long's son was leading manure with the horse and cart, and when near the Millfield Gardens he turned to get out of the way of a conveyance coming along the road. The pony backed too much and the wheel of the cart caught one of the millrace fence posts which snapped "like a carrot." As the embankment is very steep, the cart went back down into the millrace, pulling the pony with it, a drop of nearly 9ft. The boy was at the pony's head but he let go to save himself and rushed off for help.

Mr W. Long, Mr J. Clark and Mr Olvanhill were quickly on the spot and it was well they were. The pony had a narrow escape from drowning since its head was under water, held down by one of the shafts. Messrs Long and Clark got into the race and liberated the pony and they got it on the road again opposite Millfield House. A number of men, with ropes, pulled the cart out after the sluice had been put down and the race run dry; but it was a work of some difficulty.

The fence has not been in good condition of late, indeed it may be said to have been dangerous. After this demonstration, Mr Marshall (landowner) may possibly see his way to a more substantial erection.

October 17th
DOWNHILL RACERS

(Letter to the Editor): Can any of your readers inform me what is the limit of speed in riding down hill? Riders occasionally come down the steep hill on the Ambleside road, quite near to the town, at full speed, which seems extremely dangerous both to the rider and to persons – especially children – and animals on the road at the time. It will be remembered that tobogganing down this hill was stopped as being dangerous and I think police will find the new danger also needs suppression.

1897

June 19th
"THE QUALITY OF MERCY WAS NOT STRAINED"

Five lady visitors to Borrowdale, Edith Rigby, Annie Taylor, Agnes D Routledge, Mary Beesley and Alice Raynor, were summoned for riding bicycles without lights.

The clerk reported to the bench that he had received a letter in which the defendants had pleaded guilty to a breach of the law. The writer (Mrs Rigby, of Preston) stated that they pleaded for leniency because "the distance was temptingly short and the night unusually light," and they rode very slowly. There was a postscript to the letter, a quotation from Portia's address in 'The Merchant of Venice' – "In the course of justice none of us should see salvation."

Police Sergeant Dixon deposed that he came across the defendants between Grange Bridge and the Borrowdale Hotel at about 11pm. It was not a dark night but lamps should have been lighted at about 9.38.

"The quality of mercy was not strained" in as much as there were unfortunate precedents and the defendants were fined, as other ladies have been, 10s each including costs.

The newspaper excelled itself with another report of a young woman from Stockton on Tees who was fined 10s for riding a bicycle without a lamp. 'ANOTHER FOOLISH VIRGIN' was the marginally politically incorrect headline!

BONFIRE ON SKIDDAW TO CELEBRATE QUEEN VICTORIA'S DIAMOND JUBILEE

Not withstanding the heavy clouds still hung upon Skiddaw, I noticed a number of the Keswick Fire Brigade, the captain of the brigade (Mr Hull) Canon Rawnsley and others making the best of their way up Latrigg about six o'clock, carrying their rockets and coloured fire, evidently determined on a Jubilee bonfire (a celebration of the Diamond Jubilee on June 22, 1897, the 60th year of the reign of Queen Victoria). At five minutes to ten, someone sent up a rocket that exploded with a loud report, and rockets leapt up in answer from far Scawfell, from Helvellyn, from Blencathra, from Catbells, and from Grisedale Pike.

Another rocket sailed up and broke into a star of light that floated like a balloon of electric brightness, and we knew that 10 o'clock had come. There was a little pause, for the fire would not catch on. But now one of the tar barrels blazed as if the bellows of Eolus (ruler of winds in Greek mythology) were urging the flame from below, and like a huge torch the great pile shot into flame. It was answered by the fire on the "Great Man" and the huge plain beneath us seemed suddenly to twinkle into starry beauty.

Never was more heartily sung "God Save the Queen" than round that Skiddaw bonfire. At half past ten red light was burned. The rose of England would flash its love and loyalty to the Scottish Border, and three rockets, in symbol of the United Kingdom of Scotland, Ireland and England, sailed up and broke in stars of multi-coloured light. All the mountain heights round, by careful pre-arrangement, answered.

Left: Woolpack Yard from Back lane and Hudspiths' School. Drawing by Tom Wilson.

July 31st

THIBETIAN ATTENDANTS AT THE CONVENTION

Miss Annie Taylor, with her two Thibetian attendants have been the observed of all observers in the streets of Keswick during the (religious) convention. Mr and Mrs Pontsu – so unique in their picturesque oriental costumes and so unlike ordinary mortals of the Anglo Saxon type – created quite a sensation both amongst visitors and natives. Miss Taylor's work in connection with the Thibetian Pioneer Mission reads more like romance than real life, and might be a fitting complement to the "Acts of the Apostles."

August 28th

'SENSATIONAL' ENDING

To end this selection of reports for 1897 on a disturbing note, the newspaper reported, on August 28, that one young man, aged 32, committed suicide in what it described as a "sensational manner." He drank sheep dip.

1898

September 3rd

THE SAILOR AND THE WIFE

Food for gossip has been found this week in the reported elopement of a young sailor and the wife of a working man in the immediate neighbourhood. The runaways went to Liverpool, and the young man introduced the woman to friends as his wife; but the truth came out through a letter of congratulation to the sailor's mother, who indignantly telegraphed information that the woman was the wife of another and had left a family of four children.

After this it is said the erring woman had to leave her temporary home hurriedly, and that a pressing invitation from one of Her Majesty's ships cut short the spurious honeymoon of the sailor.

October 15th

DIGBY DRAMA ON GRETA BRIDGE

Yesterday (Friday) morning Mr Frank Mumberson and two gentlemen, Mr Wagstaff and Mr Teale, had a narrow escape from a serious accident. They were proceeding from town in a digby, and after they got over the Greta Bridge the pony, a young one, shied at a man sweeping the road, swerved to the right across the path and got over the river wall at a point where the coping is six to eight feet from the water. Mr Mumberson and Mr Wagstaff were pitched out but Mr Teale kept his seat and his weight saved the trap from being dragged over the wall into the river. The pony was suspended and it was necessary to cut the harness to set it at liberty. The animal, after dropping into the river, made it across and found its way to a field after passing up the Southey Hill Works mill race. Mr Wagstaff, who suffered from a sprain of the right arm and hurt to both thumbs, was attended by a doctor. The other gentlemen were somewhat but not seriously bruised.

1899

February 25th

WOMEN ATTACKED IN THE HOWRAHS

Two cases have occurred recently of young women being attacked by a ruffian in the Howrahs. In the first instance the screams of the intended victim were heard by Mr Garnett, lay reader, who was returning from his duty in the country and ran to her help. Before he could reach the place, however, the unknown scoundrel made off across the field. Mr Garnett accompanied the young woman to her home afterwards. The second case happened but a few nights ago, and although the young person struggled some time with her assailant she was not able to fix his identity.

April 29th

MUTILATED BLACKBIRDS IN CHURCH LANE

On Sunday morning in St John's churchyard lane some children found the mutilated bodies of several young blackbirds near hand to the nest. It would seem that they had been cruelly butchered with a knife. If the guilty one or ones can be discovered, a strong birching appeal should be made to their better feelings, and possibly save the hangman a job.

April 29th

THE FIRST SWALLOW

The first swallow that we have heard of having been seen in the neighbourhood this year came on Wednesday and was noted by Mr J. Black. This is about the general time of the first appearance. The late Mr W. Greenip gives the earliest arrival on April 7th, 1878.

Winter sports on the ice on the River Greta downstream from the silver bridge. The building on the right is the former pavilion. The veranda is still there and leads to the YHA building.
Picture courtesy of The George Fisher Collection.

The Greta . . . a river runs through it

May 6th

1899 SERIOUS CHARGE AGAINST ROBERT SOUTHEY'S GRANDSON

Robert Harold Southey, aged 27, grandson of the poet (and himself a writer of verse) was brought up in custody at Ystrad (South Wales) on Monday charged with obtaining 10s by false pretences from D. Thomas, ironmonger, Treorchy. The prosecutor deposed that Thomas sent 10s to the prisoner, who, in an advertisement in the *Daily Mail*, offered to send a pair of pure white kittens. Defendant advertised Persian cats for sale in the *Church Times* at 5s each. The stipendiary having intimated that the prisoner would have to go for trial, Southey made a pathetic appeal to be dealt with summarily. He said he had tried hard to find work, but failed. He was remanded in custody. It was stated that the defendant had lived in several parts of Wales.

June 24th

GOOD HEAVENS, IT'S A MOTOR CAR!

Some little sensation has been caused in Keswick during the week by the arrival of a motor car engaged by Mr Bownass, Queen's Hotel, on trial from the Lancaster and Morecambe Motor Company. It arrived shortly before midnight on Friday, 16th inst, after a five and a half hours run from Lancaster. It was out twice on Saturday as far as the Swan Hotel in the first instance and afterwards round Bassenthwaite Lake, accomplishing the run in an hour and forty minutes. It has since been out several times but the result is such as to show that further advance in the power of the engine is necessary before the invention can be regarded as equal to the requirements upon it in such a hilly district as this. The car broke down at Bassenthwaite on Wednesday afternoon through the giving way of some part of the machinery. It was afterwards dragged by a pair of horses to Keswick. The disabled vehicle was sent away by tram yesterday (Friday) morning. Two other private cars on tour have been at The George Hotel.

July 22nd

"TEDDY A FIT SUBJECT FOR THE INEBRIATE'S HOME"

"Teddy" Edmondson was on Thursday sent to prison for a month for drunkenness and disorderly behaviour in Lake Road the previous day. The magistrates considerately expressed their power to relieve him of hard labour, and put him on a better diet. The poor fellow is a fit subject for the inebriate's home.

October 21st

MARK TWAIN THE PRACTICAL JOKER

A few years ago 'Mark Twain' (Mr Samuel Clemens) passed through the Lake District with two ladies and while on his way to Derwentwater, was caught in a thunderstorm. The party sought shelter uninvitedly in the hall of one of the lodges in Lake Road, and remained there until the shower had abated. As he was descending the steps he rang the door bell sharply and then hurried away as fast as he could, almost bursting with suppressed laughter at the awkward situation in which he had landed his friends, and whom he left behind to apologise as best they could.

Pathway beside the river in Keswick's Lower Fitz Park.

1900

February 24th

BRINGING HOME A BAYONET FROM THE BOER WAR

Newspapers at this time contained a lot of material about the Boer War. Keswick organised a War Relief Fund and an appeal was made for comforts for the troops such as warm knitted goods, light drawers, socks, beef essence, chocolate, pocket handkerchiefs, pencils, soap, postcards and tobacco.

Accounts appeared of soldiering experiences and in the February 24th edition of *The Lakes Visitor and Keswick Guardian*, a Keswick man, Bombardier Thomas Stephenson was at the front and wrote home as follows: "When our infantry got among them with their bayonets and the cavalry with their lances they carried the position and drove the enemy further away. We were well to the front and I saw dozens of the enemy lying dead and wounded. I passed alongside them to supply ammunition to a maxim gun. As I passed one dead Boer I took a bayonet out of his heart. It must have been loose when the thrust was made and, of course, left the rifle. I have got it here and when I return you will see it."

Reports also appeared of those local men who had lost their lives in battle.

May 19th

BOY ON SWING FELLS WOMAN IN PARK

On Wednesday evening a young woman (servant at Mr C. Clark's) while walking in the Low Fitz approached too near a swing upon which a boy named Thwaite was enjoying himself. The boy's clog caught her on the forehead and knocked her down. She was rendered unconscious for a short time and lay where she fell. Two ladies, named Swindle and Atkinson, went to her assistance and took her to the drinking fountain near the cricket pavilion and bathed her head, and when she had come round she was escorted home by some young women.

June 2nd

"AN ODIOUS CONCERTINA"

(Letter to the Editor): Cannot something be done to make it possible for visitors to walk to Friar's Crag without being daily annoyed by an odious concertina and a worse fiddle? I would gladly subscribe to a fund to keep these poor men off the road and to give them a few comforts at home in return for their consenting to be no longer begging nuisances. Nobody should be permitted to disfigure a beautiful walk and annoy passers by. The men know they are nuisances and trade upon the fact. There should be a fund for the Keswick poor.

June 2nd
WIDOW ON CHARGE OF "SLEEPING OUT"

At the police court on Tuesday, before Mr Carrick, a woman named Mary Groves, described as a widow, aged 64, of no fixed abode, was brought up in custody on the charge of sleeping out. P.C. Dunglinson found the prisoner asleep in a wash house in Scott's Court at 11.35 on the previous night. When he took her into custody she roused the whole neighbourhood with her screams. Search revealed that she had in her possession money, pipe, tobacco, matches, and some rum in a bottle. She conducted herself in a very disorderly way throughout the night in the cell. Mr Carrick sentenced her to seven days in Carlisle gaol.

August 25th
A PAINFUL ACCIDENT

A boy, named Fred Hunter, met with a painful and somewhat serious accident at Mr Adamson's slaughterhouse on Friday night last. While he was attempting to reach for a knife, Sydney Wright was in the act of beheading a chicken and the chopper struck him across the back of the right hand. Three of the tendons were severed. The lad was taken to a doctor who succeeded, after a very tedious and trying operation, in sewing the tendons together and the wound is mending as satisfactorily as can be hoped for.

September 15th
A PORTRAIT OF SOUTHEY

Miss Bertha Hill, granddaughter of the poet Southey, has kindly sent to Canon Rawnsley, to be placed in the room at the museum dedicated to the literary association of the Lake District a most interesting small portrait in oils of her grandfather by Weigill; also two water colours of Southey's library and study at Greta Hall, as it was when he was there; and, further, the original M.S., in the poet's own writing, of the celebrated poem on Lodore waterfall.

September 22nd
OTTER HOUNDS AT BRIERY

On Wednesday morning the West Cumberland otter hounds were brought to Keswick by the 9.38 train and threw off at the Bobbin Mill, Briery. They were soon on game and had a most exciting hunt for an hour and a half in a stretch of half a mile. At last a fine dog otter was viewed near Sloe-tree holm by a single hound which seized it midstream. The others were on it immediately and, after a game fight, between them they killed it. The pack was taken further upstream where Mr Crozier was expected to meet them. They were kennelled at The Riddings (Mr Crozier's residence near Threlkeld) to be in readiness for more work on Thursday.

October 6th
MEMORIAL TO RUSKIN AT FRIARS CRAG

The memorial to the late John Ruskin on Friars Crag, will be unveiled at 2.30 o'clock this afternoon by Mrs Arthur Severn, and after a short address by Canon Rawnsley. The memorial is placed (by leave of Mr R.D. Marshall, lord of the manor) in near proximity to the place from which Ruskin beheld the view he classed as "one of the three most beautiful scenes in Europe." It is to be hoped that both visitors and townsmen alike will consider the monument as committed to their special care, and do all they can to preserve it undisfigured, in honour of Ruskin.

October 27th
BRILLIANT METEOR

Between eight and nine o'clock on Sunday evening a very brilliant meteor was observed from various points in the neighbourhood of Keswick, and from one it almost seemed to fall to earth between the hospital and the river. The same meteor was seen in many other parts of the country and during the few seconds it was in view, the light was of intense brightness.

November 3rd
KLONDYKE GOLD ON SHOW

Mr James Telford, watch maker, Station Street, has on view in his window a sample of gold washings and a number of nuggets found at Klondyke. The exhibit is an interesting one.

1901

February 9th
'COUNCIL COST ME MY TEETH'

A letter was read to a meeting of Keswick Urban District Council from Mr C. Christopherson asking for compensation for the loss of his teeth which he alleges were knocked out by his falling down a hole in Bank Street left open by the council's workmen. The committee recommend that Mr Christopherson be informed that the council repudiate all liability.

February 16th
FIGHTING IN THE STREETS OF KESWICK

Edward Rice, miner, and Henry Robinson, driver, were jointly summoned for a breach of the peace. Robinson did not appear. Supt Graham said he understood the young man (Robinson) had volunteered for active service in South Africa. Perhaps the Bench might consider recommending the withdrawal of the summons against him. The magistrates declined.

Inspt Logan deposed that at 11.10pm on the day in question he found the two defendants fighting opposite the Post Office with a crowd of people round them. They had had drink but were not drunk. It appeared that both young fellows had a 'record' in the police books, this being Rice's third appearance. The chairman said they had come to the conclusion to convict in both cases and each would be fined 10s including costs.

March 2nd
AND THEN FIGHTING THE BOERS IN SOUTH AFRICA

On Monday evening Pvt H. Robinson (see above) and Pvt B. Brunskill of the 1st V.B. Border Regiment, E Co., having volunteered for active service, took their departure from Keswick by the 6.30 train for Carlisle where they will await orders. Just before the train steamed into the station a purse containing £2 1s was presented to each of them by Capt Broatch. The money had been collected from tradesmen and friends in town by Messrs D. Melvin and J. Rigg. When the train arrived the crowd sang 'Soldiers of the King' and 'God Save the King' until the train moved off again, when 3 ringing cheers rent the air. (see RETURN OF THE SOLDIERS, June 21, 1902).

Wren's Mill. 1809.

The Greta . . . a river runs through it

May 18th

YOUNG CYCLISTS RUIN RAMBLE

Of all the pleasant rambles in the Lake District none can excel the lovely walk at eventide from Keswick to the eastern shore of Derwentwater leading to Friar's Crag to behold the grandeur of the setting sun. One thing only marred our pleasure as we quietly wandered to and fro, and that was some half dozen, half grown lads trying to ride bicycles. Surely there are plenty of good turnpike roads outside the town, where they have ample room to play their pranks without disturbing the quiet of such a pleasant road. The letter was signed 'A Frequent Visitor' and added the postscript: "The old blind man with his concertina was no nuisance at all compared to these intruders."

June 1st

PLAYING CARDS ON THE SABBATH

Joseph Price, pencil maker, Arthur Storey, miner, and William Lawson, waller, were jointly summoned for playing cards in Fitz Park on Sunday afternoon. They pleaded guilty. The chairman, Col Spedding, said it was a serious offence and one to which a stop must be put. He had reason to believe there was a good deal of this sort of thing going on out of doors on the road sides. The defendants were ordered to pay 5s each.

June 15th

'CROOK SPEAKS OUT ON THE EVIL OF GAMBLING'

At the Wesleyan Church on Sunday night the Rev Harold Crook (unfortunate surname under the circumstances) resident minister, preached a special sermon, of which the subject was "The Gambling Evil." The preacher's remarks were principally directed against the spirit of gambling, and he denounced all forms of horse racing to stock exchange jobbery. There was a good congregation.

June 22nd

SOLDIERS OF THE QUEEN

Private J.T. Nelson, son of the proprietor of the Blencathra Hotel, returned to Keswick on Monday night, after some 16 months absence in South Africa. He arrived at Southampton on Sunday evening and came forward to Carlisle with his company for dismissal. On Monday afternoon he returned with them to Penrith (the headquarters of the Regiment) where a grand reception awaited them.

After the day's rejoicing he came to Keswick, and before the engine got into the station the rumble of the train was drowned by the vigorous cheering which could be heard at his home in Southey Street. His alighting was the signal for redoubled efforts on the part of the crowd who had gone to meet him, and as they marched from the station the cheers of the youngsters were varied by singing 'Soldiers of the Queen.' The cheering was continued after Mr Nelson had entered his home, and it did not cease until after he came to the door and thanked them for the unexpected welcome.

July 6th

ELDERLY VISITOR RUNS HEADLONG INTO WALL

On Monday evening an elderly gentleman visitor, named Wright, met with a somewhat serious accident while coming down the steep slope behind Walla Crag towards Rake Foot. From what we can learn of the affair, he was proceeding too quickly, especially as he was wearing smooth-soled shoes. His speed gained upon him to such a degree that he was unable to stop, and he ran into a wall with such violence as to break some ribs. Besides this injury he sustained severe cuts and bruises on the head.

December 28th

ELIXIR OF YOUTH IS ALL IN THE PODDISH

Canon Rawnsley, the Chairman of the Keswick Old Folks Dinner read the following lines at the event.

'The Secret of Old Age'

As ah came down the Keswick street
Ah met a body of 93;
She was straight of back and strong of feet,
An' this is what she said to me-
"You ask me why so lish ah go-
'Twas poddish, barn, that made me so.
What, barn! In oor foor elders' days
When merry neets were aw the thing,
When fwoaks graaved peat to mak a blaze,
An' fiddlers went a-Christmassing,
We grew oor oats, we kept a coo,
An' supped oor poddish aw t' year throo.
"Good harden-sark our mudders mead,
We carded woo', we larned to spin.
Dress makkin' was not then the treadd,
An' household work was thowt nea sin;
Powsodies for our Cursmas do
We hed, but supped oor poddish too.
We didn't clash oorsels wi' tea.
We'd milk and havver-breed to eat,
An' that is why ah'm 93,
An t' oald fwoaks' do is still a treat.
If you wad hev your oald age so,
To poddish back again you aw must go."

Footnote: Much amusement was caused at the 'do' by Mrs Sanderson, of Brigham (going on for 80) whose feet could not resist the temptation of the fiddle's strains. The chairman thought the old lady must have been "browt up on poddish."

1902

May 10th

BARBARIC TREATMENT OF BIRDS

A correspondent writes to ask if nothing can be done to check the spirit of barbarism which yearly seems to affect the youth of Keswick, perhaps not more than at other places, in the wanton and merciless destruction of bird life. He refers indignantly to the cutting off of the heads of young birds, of throwing young birds down by the roadside to starve, taking eggs from nests and substituting marbles. While the law may be invoked to do something, our friend thinks an application of old-fashioned birch to offenders would have a better and more permanent effect. No bird is sacred to the destroyer, pheasant, partridge, wild duck, down to the robin – all meet the same treatment, and even the bonny squirrel bids fair to be exterminated.

June 7th

THE END OF THE WAR

When it became known on early Monday that the Boer representatives had accepted the terms of peace, there was on every hand an expression of gladness that the Boer leaders had at last recognised their inability to prolong with any hope of success the bitter struggle. The school children of Crosthwaite were marched up into the top square where they sang and cheered and were then dismissed for a holiday. Bunting was on display, a crowd gathered in the Market Square and rockets fired from the grounds of the Keswick Hotel. A dray was brought into the square as a temporary platform for celebratory speeches and the Temperance Band played the National Anthem.

June 14th
OVERDOING IT

Thomas Hilton, waiter, pleaded guilty to a charge of having been unlawfully drunk and disorderly on the previous Tuesday night. Sergt Dickson proved the offence. Defendant, who said he had been rejoicing over the proclamation of peace, was fined 5s and 9s 6d costs.

June 21st
RETURN OF THE SOLDIERS, HOME FROM THE WAR

Privates Bertram Brunskill, John Scott and John H. Robinson returned to Keswick on Thursday night. It will be remembered that they volunteered from the E Company for service with the Border Regiment and went out in the early part of last year. They looked fit and well after all the discomforts and hardships which they have endured.

Capt Broatch awaited the men on the platform and the Band of the Volunteers met them at the station door and played them down to the Market Square. There was not much enthusiasm at the station but at the corner of Penrith Road there was a large crowd and cheering was continuous along Station Street to the upper square where the warriors were briefly welcomed by Capt Broatch, and they moved for home. Before dismissal the band played the National Anthem.

June 21st
'DO NOT DESECRATE FRIAR'S CRAG WITH LITTER'

As a visitor of some years standing to your town may I suggest that the council or whoever is responsible for the beauty of the place, should provide long baskets or suitable receptacles for old paper, orange peel and other debris along the Friar's Crag as has been done in the park, with a strongly-worded notice to tourists that they should use it, and not desecrate one of the prettiest walks in the Lake District with the strew of sandwich papers, old letters and orange peel, such as rendered the whole place simply disgusting last Thursday morning.

I cannot but think people need only to have it suggested to them to refrain from such vulgarity and want of thought for others. My love for this beautiful place and desire that others should share in its perfection is my excuse for troubling you with this letter - G Thompson, 2 Derwentwater Place, Keswick.

The following extract, in the next column, is interesting because it includes reference to the fact that men summoned to appear before the local magistrates could chose not to appear in court but would happily send their wife along instead. The headline below is the one actually used in the newspaper at the time:

July 12th
MADE TO BEAR HIS OWN BURDEN

George Wilkes, quarryman, was summoned for "violently gesticulating" on the 22nd June. Defendant's wife appeared on his behalf and pleaded guilty, adding that her husband wanted to know if they would give him a fortnight "to pay it in" (laughter).

The Chairman asked if there was any reason why the man himself did not appear. For trivial offences he did not care to bring a man from his work, but in more serious cases he thought the defendant ought to appear. In answer to the question Mrs Wilkes said her husband was at home.

Mr Oddie (the Chairman) then intimated that unless he appeared before the court rose a warrant would be issued. Mrs Wilkes left to inform her spouse of this determination and very shortly afterwards Wilkes stood at the bar. Sergt Dickson deposed that at 10.15pm on the day in question the defendant had his coat off and shirt sleeves rolled up, challenging a man to fight. The defendant said the man came to the door and invited him out, and he went out. Fined 10s including costs.

July 26th
THE BLIND MAN ON LAKE ROAD

Two or three years ago Joseph Plaskett was summoned amongst others for being on the road (Lake Road) and was given to understand that he, being a native, would not have been interfered with only he had to be removed along with strangers to the town. This summer he has been the only one there and yet the police, about three weeks ago, ordered him to leave and he did so. The poor man naturally wonders what can be the reason for his removal; and as no one will tell him he thinks it must be the music and so he stops playing and sits there for a few days without playing; but he is ordered off again, so that it cannot be the annoyance of the music.

I want to speak for the helpless, for surely a blind man will be included amongst them. Strong, able-bodied men are allowed to play organs about the streets and beg from door to door and are never told to move on or are interfered with. Others can beg all around the streets, and yet a poor helpless blind man has to have this treatment in our town. I do not believe there can be found another town in the United Kingdom that would allow their own natives, dependant upon others for their living, to suffer any such treatment.

I think it is quite time that Keswick, as a town with many who proffer to be Christians and so many who visit the place who proffer to follow the Son of God (who was, above all, the friend of the helpless) arose to roll away this terrible reproach - C. Greenwood, Keswick.

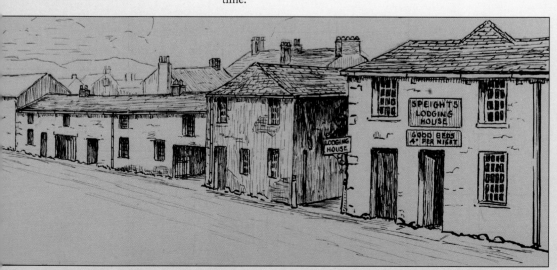

Speight's Lodging House in Back Lane, 1880. Drawing by Tom Wilson.

August 9th
BEGGAR SENT TO JAIL

David Brooks, aged 30, of no fixed abode, was apprehended in Tithebarn Street on Tuesday in the act of begging. Several complaints had been made about the scamp and PC Reid dropped upon him opportunely. He was taken before Messrs Carrick and Bromley the same afternoon and committed for fourteen days with hard labour.

August 9th
"TEDDY'S" PLEA FOR FREEDOM

Edward "Teddy" Edmondson was brought up in custody on the charge of being drunk and disorderly the previous night.

While the magistrates were considering what to do with him, "Teddy" pleaded with them not to send him to prison. He said it did not do a man any good sending him to prison again and again; it only sent him further down the hill of degradation. When he had got two or three pints the craving came upon him which he could not resist. He knew he was wrong and there was nobody sorrier than himself when he became sober. He did not want to go to prison for it put him away from the world and gave him no chance.

The Chairman (Col Spedding): "Have you any work?"

Defendant: "I have been working for three weeks and I have another place to go to."

The Chairman: "There is a case against you not settled."

Defendant: "I am aware of that."

The Chairman: "We cannot entirely ignore that. Can you keep away if we give you time?"

Supt Graham said that neither the magistrates nor the police had any desire to send defendant to prison. He had tried to advise defendant and yet he was here again.

The Chairman added that the magistrates wished to give defendant every chance, but it did not seem to be of much use. They wished to be as lenient as they could. A fortnight previously he was fined 15s; on this occasion they would fine him 5s, including costs, and give him a fortnight's time to pay or go to prison.

Supt Graham said that if defendant came again the severest penalty would be pressed for. The Chairman said that if defendant was found drunk in the meantime he would be apprehended and sent at once to gaol for the two offences. Defendant said he would try his utmost.

August 16th
HORSES TAKE FRIGHT AT CAR AND SERIOUS ACCIDENT RESULTS

A very serious accident involving injury to person and property, occurred near Bowdering End, Borrowdale, on Monday afternoon. As a laden char-a-banc of visitors at The Derwentwater Hotel was returning from Rosthwaite the horses took fright at a motor car which came suddenly round a corner some score of yards in front. The animals turned suddenly round and, in doing so, broke the pole and tore away the front body of the carriage, galloping back to Rosthwaite.

The occupants were all pitched out and all were more or less injured. The driver, Mr Fearon McCade, than whom there is not a more capable man in the district, had his left leg badly broken and injured above the ankle. An elderly gentleman, badly hurt, was taken to the Lodore Hotel and a lady was brought to the Derwentwater Hotel. Drs Crawford and Mills, having been fetched in the motor car, were quickly in attendance, as also was a squad of five members of the Ambulance Brigade. We are pleased to hear that all the injured are doing as well as can be expected.

August 23rd
"TEDDY" YET AGAIN

Edward Edmondson, who did not appear, had been summoned for having been drunk and disorderly on Sunday night, August 3rd. Sergt Dixon said the defendant was drunk, shouting and swearing in the street and refused to go away when requested. He also wanted to fight with two young men who endeavoured to get him away.

Supt Graham said the defendant had been many times before this and other courts and was fined here only 14 days ago, when he was given to understand that if he did not behave himself the warrants against him would be put in force. The charge was brought on this occasion with the view of getting him sent to an inebriates' home should it be necessary to bring him again. Supt Graham said there was an arrangement with an institution in Bristol where three or four months ago a female was sent from Cockermouth. A conviction was made of 5s and costs or 14 days in default.

Lower Main Street leading to Greta Bridge.

August 23rd
DOG KILLED BY 'FAST' CAR AT DALEBOTTOM

Edward Pears Caporn, engineer, Harrogate, was summoned for driving a motor car at a greater speed than 12 miles an hour at Dalebottom, Keswick, at about 4pm on the 29th of July.

George Fleming, farmer, Dalebottom, deposed that he was coming to Keswick with a cart containing three lambs and was accompanied by his dog. As he passed St John's (in the Vale) vicarage he heard the sound of a horn and when he got to the road end leading to his farm he saw a motor car coming in sight at the ash tree about half way up the hill. Witness said he was riding on the cart but got off and walked at the head of the horse because the motor was coming so rapidly. He had gone 103 yards from the point where he first saw the motor, and the motor had come 725 yards when they met. The distances had been measured by the inspector of police. Witness's horse walked at about three miles an hour and he would say the motor was going at about twenty. He considered it was going very fast.

His dog was injured by the motor and died shortly afterwards. He told the defendant that he might have driven at a less speed and the defendant replied that he could not avoid killing the dog. Witness admitted writing a letter to the defendant on the Saturday following demanding £10 for the loss of the dog.

William Gilpin, farm servant, deposed that the motor was going faster than he had ever seen one go before.

Mr J.W. Lowther (chairman of the bench): "Was it going as fast as the CK and P (Cockermouth, Keswick and Penrith railway line) trains. Or as 'slow' I should say." (laughter).

Witness: "I have seen bicycles go as fast, but not faster."

Jane Pritt, servant, at Causeway Foot, said she had never seen one go so fast.

For the defence, Mr Wetherhead, solicitor, Harrogate, said his case was that the car was

going at a pace between four and five miles an hour. The brakes were on and the engine was not working (engaged). It was no business of Fleming whether the car was going fast or slow. If the defendant had been at fault in killing the dog he might be civilly liable.

Edward Pears Caporn, Regent Terrace, Harrogate, engineer and expert motorist, said Mr Fleming was standing at the head of his horse when the motor was driving slowly past, because of the steep hill. The dog came from behind the cart. He thought the witness was mistaken. He always went slow down hill and did so specially on this occasion because he had seen the danger board. He would swear they were not going more than six miles an hour. Arthur Macarthy, Harrogate, said he was in the motor car and corroborated the evidence of Mr Capon.

The summons was dismissed by the bench on the grounds of conflicting evidence.

August 23rd
DRINK DENIED FOR SHEEP DOG TRIALS

Mr T. Hill, of the Salutation Inn, Threlkeld, applied for a special licence to sell intoxicating liquors on Threlkeld Common on the occasion of the sheep dog trials on the 10th of September. After consultation with his colleagues, Mr Lowther said it would be the dogs rather than the men who would need a drink and the Bench did not see their way to grant the application.

August 30th
ROYAL VISIT FOR TRUST LAND OPENING

I have heard today that HRH Princess Louise, Duchess of Argyll, will kindly come over from Lowther on October 15th to declare the Brandelhow Park Estate open. Wednesday is the town's half holiday and I am sure the townsmen will accord the daughter of Queen Victoria a hearty welcome - H.D. Rawnsley, Hon Sec National Trust. Brandelhow was the first land to be given to the fledgling Trust.

August 30th
POLITICAL INTRIGUE OVER FLOWER SHOW

(Letter to the Editor): Can any of your numerous readers tell me how it was that when the judges visited the gardens connected with the above show that one garden was vigorously searched by the secretary? Was it for plunged pots? If so, how was it that the pots in the other gardens were altogether ignored? Did the committee authorise their secretary to search this particular garden? How was it that he did not search the gardens of the winners also? I remain, yours truly, ONE WHO WOULD LIKE TO KNOW.

The silver bridge on Station Road

September 6th
TO CURE TEDDY!

Edward Edmondson was brought up in custody charged with having been drunk and disorderly on the 27th August. Asked to plead defendant said: "I don't know what to say scarcely. I cannot say 'no' or 'yes.' There's a point I cannot decide on."

Supt Graham suggested that an application might be made for the defendant to be sent to a home for inebriates. It was the fourth time the defendant had been before the court since the 19th July. He had had many chances. In none of the last cases had the fines been paid, nor had he been sent to prison. On the last occasion the chairman gave him a warning. For Edmondson's benefit it would be better that he should be sent. There was a home near Bristol with which arrangements had been made by the County Council.

Defendant: "So you want to try it with me?"

Supt Graham said it would be necessary for the defendant to be remanded until the preliminaries had been arranged.

Defendant: "I don't want to go. I want to earn some money and I will pay the fines."

He asked for another chance and offered to "sign teetotal" for twelve months; he was willing to work and would pay the fines. The chairman (J.R. Anderson) said the bench were sorry but they were convinced that it was best to send him.

Defendant again asked for another chance. Then if he failed he would be willing to go; and when he came out he hoped that neither Supt Graham nor anybody else would reap up the convictions against him because they had been paid for . . .

The chairman: "It is not a punishment."

The defendant said it would be punishment to deprive him of his liberty. It would be the same as prison.

The chairman: "You can go at present, Edmondson."

Defendant, taking up his cap: "Good morning!"

The Greta . . . a river runs through it

November 15th
VICTIMS OF DRINK

After all the temperance agitation and work during the last fifty years the bare fact remains that the total consumption of intoxicating drinks was as high as ever. It was most serious commercially – the people spend £4 16s 11d per head annually on strong drink. It would appear that Keswick spent £21,568 16s 1d per year.

In as much as the proportion of money spent on labour in the manufacture of drink is infinitesimal we had not in Keswick such dire results through drink as present themselves in larger cities; but we had too large a proportion not adequately housed or fed and conditions not conducive to morality. If the drink traffic were swept away the housing problem would be solved.

Canon Rawnsley said that he had been reading that six trains of thirty four trucks, each containing tons of solid gold sovereigns, represented the sum annually wasted in drink.

The Rev W.G. Bird observed: "No drunkard can inherit the kingdom of heaven." He was firmly convinced that there had been a diminution of drunkenness among men but on the other hand he was sorry to say that there had been an increase among women. The asylums, prisons and workhouses were largely filled by victims of drink.

December 27th
A VISIT FROM THE DARK ANGEL

The dark angel, Death, has brought deep sorrow to Keswick this Christmas. Eight deaths have happened in the space of nine days. Christmas of 1902 will long be remembered as one of unexampled sadness, and we are sure that the sympathy of the inhabitants is with the families in affliction.

1903

January 10th
INSPECTOR SCROOGE STRIKES ON CHRISTMAS EVE

Osmund Vickers and Tom Pepper, boys of about 14 years, were summoned for damaging a holly tree in Castlehead to the value of 6d. Inspector Logan deposed that he met the two boys near the library at 3.40pm on the 24th December, each carrying a bunch of holly. He took the holly from them and told them they might afterwards be summoned. The court was told that boys were in the habit of selling the evergreen.

Mr J.W. Robinson, agent for the Derwentwater estate said that latterly there had been so much damage to trees and by trespass that the case had been brought in an endeavour to put a stop to the practice which had become too prevalent. The bench were inclined to deal leniently with the defendants and would dismiss the summons if costs were paid. The boys' mothers paid the costs which amounted to 6s 6d each.

The old weir in Lower Fitz Park.

June 20th
THE END OF AN ITINERANT MUSICIAN

Jimmy Dyer, the well-known ballad-monger and itinerant musician, died in the hospital at Fusehill Workhouse, Carlisle, on Tuesday morning. He was obliged to seek the shelter of the workhouse in October last by reason of failing health. According to his autobiography, Jimmy was born at Carlisle on Christmas Eve, 1841, "ushered into the world at a very auspicious time when people are wont to eat plum pudding and roast beef, and currant cakes and mince pies and ducks and geese and turkeys and all manner of good things." Jimmy was declared to be "a little angel sent down from heaven to cheer his mother and keep her company."

At the age of two he fell down stairs and broke his nose, and the effect of the accident was a permanent disfigurement of his characterful dial.

It appears that at the close of the Crimean War he found a berth in the Navy, but he did not like it and, according to his autobiography, he simulated the fool and succeeded in gaining his discharge. He returned to Carlisle and began his career as a song writer and itinerant musician, varied with card selling at the races. He used to attend the hiring fairs at Cockermouth and Penrith. His home was principally the common lodging houses and his appearance seemed to denote that, like most dwellers in the "padding ken," his looking glass was oftener than ought else the bottom of a pint pot.

The deceased was only in his 62nd year, but his mode of life gave him a look of at least ten years older.

Jimmy Dyer is featured in the parade of local characters of Keswick in the wonderful oil painting (1870) by Joseph Brown Junior which can be seen in Keswick Museum and Art Gallery. See page 255.

August 15th
AN OLD NADDLE POSTMAN'S LAST ROUND

Mr John Musgrave, Museum Square, passed to rest on Wednesday evening, at the age of 83. The deceased in October 1860 became the first postman to serve Naddle in the Vale of St John. As time passed his round was enlarged to take in Wythburn and he daily traversed some twenty miles until arrangements were made for the Legburthwaite and Wythburn district letters to be sent by way of Grasmere. But this did not take place until Mr Musgrave was well advanced in years, and his round was shortened accordingly.

After serving the Post Office for 33 years he was reluctantly obliged to give up work, for although good in general health he was not physically capable of the exertion which his work entailed. Unfortunately, the steps were not taken which would have made Mr Musgrave more than an auxiliary and 33 years of faithful service did not meet with a pension. His wage was not such as to enable him to provide for a "rainy day," but when his walk did not occupy the whole of his time he worked at his trade as a tailor and so was able to save something from which to preserve a sturdy independence for ten years.

Latterly the brave old man had perforce to keep to his bed till, nature worn out, he "fell on sleep." He leaves a widow close upon his own age, three sons and two daughters. His remains will be interred at Crosthwaite this (Saturday) afternoon at two o'clock.

August 22nd
GARDEN A 'BLAZE OF BEAUTIFUL COLOURS'

Mr Hayes' gardens on Lake Road are in the pink of condition and their attractiveness lends an additional charm to the road to the lake. Some two or three years ago "Little Hills Fields" was a piece of pasture with nothing beyond the somewhat bare greenery. Now it is a blaze of beautiful colours, blended with rare taste. Heathers, in which Mr Hayes is first among his fellows, are a splendid lot and in many varieties; Alpine plants, in which Mr Hayes justified his claim to be a specialist, in their profusion and beauty cannot fail to gain the admiration of all connoisseurs. Begonias, phloxes, carnations, and other flowers present a brave show, while the young fruit and ornamental trees and shrubs are such as to fill the arborist's heart with envy. In the garden on the north side of the road will be found a collection of rare and hardy ferns of almost infinite variety, as well as rare and interesting flowers.

The town is indebted to him for providing a display which one thinks cannot be excelled in beauty by any other horticulturist in the Kingdom.

The Oddfellows Hall.
Drawing by Tom Wilson.

1904

February 20th
FINED FOR PLAYING PITCH AND TOSS ON SUNDAY

Henry Robinson (he of Boer War fame?), Joseph Lawson, Patrick Morgan, James Richardson and Ernest Dalzell were jointly summoned for playing pitch and toss in Castlehead Wood on Sunday, January 31st. Robinson pleaded not guilty but the others admitted the offence.

PC Lindsay deposed that while on duty in plain clothes he saw the whole of the defendants playing pitch and toss at 3.30pm on the day named. When charged with the offence Robinson admitted it. In the witness box Robinson denied playing. He was supported by Morgan and the others were ready to corroborate. Robinson was discharged but was told the case was suspicious. The others were fined 15s each, including costs.

June 4th
MOTORISTS COME TO GRIEF ON CHESTNUT HILL

On Sunday evening a couple of gentlemen were approaching Keswick in a motor car and at a good speed. As they were coming down Chestnut Hill the brake is said to have gone wrong, whereupon the driver turned into the hedge with the result that the car was upset, both occupants were pitched out, and one unfortunately broke his arm. The car, which was comparatively uninjured, was afterwards driven into Keswick by Mr G.D. Abraham. Dr Barnett attended the injured man.

High Hill and the Greta.

August 5th
THE CIRCUS COMES TO TOWN

After an interval of six years this world renowned travelling "zoo" will visit Keswick on Monday and stand in the Carding Mill Field, near Greta Bridge. Greybeards remember Wombwell's as a familiar name in their boyhood, and were not only curious to see the many and various animals gathered together by the famous George Wombwell (who began his collection with a solitary monkey) but were eager to walk miles to meet the caravans and admire the splendid teams of horses.

The show has always been considered an educational institution and, outside the Royal Zoological Gardens, London, the collection of animals the most complete which energy and money could put together. The latest addition is the horse "Linus" with a tail 17 ft long and a double mane of 13ft on each side. Another important addition is a pair of rare sea lions which have to be accommodated with a travelling tank. These animals are representatives of a class nearing extinction through the merciless manner in which they have been hunted for the sake of their fur. As may be expected there are performances with various wild animals.

1905

May 13th
MAN WAS STARK NAKED AND EVIDENTLY OUT OF HIS MIND IN CO-OPERATIVE SOCIETY DOORWAY

At three o'clock on Tuesday morning inhabitants in the neighbourhood of St John's Street were awakened and startled by a succession of loud and sustained yells. A number of them rose from their beds, dressed and went out to learn the cause of their rude awakening, and they found a man, evidently out of his mind, standing stark naked at the Co-operative Society's doorway.

They fetched a police constable on the scene, but the man, who is of powerful build, was violently opposed to any attention from the representative of law and order. Ultimately Messrs Peascod, Mandale and Hudson sent the constable down to the police station to inform Inspector Logan of the circumstances. Meanwhile they succeeded in pacifying the unfortunate man and escorted him to the police station where he was taken charge of.

Supplied with a night shirt he was put to bed in one of the cells. Later on he was induced to write his name – he would not speak it – W.F. Sadler. His clothing was found five miles away near Thirlmere. He had tramped without food or stockings and his feet were quite sore in consequence. In the afternoon the usual legal formalities were observed and an order was made for the man's removal to the Garlands Asylum, Carlisle, where he was taken by the 3.50 train.

He is a muscular, fine built man, of gentlemanly bearing, and is believed to have served as an artificer on HM ship Bacchante. His clothing was in good order and he had quite a respectable appearance. From particulars we have learned he was 44 years of age, that he ran away from home when he was 21, and his father, who is an invalid, and his sister have not seen him since. He enlisted in the army and was afterwards bought off. It appears that he is subject to mental depression after drinking bouts and possibly he may very recently have been in one of his dissipated moods, though he hardly looked it and certainly his talk was not that of a blackguard.

It appears that a man, whose description and photograph answers exactly that of Sadler, has been missed from Ingleton since Monday morning and the police there have been searching the hills. He had been staying there for the weekend and, after paying his bill, went out, leaving a bag, and did not return for it. It is thought he must have travelled by train to Windermere and afterwards wandered off the road.

July 1st

"BLIND JOE" IN TROUBLE AGAIN

Joseph Plaskett was summoned for unlawfully placing himself in Lake Road for the purpose of gathering alms. The defendant had been frequently before the bench on similar charges, and the police had done all they could to persuade him to go away. There had been numerous complaints from respectable people of the nuisance they experienced from the constant playing of a concertina. Plaskett played and sang while sitting on a stool and had a little tin mug on a box in front of him. A conviction was registered but the bench remitted both fine and costs.

September 2nd

"A LADY LINGUIST"

Before Messrs Carrick and Mitchell-Dawson at the police court on Wednesday afternoon, Annie MacDonald, a widow of no fixed abode, was charged with using obscene language in Penrith Road, at 11.30 the same morning. As the prisoner had not a good record, she having been committed previously for other offences, she was sent to prison for a month in lieu of a fine of 40s and costs.

1906

March 24th

"THE RULING FASHION"

Andrew Lowther Jnr, William Lowther, Thomas Thwaite, Tom Pepper, William Hutchinson and John Hutchinson were summoned for playing football in Back Lane – some on Sunday the 4th and others on the 7th. Sergt Louis deposed they were kicking a ball about the street and bawling and shouting at the top of their voices. He had cautioned them repeatedly and they took no notice whatsoever. They were ordered to pay costs.

The pavilion veranda and the YHA building on the left, leading the river round to what was the weir in Lower Fitz Park.

June 16th

BLIND JOE AND HIS CONCERTINA AGAIN

Joseph Plaskett was summoned for unlawfully having been in a certain public place for the purpose of gathering alms. The clerk said there had been a letter of complaint to the police, from which the following was an extract: "May I ask in the name of the visitors that the nuisance of concertina music by which we are tormented be held in reasonable check and, if possible, removed altogether? I came to Keswick for rest and quiet and in the hope of doing literary work, and the above infliction has not aided either my recovery or my literary efforts. Others feel the annoyance even more than I do. It is all very well for those who stroll past the nuisance once or twice a day to look on him with tolerant eye, but those who live within range of his noise feel very differently about it.

"Even if he is compelled to play for his bread, which I believe is not the case, it would surely be possible for him to obtain a less aggressively strident instrument and to refrain from jauntily irreverent renderings of well-known hymn tunes. He frequently repeats the same hymn tunes seven or eight times in succession and never once correctly.

"For the sake of invalids and students reading I have to request that this nuisance be put a stop to or at least abated. An auto-harp or other more gentle instrument of torture would not cause anything like the annoyance."

PC Pendrey deposed that at about noon on the 4th he saw the defendant in Lake Road sitting on a chair and playing a concertina. On the concertina box beside him was a small tin into which he saw several people drop coppers. Plaskett was fined 2s 6d, including costs.

August 11th

LEGAL VICTORY FOR BLIND JOE

Plaskett was back before the court, summoned for unlawfully placing himself in Lake Road for the purpose of gathering alms. Mr Hodgson, solicitor, Kendal, appeared for Plaskett and successfully argued that the money his client received in return for playing his concertina could not be regarded as "alms." The summons was dismissed.

It would appear that someone in the town (perhaps it was C. Greenwood who wrote in support of Plaskett on July 26th, 1902) had decided to give their support to the blind concertina player and hired a leading local solicitor to represent him. Their success in court would, clearly, be a punch in the eye for the letter writer who complained to the police about the "torment" of Plaskett's concertina playing and hymn singing.

"TEDDY"

Unfortunately I could not find any further references to that other regular visitor to the magistrates court, the hapless "Teddy" Edmondson. Perhaps he was, after all, sent to the home for inebriates in Bristol, never to return, or, alternatively, drank himself to oblivion. Or, less likely, signed the pledge and did, indeed, finally live up to his oft-stated intent to go teetotal for the rest of his days on earth.

1907

March 30th

COD AND DAFFODILS

Those who have been privileged to see the window of Mr P.S. Todd, fishmonger, must have been struck by the ingenious manner in which salmon, halibut, cod, hake, soles etc have been arranged, so as to give what are generally very modest windows a great attraction. Daffodils, carefully and becomingly placed, complete a sight which is well worth viewing.

August 24th
DRUNK IN CHARGE OF HORSES

At about 7pm on Thursday there was an exciting scene at the Royal Oak corner when the leading horse of a team of three spirited bay horses mounted the bonnet of a motor and damaged the offside wing. The affair ended in the best way, as no personal injury was sustained, nor did the horse suffer any hurt. The motor car, the property of Mr Crone, of Roker, Sunderland, was returning from Grasmere Sports and the charabanc was being driven up Main Street by a driver named Davies. The police took some note of the circumstances and as it is possible that proceedings will follow (see below) it would be unfair to make further remark.

September 7th
DAVIES FINED

Fred Davies, licensed driver, was summoned for being drunk while in charge of three horses and a charabanc. He was fined £2 including costs.

December 14th
GROCER SECRETARY OF RATEPAYERS' ASSOCIATION MADE TO EAT HIS WORDS

A ratepayers' association for Keswick was formed and at the formative meeting Mr J.H. Wilson, grocer, who was appointed secretary, said that he recalled one or two instances in which he thought the council had shown incompetence.

"Some five or six years ago," he said, "a certain estate (in which the council own large interests) was on the market for sale. They (the council) took no action whatever with the result that it fell into the hands of a private individual. The council's legal adviser (Mr Broatch) acted for a third party and knew full well the interests of the council. The result today is that we are saddled with a cost of £2,197 16s 3d."

Mr Wilson said that they met together to consider the advisability or otherwise of forming a ratepayers' association for the protection of their interests and more especially to devise means of checking, to his mind, an incompetent and spendthrift Urban Council.

Shortly afterwards the newspaper printed, under the simple headline APOLOGY, the following: "I much regret that a speech of mine read from a manuscript at a meeting for the formation of a Ratepayers' Association in Blackman's School, Keswick, on the 10th of December last year, reports of which appeared in the *Mid Cumberland and Westmorland Herald* and the *English Lakes Visitor* of the 14th of December, and possibly in other papers, imputes to Mr Joseph Broatch, solicitor, of Keswick, dishonest and unprofessional conduct as legal adviser of the Keswick Urban District Council.

"I freely admit that there is no foundation whatever in fact for any imputation of the kind upon that gentleman and that statements made by me were made upon information I had failed to verify. I unreservedly withdraw all such statements and deeply regret that any words of mine, capable of above construction, should have been uttered." - John H Wilson, Grocer, 44 Main Street, Keswick.

1908

April 4th
OLD SOLDIER DRUNK

William Henry White, who described himself as an old soldier, was found drunk and incapable in Woolpack Court on Tuesday night. PC Maher stated that the prisoner was so incapable that he had to be brought to the station on a wheelbarrow. Prisoner, in excuse, said that as he "had not been able to get a wink of sleep for a fortnight he had taken a little drink to help him and had 'over drownded' it."

An empty pint whisky bottle was produced as having contained the soporific. He was committed for seven days in default of a fine of 10s.

May 30th
THE VOTE FOR WOMEN

A Women's Suffrage Association has been formed in Keswick. The object for which it will work is the franchise for women on the same terms as it is, or may be, granted to men.

Painters go to work on the bridge in Lower Fitz Park. Picture courtesy of The George Fisher Collection.

The Greta . . . a river runs through it

August 15th

THE RUNAWAY BOY WHO DREAMED OF FINDING GOLD

On Saturday last a bonny, bright-eyed, intelligent lad, ten years old, named James Dempsey, went up to PC Greenhow and told the officer that he had run away from home with another boy of fifteen years to seek their fortunes, and that he wished to go home again. They had tramped from Morecambe, through Kendal and Windermere to Keswick "in search of the biggest mountain" in which they believed there was a "great lot of gold hidden."

From the time they had left home they had slept at night under hedges, and while at Keswick had frequented the lake shore. The boy was hungry and the police officer kindly provided him with food. In the meantime the boy's father, who lives in Back Pedder Lane, Morecambe, was communicated with by telegraph, and a reply message came with the request to put the boy on the train, stating that his fare should be paid at Morecambe.

The police acted upon the instruction and the youngster was restored, greatly to the joy of his parents. It is not known what became of the elder boy.

Below. KESWICK STREET 1870, painted by Joseph Brown Jnr. Painting courtesy of Keswick Museum and Art Gallery.

It is difficult to pinpoint precisely who is who but the characters here include (from left to right): J.F. Crosthwaite, a prominent townsman, bank manager and postmaster; Jimmy Dyer, a strolling player; John Glaister, a noted pig keeper; Mary Sowerby; Joe Spencer, earthenware dealer and fruiterer; Sarah Skurr, weighing machine attendant; Isaac Hodgson, verger, bellringer and sexton, Crosthwaite Church; Mary Addison; Mark Shearman, cabinetmaker and Station Hotel; William Gaspey, writer and poet; Sim Fisher, of Braithwaite, straw beehives maker; Tom Fallows, barber and coach agent; Tom Howe, retired farmer; Neddy Thwaites, travelling draper; John Crow, crowing for coppers; Willie Coulthard, lamplighter; Mr Denton and Mr Langton; John Coward, shoemaker; Sam Gordon and friend; Joseph Johnson, a tailor; John Adamson, miller; Dr Brown; Police Sergeant Rooney; Joe Sparks, an old miner; Willie Hogarth, shoemaker; Tom Temple, grocer; The Skiddaw Hermit or 'Doddy' who lived on Dodd in a hut made with moss (he was also an accomplished portrait painter); John Knowles, tinsmith; Robert Makinson, shoemaker; West Walker, guide and boatman; John White, nail maker; John Fleming, bellman; Tom Atkinson, barber; Billy Bowe, boatman; quarter master Nixon; Abraham Wigham and his donkey, the town's cleaning department (or scavenger as it was at one time known); Sandy Coulthard, an old horseman; Isaac Weightman, or 'Tisem', an old weaver; George Holmes, upholsterer and bell ringer at Crosthwaite Church; George Todhunter, cooper; Bob Raven; Mark Rook; Abel Banks and his fiddle; Mary Jane Wise.
The buildings shown include (left to right) Old Poorhouse; the lockup; Papes; Woolpack; Luptons; Queen's; George Hotel; Moot Hall; I. T. Atkinson; Wagon and Horses (the Bank Tavern); Woods, decorators.

Many thanks

I never know where to begin when thanking people and organisations for their help with a book, so I think it is best to start at the beginning of *The Greta* and swim my way downriver from there.

The energetic Ian Creighton, of the West Cumbria Rivers Trust, accompanied me on many of the walks along the tributaries and various becks leading in to the Greta. Particularly memorable was the trek through the snow and ice to Sharp Edge to trace the source of the Glenderamackin.

The opening chapter developed into a closer examination of the story behind the Hawell Monument near Whit Beck on Skiddaw and I am indebted to the work of Canon Hardwicke Drummond Rawnsley for his account of the Hawell family and their place in local shepherding folklore. A great chronicler and observer of his day, his literature also proved invaluable in other areas of the book.

A big thank you to all the local people, Bainbridges, Paxons and Wilkinsons in the main who subjected themselves unflinchingly to my unique interviewing technique for the chapter on "River Dwellers" and who kindly allowed me to use family photographs and other illustrations. Some of the old black and white photographs provided by Doris Price (nee Bainbridge) were of the highest quality (see page 42) and I think Doris may have missed her true vocation in life, that of a portrait photographer! Thanks also to the Wilkinson family for the use of the superb 'Wilk' cartoons that provide a tremendous flavour of the times and local characters, especially those who frequented the Twa Dogs Inn in the days of Gerald Hayes. My thanks also to Peter Harding, current landlord of the Twa Dogs for being very helpful and hosting some very important interviews with local anglers over several pints of Jennings beer.

And to Jill (nee Wilkinson) and Rod Donington-Smith, a special thank you for the almost continual supply of chocolate biscuits and tea at Greta Cottage. Adam Paxon, at Toll Bar Cottage, went beyond the call of duty by keeping a diary of his sightings at Calvert Bridge while working on the creation of jewellery in his riverside studio.

Thanks to Mirehouse Historic House and Gardens for permitting me to use the stunning 1835 painting by Henry Gastineau (1791-1876) of Calvert Bridge, the Toll Bar Cottage and Penrith Road and, similarly, my gratitude to The Wordsworth Trust for providing a series of drawings and paintings through their archive at the Jerwood Centre, Grasmere.

The work of the late Mike Davies-Shiel was invaluable in the research work for the chapter on mills and industry along the river. My thanks also to Keswick Historical Society and Dorothy Hind for providing the documentation and to Mike's widow, Noree, for her approval of its use in the book.

The chapter on industry on the river also contains the earliest Ordnance Survey maps of Keswick and area (1864) and these are reproduced courtesy of Cumbria Archive Centre, through their offices at Lady Gillford's House, Carlisle.

It was fascinating to compare the lives of Robert and Edith Southey with those of the current residents at Greta Hall, Jeronime and Scott. By an amazing coincidence the respective families, with 200 years separating them, each had seven children at Greta Hall; although some of the 21st Century family were born in Hong Kong and not at Greta Hall. Scott and Jeronime were enormously helpful, and thanks to Scott for the impromptu tour of the house and the visit to the roof. Greta Hall is highly accessible to the public both as a centre for the arts and for accommodation. Further information can be found on www.gretahall.net

Some of the wildlife images I have used were provided by various national agencies and these and the names of the photographers are credited on the pages where they appear. Similarly, books I have referred to in my research are listed in the pages of the book.

In some instances it has proved impossible to discover the origins of all images, photographic and otherwise. A case in point is the painting of a steam train passing over a bridge on the Greta. A print of this painting is displayed in the Twa Dogs. I have tried extensively to ascertain the name of the artist, but to no avail. If, in the course of the publication of this book, light can be shone on any areas of uncertainty, such as this, then I would be happy to acknowledge the fact and include relevant information in any future editions of the book.

Stuart Holmes, of Keswick, provided striking images of the flooding that has affected Keswick in recent years and many local people have helped enormously with other images. They include the George Fisher Collection, Sue Steinberg, and Jeff Taylor.

My thanks also to the artist Carry Akroyd for kindly allowing me to use her illustration entitled 'Pink River' (www.carryakroyd.co.uk). The image of the heron flying up stream with the road on the rise in the background reminded me very much of the Greta and our resident herons.

Local anglers Mick Tinnion, Terry "The Heron" Appleby and Bruce Frampton showed that they are naturals when it comes to photographic fishing shoots on the River Greta. My thanks to them for taking time out in Town's Field and to Terry for telling some wonderful stories relating to local anglers; most of which I actually believed. Thanks to all the other people and anglers who provided material, sometimes unwittingly, for the book. Thanks also to Keith Bowen for permitting me to use the pastel drawing of an angler on the River Greta and to Chris Pilling for his poem *A Good Day's Fishing* (Bookcase 2009) about the old fisherman practising his casting in the garden and field.

I am thankful to the Theatre by the Lake, Keswick, for their help in respect of events relating to the launch of this publication at the theatre.

An enormous amount of the research work for this book, and especially for 'The History Files' was carried out at Keswick Museum and Art Gallery with the co-operation and tea and biscuits of the people there Charlotte, Nicky, Tricia and Pat, who also kindly provided many images from the museum's archives. Keswick Historical Society, as mentioned previously, was also very helpful.

If only they were still around I would have personally thanked the editor and staff of the *Lakes Visitor and Keswick Guardian* (first published 1877) who produced a magnificent newspaper and which proved invaluable in giving me a fascinating, entertaining and rich historical source of information to help with the theme of how the river runs through the life and times of Keswick and its people.

Thanks to Malcolm Rigg, of Keswick, who only accepted the design work for this book on the understanding that he would be selected to play for Keswick Cricket Club in the summer of 2013. Seriously, Malcolm has done an excellent job; my thanks also to Ross Brewster for his proof reading and to Richard Cook and the printers, Amadeus, of Cleckheaton in the good old UK.

Last, but most definitely not least, my eternal thanks as always to the photographic genius of Val Corbett. Her images for this book are wonderful, as they have been for its predecessors *Ivver Sen*, *Joss* and *Jack's Yak*. Val's picture in *The Greta* of youngsters wild swimming in the river at Town's Field, is a remarkable image showing tremendous composition, light and energy. It is nothing short of a masterpiece; but then much of Val's photographic work warrants that description.

Keith Richardson, September 5th, 2012

The Greta . . . a river runs through it

By the same Author

RIVER
GRETA
WRITER

Companions of a kind
  Short Stories.

Ike
  Biography of the West Cumbrian Rugby League player Ike Southward.

Ivver Sen
  Lake District. The life and times of the men and women who work the land.
  (all three above books currently out of print).

Joss
  The life and times of the legendary Lake District fell runner and shepherd
  Joss Naylor.

Jack's Yak
  A unique journey through time with the special trees of the Lake District
  and Cumbria and the remarkable stories they have to tell.

The Greta
  The story of a Lakeland river as it flows through the life and times
  of Keswick and its people.

To find out more about River Greta Writer and its publications go to:
www.rivergretawriter.co.uk

Index

The Greta

The Greta

The Greta . . . a river runs through it

Skiddaw slate at the water's edge below Brundholme Woods, opposite bank to the Pigfields, River Greta.

Following pages: The river races through the Pigfields.